Socioeconomic

Background and

Educational

Performance

by

Robert Mason Hauser

Department of Sociology
The University of Wisconsin, Madison

Published for the Arnold M. and Caroline Rose
Monograph Series, American Sociological Association.

THE ARNOLD AND CAROLINE ROSE
MONOGRAPH SERIES IN SOCIOLOGY

A gift by Arnold and Caroline Rose to the American Sociological Association in 1968 provided for the establishment of the Arnold and Caroline Rose Monograph Series in Sociology. The conveyance provided for the publication of manuscripts in any subject matter field of sociology. The donors intended the series for rather short monographs, contributions that normally are beyond the scope of publication in regular academic journals.

The Series is under the general direction of an editorial board appointed by the Council of the American Sociological Association and responsible to the Publications Committee of the Association. Competition for publication in the Series has been limited by the Association to Fellow, Active and Student members.

Library of Congress Number 73-183120
International Standard Book Number 0-912764-01-5

© American Sociological Association
1722 N St. N.W.
Washington, D.C. 20036

Acknowledgments

This monograph is a revision of my doctoral thesis at the University of Michigan. I offer what I did with gratitude to those who are responsible for its merits. Its faults are my own.

Albert J. Reiss, Jr., and Albert Lewis Rhodes allowed me to use their Nashville data files. It is remarkable that such a rich and relevant body of data was collected several years before the present level of scientific and popular interest in the schooling process developed. I must admit to using only a small fraction of their data, and the errors of omission and commission in the use of the data are my responsibility.

A "brown bag" presentation by Otis Dudley Duncan in the autumn of 1966 suggested to me both the subject matter and the method of the study. While he was serving as chairman of my doctoral committee at the University of Michigan, his incisive criticism and personal encouragement were invaluable resources. My thanks go also to the members of my doctoral committee, Jerald G. Bachman, Edward O. Laumann, and Albert J. Reiss, Jr., each of whom read at least two drafts of the manuscript, and whose frank criticism marked the course of its evolution.

During 1966-67, when I began to work on this problem, I was supported by a National Institutes of Health traineeship in social organization and human ecology at the University of Michigan. At Brown University, from the fall of 1967 through the spring of 1969 my support came from the Population Research Laboratory. I owe particular thanks for the support and advice of my former colleagues at Brown University, especially Harold Organic, Harold W. Pfautz, Sidney Goldstein, James Sakoda, Richard Taub and Basil Zimmer. During the past two years my senior colleague, William H. Sewell, has patiently suffered my intermittent preoccupation with revision of the manuscript. Since I have been at Wisconsin, my work has been supported in part by the National Institues of Health, U. S. Public Health Service (M-6275) and by the Social and Rehabilitation Service, U. S. Department of Health, Education and Welfare (CRD-314).

Joseph R. Garrett, of the Metropolitan Board of Education of the City of Nashville and Davidson County, Tennessee, was most helpful in locating a long-lost set of school district boundaries. Tabulations were carried out at the University of Michigan Computing Center, the Sociology Computing Laboratory of Brown University, and the University of Wisconsin Computing Center. J. Michael Coble and N. Roy Kass gave efficient user-oriented programming services at Michigan and at Brown, respectively.

Able statistical clerking was provided by Ruthe Sweet and Greer Litton at the University of Michigan, by Bonnie Blodgett at Brown University, and by Mark Evers at the University of Wisconsin. I also offer my thanks to Helen MacGill Hughes for her expert editing of the final copy, to Jan Slote and Kathleen Yapuncich for typing drafts, and to Becky Heideman for typing the final manuscript.

My wife, Taissa, did much of the real work with consummate skill: keypunching, operating computing machinery, setting up tabulations, organizing and documenting data files, finding and checking references, editing and typing. Her energy and patience kept me going, too.

Robert M. Hauser
Madison, Wisconsin
June, 1971

TABLE OF CONTENTS

LIST OF TABLES

LIST OF FIGURES

Figure   Page

SCHOOLS, SCHOOLING, AND THE STRATIFICATION PROCESS

The study here reported is an investigation of the role of socioeconomic factors in the process of secondary education in a metropolitan community. Two questions guide the inquiry:

To what degree is the influence of socioeconomic background on performance in school an adequate theory of educational performance?

How much does a student's educational performance depend on which school he attends?

These two questions cannot be answered independently, and numerous substantive and methodological issues must be faced before either can be answered. In the course of the study three educational performances—academic achievement, course marks and aspirations—are examined and the influence of several home, school and neighborhood factors is measured and interpreted.

In this first chapter the role of education in the process of stratification is outlined, some relevant research on educational performances is examined, and an overview of the study is presented. While much of the analysis that follows is descriptive and inductive, it is guided by an explicit frame of reference and research strategy. We conceive of the analysis as an elaboration of a basic model of the process of stratification which has been proposed by Blau and Duncan (1967:Chap. V. See also Duncan and Hodge, 1963; Duncan, Featherman and Duncan, 1968:9-16, 50-58). An incremental strategy of model building is used in an effort to construct explicit, coherent and internally consistent multivariate interpretations (Duncan, Featherman and Duncan, 1968:16-22).

Schooling is part of the life-long process of stratification which Duncan (1967:87) has termed "the socioeconomic life-cycle":

> In the career of an individual or cohort of individuals the circumstances of the family of orientation—its size, structure, socioeconomic status, stability, and so on—provide a set of 'initial conditions' whose effects are transmitted through subsequent stages of attainment and achievement.

The conceptual framework is concerned explicitly with "distributive" variables (Moore and Sheldon, 1966:144-149): education, occupation and income, but it also invites interpretation of major segments of the cycle in terms of intervening processes or mechanisms. One catalog of mechanisms of stratification includes ascription, inheritance, genetics, socialization, access to opportunities, environments and differential association (Duncan, 1968b:683-685). A major task of research on stratification is to assess the importance of each of these mechanisms in producing the correlation between statuses of origin and of destination.

This study is concerned with intervening mechanisms in two ways. First, the process of schooling may be interpreted as an early career contingency which links characteristics of the family of orientation with adult achievements, a viewpoint which makes salient the overall relationship between family background factors and educational outcomes. Second, components of these overall relationships may be identified with specific processes of socialization and selection. Here, we shall be especially concerned with the degree to which academic performances mediate the effects of social origins on the ultimate outcomes of schooling.

Educational Outcomes: Attainment and Performance

Among the most obvious properties of the educational system in the United States are the nearly universal exposure of children to a minimum of schooling and the use of age-grading to define level of advancement within the system. These properties make it hard to distinguish the effects of schooling from those of other processes of socialization and selection (Parsons, 1959). Two ways of conceiving of the outcomes of education correspond roughly to the effects of socialization and of selection. The first is success in internalizing various cognitive or moral attributes. The second is success in completing work at a particular age-grade level of the system. We shall refer to the former set of outcomes as educational performance and to the latter as educational attainment or years of schooling (Jencks, 1968:282). The differences between the two concepts of educational success have important effects on their use in research on stratification. For example, it is difficult to measure educational performance of students not currently enrolled in school, while educational attainment is a valid indicator of educational differentials only among persons who have completed their schooling. Roughly speaking, educational performance refers to the quality of education and educational attainment to the quantity of education, but we shall see that the conceptual distinction cannot be maintained empirically.

Conflicting judgments about the role of education in the process of stratification are associated with the choice of educational indicators. The most salient comparison is that between the retrospective national household survey, "Occupational Changes in a Generation" (Blau and Duncan, 1967), and the massive school survey mandated by the Civil Rights Act of 1964 (Coleman et al., 1966). Choosing years of schooling as their indicator, Blau and Duncan (1967:201) concluded that the educational system is a major source of social mobility:

> Far from serving in the main as a factor perpetuating initial status, education operates primarily to induce variation in occupational status that is independent of initial status. . . . This is not to gainsay the equally cogent point that the degree of 'perpetuation' . . . that does occur is mediated in large part by education.

At nearly the same time *Equality of Educational Opportunity ("EEO",* Coleman, *ibid.,* p. 325) concluded

> that schools bring little influence to bear on a child's achievement that is independent of his background and general social context; and that this very lack of an independent effect means that the inequalities imposed on children by their home, neighborhood, and peer environment are carried along to become the inequalities with which they confront adult life at the end of school. For equality of educational opportunity through the schools must imply a strong effect of schools that is independent of the child's immediate social environment, and that strong independent effect is not present in American schools.

In our view the Blau and Duncan statement is a more accurate characterization of the American educational system, and it is not at all inconsistent with the empirical findings of the school survey. The conceptual and empirical arguments supporting this conclusion merit some attention, for they provide the theoretical context of the present study.

Educational Attainment and Stratification

The role of educational attainment may be summarized by reference to the basic model of the process of stratification proposed by Blau and Duncan. In the model it is assumed that a father's educational and occupational statuses influence his son's educational attainment and occupational achievement and that the son's educational attainment also influences his occupational achievement. For the cohorts represented in the 1962 survey, the influence of socioeconomic origin on the son's occupational achievement is mainly indirect, by way of educational attainment. That is, once schooling has been completed, a father's educational and occupational statuses are only a minor handicap or advantage to his son. Moreover, most of the variation in the son's educational attainment must be explained by factors unrelated to his father's statuses. The effect of the son's educational attainment on his occupational achievement nearly exhausts the influence of paternal statuses, and at the same time that effect is largely an indication of the impact of educational opportunity on occupational achievement. With some variation in detail the same pattern holds when additional indicators of social background are introduced, and it holds in the case of cohorts completing school throughout the present century. This basic model provides a framework for interpreting the role of educational performances in the process of stratification.

The relationship between educational attainment and educational performance and their relative importance as determinants of adult achievement are problematic. There is a manifest relationship between level of attainment and the presumed level of difficulty and specialization of educational materials. Consequently, to the extent that past performance determines continuation in school, we expect attainment and performance to be correlated in cohorts which have completed their schooling. On the other hand, the relationship between level of attainment and demand for performance is probably loose. Schools may differ in standards of successful performance and in policies with regard to retarding students. Various curricula require varying aptitudes (Wilson, 1963; Ginsberg, 1961; David et al., 1961:123; Perrucci, 1967:115; Jencks, 1968:284-286; Davis, 1966). More important, factors other than educational performance, however broadly that term may be defined, enter the process of selection (B. Duncan, 1965; Folger and Nam, 1967:33-75; Sewell, Haller and Portes, 1969).

Despite these arguments for imperfection in the relationship between educational performance and educational attainment, the introduction of measures of the quality of education is unlikely to produce substantial change in the interpretation already advanced. First, there is little room for more of the effects of initial statuses on adult achievements to be mediated by indicators of educational quality. The importance of educational success as an intervening variable is fully established in the Blau-Duncan model. Second, even a moderate correlation between attainment and educational performance would make it unlikely that performance would account for much more variation in occupational achievement than educational attainment alone (Blau and Duncan, 1967:188-194, 203; Jencks, 1968:281; Sewell and Shah, 1968a). To add anything to the explanation the relationship between educational quality and occupational achievement would have to be quite strong. Third, there is reason to suspect that the relationship between educational quality and occupational achievement is weaker than that between educational attainment and occupational achievement. For example, Lavin (1965:Introduction) has remarked on the paucity of evidence relating college grades and other measures of educational performance to adult occupational achievement. On the other hand, the presumed monopoly of the educational system on the provision of credentials for employment is the subject of frequent comment by social critics (Goodman, 1964), and we have already noted the observation of several authors that the "certification effect" of college training may outweigh the supposed effects of differences in school quality (Eckland, 1965). It is ironic that imputed differences in the quality of schools at the college level are interpreted as conducive to social mobility, while at the secondary level they are interpreted as obstacles to the creation of equal opportunity.

In an effort to be more explicit, O. D. Duncan (1968a) has argued that intelligence at maturity is one appropriate index of educational quality and he incorporated it in an extended model of the process of stratification. The model interprets the effects on occupational achievement and earnings of the status of the family of origin, early intelligence, intelligence at maturity, and educational attainment. Two aspects of the interpretation are of special interest here. First, early intelligence has a strong direct influence on educational attainment, beyond the effects of family background factors. Second, later intelligence is of less direct importance than educational attainment in the determination of occupational status. Duncan concluded (*ibid.,* p. 9):

> For the most part, though not entirely, ability influences achievement insofar as it is translated into training or skill and is certified by a formal educational system.

Duncan's interpretation is based on data from heterogeneous sources, so it is encouraging to see similar findings emerge from recent studies of a large statewide cohort of high-school graduates (Sewell, Haller and Portes, 1969; Sewell, Haller and Ohlendorf, 1970).

Studies like the present, which are concerned with the determination of measures of educational performance, are more likely to succeed in refining and adding detail to the basic model described above than in producing novel interpretations of the role of education in the process of stratification.

Studies of Educational Performance

We have outlined the role which educational attainment plays in a model of the process of stratification and argued that the introduction of indicators of educational performance would not greatly change our interpretation of the model. Why, then, do studies of schools often produce findings in apparent conflict with the model? There are at least five reasons, each of which is developed briefly below:

(1) *Choice of Inappropriate Populations.*

The population unit to which we ordinarily want to generalize in research on stratification is the birth cohort, that is, persons who are born in a single year or short span of years and who grow up under common historical conditions (Ryder, 1965; B. Duncan, 1968). Differentials in the timing and selectivity of education make it difficult to generalize from findings about the performance of enrolled persons to the progress of birth cohorts through the educational system. For example, the range in the ages at entering school and at leaving it and variations, too, in the pace of passing through the grades make it unlikely that enrolled persons in any grade exhaust or represent any birth cohort. Yet most large-scale studies of educational performance have been based on cross-sectional samples of students (Coleman *et al.,* 1966; Flanagan *et al.,* 1962; Edwards and Wilson, 1961; Wilson, 1967; Sewell and Shah, 1967) although the virtues of longitudinal analysis do not compensate for this intitial problem of selection.

Also cross-sectional studies do not provide representative samples of students' ultimate educational performances because they are measured at varying points in students' careers. Years of schooling is the maximum of one kind educational achievement in an adult, but the same cannot be said of his performance in an arbitrarily chosen grade. Achievement in the tenth grade may be the zenith of performance of a boy who leaves school at the age of 16 but meaningless as a description of the performance of an eventual college graduate. Relative success within a cohort at one level of attainment increases the chances of similar standing at higher levels, but its effect on ultimate standing is mediated by experiences of learning and retention in school.

Of course, it is operationally difficult to obtain appropriate measurements of educational performances. Follow-up and follow-back studies of individuals and the testing of samples of the general population may not always be feasible, but such efforts are required in principle if we are to secure complete sets of data. Whatever may be the substantive deficiencies of years of schooling as an educational indicator, at least it can be ascertained in representative samples of birth cohorts.

(2) *Lack of Rationale in Choice of Indicators.*

There is no measure or set of measures of educational performance in a given grade whose relationships with background statuses provide unequivocal evidence of more or less equal opportunity. Among the heterogeneous measures which have been interpreted as indicators of opportunity are intelligence quotients, academic achievement test scores, course marks, grade-point averages, educational and occupational aspirations, expectations or plans, and a variety of less easily described attitudinal measures (Coleman *et al.,* 1966; Flanagan *et al.,* 1964; Charters, 1963:740). There has been relatively little effort to order these indicators in a model of the relevant portions of the process of achievement. In the absence of such a model, interpretation of the indicators is equivocal.

(3) *Lack of Criteria of Adequacy of Explanation.*

Analyses of educational opportunity have usually gone no further than to demonstrate that differentials in educational performance are associated with one or more socioeconomic background characteristics. However, there are great differences among the conclusions: (a) that a postulated relationship exists; (b) that it is of a given size; and (c) that it is a sufficient explanation of the phenomenon of interest. While interpretations of the influence of initial social statuses on educational performance frequently require the last-named (c) type of evidence (Warner, Havighurst and Loeb, 1944; Hollingshead, 1949; Sexton, 1961; Hodgkinson, 1962; Wilson, 1959, 1967), most evidence of educational stratification is of the first two kinds (a or b) (Coleman *et al.,* 1966; Lavin, 1965:122-124; Boocock, 1966). We do not know whether socioeconomic background would account for the observed similarity of a student's scores in more than one measurement of educational performance, but it is implicitly so assumed in the contention that socioeconomic background "explains" educational performance.

(4) *Preoccupation with Quality of School.*

There is a voluminous sociological literature dealing with the quality of secondary schools (Coleman *et al.,* 1966:290-325; Bowles and Levin, 1968; Coleman, 1968; Boyle, 1966a; 1966b; Coleman, 1961a; 1961c; Krauss, 1964; McDill, Meyers and Rigsby, 1967; McDill, Rigsby and Meyers, 1969; Michael, 1961, 1966; Sewell and Armer, 1966a, 1966b; Shaycoft, 1967; Turner, 1964, 1966; Wilson, 1959, 1963, 1967; Cleveland, 1962; Dyer, 1968). In part the preoccupation with school quality has resulted from an erroneous identification of the effects of the school with those of schooling as a process. While some educational inputs may be indivisible below the aggregate level of the school, the learning experience of individual students is not. Moreover, schooling is differentiated temporally, not territorially. Throughout from 10 to 20 years of formal education most students are exposed to a variety of educational environments, and their being "in" rather than "out" of school is far more important than which schools they attend.

Why has there been so much interest in school effects? Perhaps it is because school characteristics — physical plant, expenditure, curriculum, teachers' credentials, methods of teaching, the composition of the student body and so on—are within the realm of legitimate public action. For example, the fact that schools are highly segregated by race invites interpretation of differentials in the performance of black and white students in terms of school quality although the differentials are present at the age of entering school (Coleman *et al.,* 1966: 221-222). Moynihan (1968:30) has suggested that in doing research social scientists have "a predisposition, confirmed and strengthened by the larger society, to direct attention in education toward the 'neutral' strengths and weaknesses of school-related characteristics, rather than student-related characteristics, in ascribing responsibility for inadequate achievement levels." For example, Wilson (1968:

80) argued, "The effects which differences between schools may have upon students' academic development acquires (sic) special public salience, then, even though this effect may be much smaller than the effects upon achievement of family socialization or the differences between pupils within schools."

Investigations of the quality of the school have been unproductive for at least three reasons: (a) School effects are small. There is a great deal of overlap among student bodies in educational performance, and the processes determining educational performance are much the same in any school. That is, differences among schools contribute little to the individual differences in educational performance which are to be explained in distributive research in stratification. (b) Differences in levels of educational performance from school to school may overstate differences in educational quality because the composition of student bodies varies in respect to variables which antedate educational performance. Net differences among schools may be identified with school quality after composition on prior factors has been controlled statistically. The imposition of such controls amounts to the adoption of a model of the determination of differntial performance within schools, and one who proposes such a model should be prepared to take it seriously. (In later chapters we show that a socio-economic theory of educational performance is not adequate from this point of view.) (c) At the same time, differences in the quality of educational experience may occur within a school, and these are ignored in studies of the quality of schools.

(5) *Failure to Link Educational Performance with Later Events in the Process of Stratification.*
We know little about the effects of educational performance in given grades on the later achievement of representative cohorts (Lavin, 1965: Introduction). Sewell's panel data on 1957 Wisconsin high school seniors provides valuable documentation (Sewell and Shah, 1967; Sewell and Shah, 1968a, 1968b; Sewell, Haller and Portes, 1969), but it is limited to high school graduates in a single state. The follow-up studies of Project Talent are of doubtful value because of low rates of response (Shaycoft, 1967; Folger, Astin and Bayer, 1970), and no panel studies can be made with the data from the *Equality of Educational Opportunity* survey (Coleman *et al.,* 1966; Sewell, 1967; B. Duncan, 1968). Other panel studies suffer from defects in scope, size of sample, coverage of population or in method (Havighurst and Rodgers, 1952; Havighurst *et al.,* 1962; Davis and Hess, 1963; Nam and Cowhig, 1962). In short, most of the evidence that indicators of educational performance are relevant to the process of stratification consists of their correlations with socio-economic background variables. The influence of educational performance on adult achievement is poorly documented and poorly understood. Yet the importance of educational indicators in the process of stratification is not established unless they have both antecedents and consequences in the system of stratification.

Overview of the Study

This study is an effort to interpret differential educational performances among white students enrolled in the public secondary schools of Davidson County, Tennessee, in 1957. We are especially concerned with the adequacy of socioeconomic theories of educational performance and with the interpretation of school effects. The preceding discussion makes it clear that no far-reaching conclusions about the process of stratification can be drawn from the data. At the same time, a thorough analysis of the determination of educational performances is not without interest—or complexity. An adequate treatment of this limited aspect of the role of education in stratification requires attention to (1) the role of the student's background in the differentiation of educational performances within schools; (2) the role of urban residence in determining the composition of student bodies; and (3) the logical implications of those findings for the interpretation of differences in performance among schools.

The interpretation of school effects is treated here as a special case of the more general problem of interpreting explanations at differing levels of aggregation. In order to prepare the way for the statistical analysis in later chapters, we examine in Chapter II the logical and substantive issues in aggregation, and arrive at the conclusion that the analysis of covariance is an appropriate statistical model for the simultaneous interpretation of individual and aggregate relationships. Unlike several *ad hoc* techniques of multi-level analysis which have been suggested in the past, the analysis of covariance permits the simultaneous examination of all relevant aspects of the data within a single analytical framework.

The study population and the variables used in the analysis are described in Chapter III. There were nearly 17,000 students in the study population, and separate analyses were run for subgroups defined by sex and grade. Because several of the variables were ascertained from school records, missing data posed a substantial problem, and their sources and consequences are discussed. In Chapter IV we survey the substantive findings of previous studies of the effects of secondary schools and present some preliminary findings about the size and persistence of differences among schools in the Davidson County study population.

In the following three chapters, detailed analyses of academic achievement, course marks and aspirations are presented. We start with the minimal assumption that the student's background influences his academic achievement and we exhaust the implications of that assumption for the determination of course marks and aspirations. In interpreting the determination of these educational performances we are less concerned with the size and direction of relationships then with the adequacy of explanations based on commonly accepted assumptions. In general, we find that the explanations used to rationalize statistical controls in studies of the effect of the school are incapable of accounting for the covariation in similarly determined educational performances, but they do account for substantial portions of differences in performance among schools. In these chapters the effect of residential segregation on the composition of student bodies and on other aspects of school quality are also examined, and we find that their importance has frequently been overestimated. In the concluding chapter our major findings and their implications are recapitulated.

As we have already noted, there are several limits to the contribution this study can make to our understanding of the role of educational performances in the process of stratification. The analysis is based on cross-sectional data. Neither race nor integration can be treated as variables nor is the study population necessarily representative of white students in the United States. Furthermore, the variables treated in the analysis exhaust neither the universe of potentially relevant factors nor the wealth of material ascertained in the survey of which this is a secondary analysis. Finally, since we have no data on the achievement of these cohorts of high school students in early adulthood, we can offer no direct assessment of the implications of our interpretations for later stages of the process of achievement.

These remarks are not offered as an apology. The goals of the study were to define and investigate a specific set of problems relevant to a more extensive process. If the limitations of the study are obvious, then, at least, the first of our goals may have been achieved.

II

SOCIAL CONTEXTS
AND THE ANALYSIS
OF COVARIANCE

While this study focuses primarily on explaining performance in school, the measurement and interpretation of school effects exemplify problems of aggregation which occur frequently in sociology and deserve to be examined at a general level. Thus, this chapter begins with a brief history of the use of the analysis of covariance in interpreting individual and group data, after which its use as a technique of interpretation is discussed in detail. The several parameters of an analysis of covariance are derived, and the results are presented in terms of the graphic and notational conventions of path analysis. We show that covariance analysis provides an explicit treatment of procedures and problems of interpretation in contextual analysis. We conclude that contextual analysis often leads to purely speculative or artifactual interpretations.

Ecological Correlation and Contextual Analysis

Two decades have passed since the publication of W. S. Robinson's well-known article, "Ecological Correlations and the Behavior of Individuals" (1950), but sociologists have not yet fully exploited the insight it provides into the interpretation of relationships at different levels of aggregation. Robinson (1950:351) defines an individual correlation as "a correlation in which the statistical object or thing described is indivisible", and an "ecological correlation" as one where "the statistical object is a group of persons." Using the algebra of the analysis of covariance to demonstrate the mathematical relationship between individual and ecological correlations, Robinson presented analyses of areal data in which ecological and individual correlations differ in magnitude or sign. He argued that ecological correlations had been used in place of individual correlations where individual variation was actually the object of explanation, but individual data were unavailable. Robinson (*ibid.*, 357) concluded, "the only reasonable assumption is that an ecological correlation is almost certainly not equal to its corresponding individual correlation . . . The purpose of this paper will have been accomplished . . . if it prevents the future computation of meaningless correlations and stimulates the study of similar problems with the use of meaningful correlations between the properties of individuals."

In response to Robinson's article several investigators used the framework of the analysis of covariance to suggest ways of estimating individual relationships from data on aggregates. Goodman (1953) noted that the between-areas regression coefficient is an estimator of the total regression coefficient of the relationship between two dichotomous attributes if the category-specific rates of the dependent attribute can be assumed identical in each areal subdivision. Duncan and Davis (1953) demonstrated that the marginal distributions of areal units imply upper and lower bounds of the total individual correlation. In a second article Goodman (1959) extended his earlier discussuon to the determination of the total correlation coefficient. He discussed in some detail the assumptions under which his procedure was justified, its application to m x 2 classifications and continuous bivariate distributions, and possible modifications of it where the zero-order between-area regression coefficient could not be assumed equal to the total regression coefficient. Duncan, Cuzzort and Duncan (1961), departing from their earlier concern with estimation of the total regression coefficient or total correlation coefficient from incomplete data, used the covariance algebra to illustrate the complexity of procedures for aggregating data over areal units. More important, they applied the analysis of covariance to a variety of problems in the explanation of areal variation (Duncan, Cuzzort and Duncan, 1961:64-67, 99-113, 136-146, 166-168). Bogue and Harris (1954), Taves (1950) and Schuessler (1969) have proposed its use in studying areal variation, time series and scale analysis.

Robinson's article was directed specifically at the use of between-group correlations in areal data, as indicated by his examples and by his use of the term "ecological" to denote between-group correlations. It has been pointed out by several critics (O. D. Duncan, 1959: 680; Duncan, Cuzzort and Duncan, 1961:27; Riley, 1964:1020) that this terminology "perpetuates a usage of the term 'ecological' in a meaning that has no generic connection with ecology or human ecology." The same problem occurs whenever relationships among the characteristics of aggregates are interpreted as relationships among those of individuals. Yet, although Robinson's and Goodman's works have been cited in discussions of related topics (Blau, 1960:190; Davis, Spaeth and Huson, 1961:222; Tannenbaum and Bachman, 1964:591-592; Riley, 1964:1020-1021), sociologists generally have not used the analysis of covariance to interpret differences among social aggregates. Duncan, Featherman and Duncan (1968) have already applied the method used here to the interpretation of school differences. Wilson (1963, 1967) has used covariance analysis in studies of school effects without avoiding several pitfalls in his interpretations. Within-school and between-school correlations were analyzed in the Plowden Report (Central Advisory Council on Education, 1967), but no effort was made to adjust for differences between schools in the composition of their student bodies. *Equality of Educational Opportunity* (Coleman *et al.,* 1966) presented correlation ratios for some indicators of academic achievement but resorted to partial correlation in the interpretation of differences between schools. One report of Project Talent (Flanagan *et al.,* 1962: Chapter V) included an algebraic exposition of the analysis of covariance, but little use was made of it in the reported analyses of differences between schools.

This is not to say, however, that sociologists have shown no interest in interpreting differences among groups. Several expositions of techniques for isolating "structural effects", "contextual effects", "social climates", "compositional effects", or "institutional effects" have appeared within the last fifteen years (Blau, 1957; Lazarsfeld, 1959; Blau, 1960; Davis, Spaeth and Huson, 1961; Tannenbaum and Bachman, 1964; Riley, 1964). None has included an explicit mathematical rationale, and several difficulties in their application have been overlooked. The common feature of these techniques was clearly stated by Blau (1957:63):

> To isolate a structural effect, the relationship between a group attribute and some effect is determined while the corresponding characteristic of individuals is held constant.

The history of analyses based on this technique may be traced to a famous example of relative deprivation in *The American Soldier* (Stouffer *et al.,* 1949:252), to interpretations of that and similar findings by Merton and Kitt (1950:82-83) and Kendall and Lazarsfeld (1950:186-196), or even to some parts of Durkheim's (1951:151-170, 259-276) analysis of suicide rates. Numerous applications of "contextual analysis" in a variety of substantive areas have appeared in recent years (Bachman, Smith and Slesinger, 1966; Davis, 1961a, 1961b; Levin, 1961; Meltzer, 1963; Nasatir, 1963, 1968). Contextual analyses of differences between schools are discussed in Chapter IV.

Contextual analysis is based on a misunderstanding of statistical aggregation and of social process which is rooted in the identification of differences among groups with the social, and differences among individuals with the psychological. For example, Blau (1960:178, 191) states:

Even socially acquired or socially defined attributes of individuals are clearly distinct in their effects from attributes of social structures . . . If a structural effect is observed, it invariably constitutes evidence that social processes originating outside the individual personality are responsible for the differences in the dependent variable, since the influences of psychological processes have been controlled in the analyses.

Coleman (1961b:607) begins a commentary on studies of "climates of opinion" with the observation:

The answers to interview questions, punched on IBM cards and crosstabulated, gave rise to peculiarly individualistic studies. The typical survey analysis inferred causes and processes internal to the individual, simply because the variables being cross-tabulated were attributes of the same individual.

In a later study (Coleman *et al.,* 1966), Coleman used the "method of residues" to study differences among schools. He had earlier (1964:522) characterized that method as "used to factor out the sociologically trivial, leaving as residue the sociologically interesting." In a discussion of "contextual propositions", Lazarsfeld (1959:72) writes, "This is a type of proposition which has an especially strong sociological flavor."

Perhaps the ultimate extension of these points of view would be the identification of intra-societal variation with the psychological, and intersocietal variation with the social. Clearly, levels of aggregation are not a fruitful basis for distinguishing social from psychological explanations. The distinction is better made in terms of the mechanisms by which variables are presumed to influence one another. The reality of the individual or the group need not be at issue in sociological explanation. We may agree with Duncan and Schnore (1959: 144), "that both are abstractions and thus unreal in equal degree." In the initial contributions to the literature on "ecological correlation", the mechanisms by which variables were related were not an issue, except in Robinson's apparent denial of the legitimacy of investigating interrelations of structural characteristics. Such relationships, it can be argued, reflect the basic interest of sociologists in social organization (Menzel, 1950), and they are consistent with a variety of social or psychological mechanisms (Duncan and Schnore, 1959; Schnore, 1961; Duncan, 1964).

Similarly, there is room for variety in the interpretation of relationships among individual variates. For example, the interest of demographers in the effects of composition is hardly motivated by a theoretical commitment to psychological explanations, or even to the treatment of persons as indivisible units of analysis in any given analysis (Hauser and Duncan, 1959:4; Taeuber and Taeuber, 1965:78-95; Duncan, Cuzzort and Duncan, 1961: 136-141). It would be difficult to convince a sociologist that Robinson's example of the individual relationship between color and literacy is based on a psychological causal framework which could be separated from manifest properties of American social structure. The long-standing controversy between the advocates of heredity and environment is rooted in more substantial problems than a choice of indicators of individual attributes (Eckland, 1967). Clearly such examples can be multiplied at will. The interpretation of relationships among individual attributes is compatible with the most varied forms of explanation, including those with a particular concern for effects of social structure. Indeed, social structure may be defined convincingly in terms of the social forces that actually impinge on the life-space of the individual. In the words of Campbell and Alexander (1965:284):

> It is necessary to consider the position of the individual within the social structure—defined in terms of his specific relationships to other members of the collectivity—before attributing causal relevance to characteristics of the total collectivity.

This is not to say that irreducible structural characteristics of groups have no power to determine other group or individual characteristics or to modify social processes within groups. It does require that attention be paid to the mechanisms by which aggregate social structures come to exert such influence.

Contextual analysis suffers from problems other than a confusion of levels of aggregation with levels of explanation. It also encourages faulty analysis and interpretation of data, as we shall show by examining the analysis of covariance in some detail.

The Analysis of Covariance

The treatment of the analysis of covariance in most statistics texts focuses on problems of statistical inference (Walker and Lev, 1953; Brownlee, 1960; Blalock, 1960). While the issues in our analysis are formally identical, our major concern is the interpretation of population data, and we ignore the distinction between sample estimates and population parameters.

Let x_{ij} and y_{ij} be defined as a predetermined variable and consequence of that variable, respectively, where the subscripts i and j refer to individuals and groups, respectively. In this interpretation, j can refer to cities, census tracts, work groups, regions, cliques, schools, or any other relevant basis for aggregation, and i to distinguishable units within the group. We let x_{ij} be the observed value of x for the ith individual in the jth group, $\bar{x}_{.j}$ be the mean of x for the n_j individuals in the jth group, and $\bar{x}_{..}$ be the weighted grand mean of x, and similarly for y, where $\sum_j n_j = N$.

The analysis of covariance interpretation is based on the identity

$$y_{ij} = (y_{ij} - \bar{y}_{.j}) + \bar{y}_{.j}, \tag{2.1}$$

where

$$(y_{ij} - \bar{y}_{.j}) = b_w(x_{ij} - \bar{x}_{.j}) + e_{ij} \tag{2.2}$$

and
$$\bar{y}_{.j} = b_w(\bar{x}_{.j} - \bar{x}_{..}) + \bar{y}_{.j}^*. \qquad (2.3)$$

Equation 2.1 states that the value of the dependent variable for any individual is the sum of the mean of his group and a deviation from it. Equation 2.2 states that the deviation, or within-group component of y is determined by a linear combination of an analogous within-group component of x and an error term. The average within-group regression coefficient, b_w, is determined by ordinary least squares, which means that the error term, e_{ij}, is uncorrelated with the predetermined variable, $(x_{ij} - \bar{x}_{.j})$. Equation 2.3 states that the group mean, or between-group component of y is the sum of a compositional component and an error term. The compositional component of the group mean of y is given by the product of the average within-group regression coefficient and the deviation of the group mean of x from its grand mean. That is, the composition term is the amount by which the group mean of y would change if the composition of the group on x were made equal to that of all individuals. The error term, $\bar{y}_{.j}^*$, is the adjusted y-mean, that is, the mean the jth group would have if its composition were the average of all groups. The adjustment for composition, or covariance adjustment, is shown graphically in Figure 2.1. Because the previously determined within-group regression coefficient, b_w, is used as a primitive term in equation 2.3, the ordinary assumption of linear regression that the error term be uncorrelated with the predictor variable does not hold. Since b_w and $\bar{x}_{..}$ are constants, it implies that $\bar{x}_{.j}$ and $\bar{y}_{.j}^*$ may be correlated. As explained below, this feature of the model

Figure 2.1.—Illustration of covariance adjustment

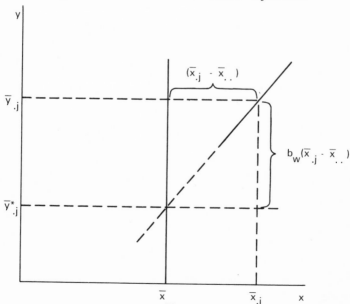

SOCIAL CONTEXTS AND THE ANALYSIS OF COVARIANCE

is the basis for the most common form of "contextual effect". Finally, it is convenient to write an equation like 2.1 for the determination of x_{ij}:

$$x_{ij} = (x_{ij} - \bar{x}_{.j}) + \bar{x}_{.j} \qquad (2.4)$$

This allows the model to reproduce the total correlation between x and y without having postulated more relationships than can be estimated from the data (Blalock, 1967a).

The covariance analysis is summarized graphically in a path diagram in Figure 2.2. The straight paths symbolize direct causal influence in the

Figure 2.2.–Path diagram of analysis of covariance model

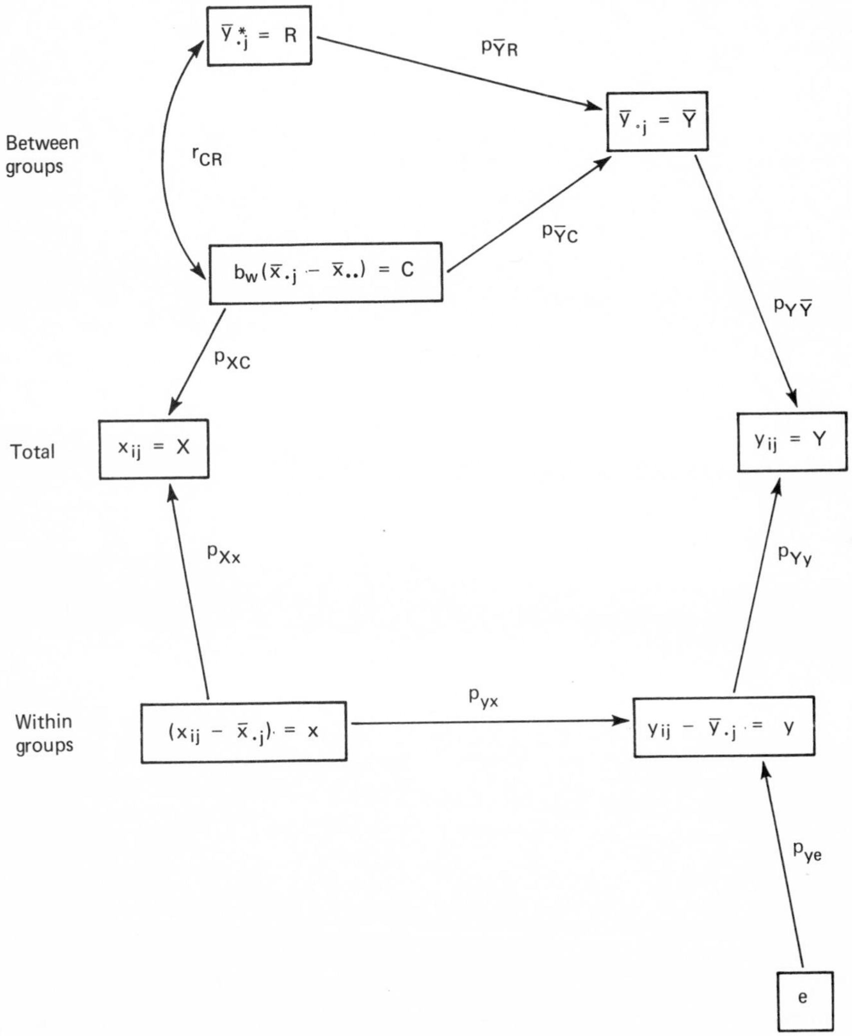

direction indicated by the arrow. The curved two-headed arrow depicts an unanalyzed relationship, that is, a possible correlation about which no causal assumptions have been made (Duncan, 1966). Path coefficients indicate the net effect of one variable on another where both variables are in standard form. For example, p_{yx} is the size of the change in the within-school component of y (in standard deviations) associated with a one standard deviation change in the within-school component of x. It is conventional to list the subscript of the dependent variable prior to that of the predetermined variable on path coefficients. The order of subscripts on correlation coefficients is arbitrary. For convenience in the manipulation of subscripts, some notational equivalents are indicated in the diagram. Given coefficients for all of the paths shown in Figure 2.2, it is possible to reproduce the correlations among all of the variables in the system.

Subtracting $\bar{y}..$, the grand mean of y, from both sides of equation 2.1, squaring, and summing over all observations, we obtain

$$\sum_j \sum_i (y_{ij} - \bar{y}..)^2 = \sum_j \sum_i (y_{ij} - \bar{y}_{.j})^2 + \sum_j n_j(\bar{y}_{.j} - \bar{y}..)^2, \qquad (2.5)$$

since the cross-product terms on the right-hand side sum to zero. Following the notation of Walker and Lev (1953:Chapter XV) and the presentation of Duncan, Cuzzort and Duncan (1961:64-67), we denote the three terms in equation 2.5 by C_{yyT}, C_{yyw} and C_{yyb}. These are the total sum of squares and the independent within-group and between-group sums of squares, respectively. The sums of squares for x and the sums of cross-products can be expressed in analogous notation. We can then write the total, within-group and between-group (or ecological) correlations, r_{xyT}, r_{xyw} and r_{xyb}, using expressions of the form:

$$\frac{C_{xy}}{\sqrt{C_{xx} C_{yy}}} \qquad (2.6)$$

and the three regression coefficients, b_T, b_w and b_b, by:

$$\frac{C_{xy}}{C_{xx}}. \qquad (2.7)$$

We can also write the two squared correlation ratios:

$$E_{XG}^2 = \frac{C_{xxb}}{C_{xxT}} \qquad (2.8)$$

and

$$E_{YG}^2 = \frac{C_{yyb}}{C_{yyT}}. \qquad (2.9)$$

The path coefficients in Figure 2.2 can be calculated directly if all of the sums of squares and cross-products are known. Since y_{ij} is completely determined by the sum of its within and between group components (Duncan, 1966:8), we can write

$$p_{Y\bar{Y}} = \frac{\sigma_{\bar{Y}}}{\sigma_Y} = \sqrt{\frac{C_{yyb}}{C_{yyT}}} = E_{YG} \tag{2.10}$$

and
$$p_{Yy} = \frac{\sigma_y}{\sigma_Y} = \sqrt{\frac{C_{yyw}}{C_{yyT}}} = \sqrt{1 - E^2_{YG}}. \tag{2.11}$$

This formalism does not hold for the determination of x_{ij} because of the transformation of $\bar{x}_{\cdot j}$ in the between-group model. Nonetheless, the computing forms are analogous to equations 2.10 and 2.11 because C is a linear transformation of $\bar{x}_{\cdot j}$. We can write:

$$p_{XC} = \sqrt{\frac{C_{xxb}}{C_{xxT}}} = E_{XG} \tag{2.12}$$

and
$$p_{Xx} = \sqrt{\frac{C_{xxw}}{C_{xxT}}} = \sqrt{1 - E^2_{XG}}. \tag{2.13}$$

Since x is the only measured determinant of y in the within-group segment of the model, we can write:

$$p_{yx} = r_{xyw} \tag{2.14}$$

and
$$p_{ye} = \sqrt{1 - r^2_{xyw}}. \tag{2.15}$$

In the between-group segment of the model we also have an additive decomposition, since the $\bar{y}^*_{\cdot j}$ are determined residually. Thus, we can write:

$$\bar{Y} = p_{\bar{Y}C}C + p_{\bar{Y}R}R, \tag{2.16}$$

where
$$p_{\bar{Y}C} = \frac{\sigma_C}{\sigma_{\bar{Y}}} \tag{2.17}$$

and
$$p_{\bar{Y}R} = \frac{\sigma_R}{\sigma_{\bar{Y}}}. \tag{2.18}$$

Since $\sigma_C = b_w \sigma_{\bar{x}}$ it is easy to determine that:

$$p_{\bar{Y}C} = b_w \sqrt{\frac{C_{xxb}}{C_{yyb}}}. \tag{2.19}$$

From equation 2.16 and the basic theorem of path analysis (Duncan, 1966: 10), we can write:

$$r_{C\bar{Y}} = p_{\bar{Y}C} + r_{CR}p_{\bar{Y}R}, \tag{2.20}$$

$$r_{R\bar{Y}} = p_{\bar{Y}R} + r_{CR}p_{\bar{Y}C}, \tag{2.21}$$

and
$$r_{\bar{Y}\bar{Y}} = 1 = p^2_{\bar{Y}C} + p^2_{\bar{Y}R} + 2p_{\bar{Y}C}r_{CR}p_{\bar{Y}R}. \tag{2.22}$$

On the earlier argument, $r_{C\bar{Y}} = r_{xyb}$, and equation 2.20 can be solved for $r_{CR}p_{\bar{Y}R}$. Substitution of this result in equation 2.22 yields an equation in $p_{\bar{Y}R}^2$, from which an arbitrarily positive solution for $p_{\bar{Y}R}$ can be obtained. Equation 2.21 can then be solved by substitution for $r_{R\bar{Y}}$. Equation 2.22 provides a convenient decomposition of between-group variance in y into net effects of composition on x, net effects of unmeasured variables, and joint effects of composition and unmeasured variables. The procedure can easily be extended to the case where there is more than one covariate or predetermined variable (Hauser, 1968:32-34).

Interpretation of Contextual Analysis

We are now prepared to interpret contextual analysis in some detail. While the same observations hold where there are multiple covariates, it is easier to present the issues in the case of a single covariate, x_{ij}, and a single dependent variable, y_{ij}.

Within- and Between-Group Variation

Absolute upper limits to the variation in x and y that lies between groups are given by the correlation ratios, $p_{XC} = E_{XG}$ and $p_{Y\bar{Y}} = E_{YG}$. Their complements, $p_{Xx} = \sqrt{1 - E^2_{XG}}$ and $p_{Yy} = \sqrt{1 - E^2_{YG}}$, are absolute upper limits to the within-group variation. Because the within- and between-group components determine x_{ij} and y_{ij} completely, any variable which acts on x_{ij} or y_{ij} must do so through their within-group or between-group components. Because the components are orthogonal, a variable can act only on one of the components. This is indicated by the absence of any direct connections between the within- and between-group segments of the path diagram in Figure 2.2.

While the correlation ratios have been described above as the square root of the ratio of between-group to total variance, their interpretation may be clearer if it is noted that E_{YG} is the Pearsonian correlation (over individuals) of the individual scores, y_{ij} and the group means, $\bar{y}_{.j}$. It is instructive to consider what is being explained in contextual analysis from this point of view. Since contextual variables are properties of groups, the maximum possible effect of those properties on the values of the dependent variable for individuals is given by the correlation ratio, which describes the variability of the dependent variable among groups. This maximal relationship can be observed only where the correspondence between the contextual antecedents and the group means on the dependent variable is perfect, and its value can be determined without reference to the variables assumed to influence y in either the within- or between-group segments of the model.

The same point applies to the problem of measuring contextual variables from individual characteristics. Discussions of this problem have frequently ignored the mathematical relations between classes of indicators (Kendall and Lazarsfeld, 1950; Lazarsfeld, 1958). Confusion on this issue leads to the kind of exchange observed between Sewell and Armer and their critics. Sewell and Armer (1966a:161) noted, "there is an element of *contamina-*

tion (emphasis supplied) in the neighborhood or school environment variable measured by school socioeconomic status because both the school status and the family status indexes are based on the same information." Turner (1966:698) replied briefly, "because the number of cases in each school is large, contamination with family socioeconomic status should not be excessive," and Michael (1966:702; see also Michael, 1961:585) responded in a lengthy footnote, also claiming to show that "the independence of the collective (i.e., school) measure from individual data varies with the size of the collectivity." The degree of "contamination" may readily be expressed as the correlation between the individual scores and group means of x, as described above, which is identical to the correlation ratio of x. Thus, the amount of "contamination" depends not on the size of the groups, but on the degree of segregation of x values among groups. To argue that a contextual variable is "uncontaminated" in this sense is to argue that it does not vary among groups, in which case it cannot account for between-group variation in some other variable.

Additive Contextual Effects

There are two kinds of contextual effects: additive effects and nonadditive effects. The first occur when there is non-random variation in the adjusted group means, and the second occur when the relationship between the covariate and the dependent variable changes from group to group. In observational data the size of either kind of effect may be related to group composition on the covariate; the claim that such correlations are readily interpretable is a distinctive feature of contextual analysis. The first type has been characterized elsewhere as a "direct" or "inverse structural effect" or as a "compositional effect on the between-group difference," and the second type has been described as a "contingency effect" or as "a compositional effect on the within-group difference" (Blau, 1960; Davis, Spaeth and Huson, 1961). The first type is a degenerate case of the observation of a difference in adjusted means in experimental application of the analysis of covariance, and the second is an interaction effect of treatment and covariate.

Four possible configurations of data for a covariance analysis are illustrated in Figure 2.3. The solid lines depict segments of within-group regression lines, and the dots are group means of x and y. The graphs are purely schematic; in real data there is almost always a great deal of overlap among groups in the observed values of x and y. In panel A the slopes of the within-group regression lines are identical, and all of the within-group regression lines lie on a single total regression line which also connects the group means. The adjusted y-mean of each group is equal to the grand mean of y. In this situation there is no "contextual effect" of either sort, although the possibility of observing "that the distribution of X in a group is related to Y even though the individual's X is held constant" (Blau, 1960:64) still exists if the data are examined in a simple cross-tabulation with inadequate controls (Tannenbaum and Bach-

Figure 2.3.—Some possible configurations of data in covariance analysis

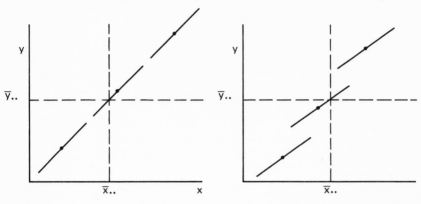

A. Composition accounts for variation in $\overline{Y}_{.j}$

B. Additive net effects of groups correlated with composition

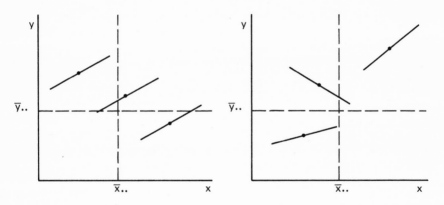

C. "Inverse Structural Effects"

D. Nonadditive group effects

man, 1964). In Figure 2.2 the configuration of panel A would be manifested in a zero correlation between C and R. That is, since $b_w = b_b$ in the present case, we can write

$$p_{\overline{Y}C} = b_w \sqrt{\frac{C_{xxb}}{C_{yyb}}} = b_b \sqrt{\frac{C_{xxb}}{C_{yyb}}} = r_{xyb}. \qquad (2.23)$$

But from equation 2.20,

$$r_{xyb} = r_{C\overline{Y}} = p_{\overline{Y}C} + r_{CR}p_{\overline{Y}R} = r_{xyb} + r_{CR}p_{\overline{Y}R}, \qquad (2.24)$$

and the product $r_{CR}p_{\overline{Y}R}$ must be equal to zero. In the present example the

SOCIAL CONTEXTS AND THE ANALYSIS OF COVARIANCE

between-group correlation is obviously unity, and both members of the product term are zero. In real data there is no necessity for the between-group correlation to reach unity when $b_w = b_h$. There may be 'random' scatter in the group means about the single regression line. Even in that case there would be no "effect" of the group values of x on y, if the individual values of x were controlled properly. The example of panel A and the modification just described correspond, respectively, to the observation of no treatment effect and to that of an additive treatment effect in the experimental use of the analysis of covariance. In experimental work the zero correlation of C and R in the between-group segment of the model is achieved by assigning individuals randomly to treatments. In observational studies it may be ascribed to good fortune or good explanation. While it need not account for all of the between-group variation in y, these configurations of data allow us to exhaust the effects of x on y without going beyond the assumption of an effect of x on y within groups.

In panel B the within-group regression lines are parallel, but they do not form segments of a single line. Further, the slope of the regression of group means is greater than the slope within groups. In this instance the adjustment on within-group regression lines to the grand mean of x preserves a set of differentials in the adjusted y means which are positively correlated with composition on x. This kind of "contextual effect" would appear in a cross-tabulation of y by group and individual values of x even where the marginals were controlled properly. Algebraically, the observation that $b_w < b_h$ imples that

$$p_{\overline{Y}C} = b_w \sqrt{\frac{C_{xxb}}{C_{yyb}}} < r_{xyb}. \tag{2.25}$$

Thus, the product $r_{CR}p_{\overline{Y}R}$ must be greater than zero, and the assumption that $p_{\overline{Y}R} > 0$ implies $r_{CR} > 0$. This is a degenerate case of the analysis of covariance from the experimental point of view because it would not appear if individuals were assigned randomly to groups.

As indicated by the representation of r_{CR} as an unanalyzed relationship in Figure 2.2, it is misleading to interpret $r_{CR}p_{\overline{Y}R}$, the indirect component of the between-group correlation, as a "contextual effect" of x on y. Because R is a residual, its content can not be defined except in residual terms, as "the effect on the group means in y of variables not directly measured." The substantive interpretation of a "contextual effect" of this kind invariably requires the identification of the residual variable with a particular set of unmeasured variables.

In the studies of "school socioeconomic contexts", for example, a situation like that in panel B is commonly interpreted as evidence of the influence of normative climate or peer interaction in the school or neighborhood (Michael, 1961; Coleman et al., 1966; Pettigrew, 1968; Wilson, 1967). While it may be difficult to measure and interpret such factors, they are accessible to direct empirical treatment (Duncan, Haller and Portes, 1968; Campbell and

Alexander, 1965); the identification of residual variation with effects of particular variables places the investigator under some obligation to demonstrate that those variables perform as advertised. The place to begin is not the between-group segment of the model, but the within-group segment. Neither normative climates nor peer groups are homogeneous within schools. This form of "contextual" analysis depends on the explicit assumption of a particular relationship among at least two variable characteristics of individuals. The observation that such a relationship does not account for a pattern of intergroup differentials is not a license for speculative *post hoc* explanation; it is an indication of unsatisfactory explanation.

An additional example is given in panel C of Figure 2.3. It is an extreme form of that in panel B where the within-group regression lines are still parallel, but b_w and b_b differ in sign. It is easy to show in this case, that of the "inverse structural effects" described by Blau (1960:182-183, 191-192), that $r_{CR} < 0$ if we assume $p_{\bar{Y}R} > 0$. Panel C corresponds to the famous example from *The American Soldier* (Stouffer et al., 1949:252): the individual soldier's satisfaction with policies of military promotion varied directly with promotion within units, while average satisfaction varied inversely with promotion rates between units. To interpret this and similar findings in terms of relative deprivation or reference group theory requires one to postulate that the variable, internalized level of expectation intervenes between individual promotion and level of satisfaction (Merton and Kitt, 1950: 45-46). The theory is not proved valid by a negative between-group regression; its validation requires measurement of the intervening variable.

The argument up to this point may be summarized by decomposing the total correlation between x_{ij} and y_{ij}. We can write

$$r_{xyT} = r_{xyw} \sqrt{1 - E^2_{XG}} \sqrt{1 - E^2_{YG}} + E_{XG}E_{YG} (r_{xyb}) \qquad (2.26)$$

or

$$r_{XY} = r_{xy}p_{Xx}p_{Yy} + p_{XC}p_{Y\bar{Y}} (p_{\bar{Y}C} + r_{CR}p_{\bar{Y}R}). \qquad (2.27)$$

That is, the total correlation of x and y is a function of the within-and between-group relationships of x and y and the degree to which x and y values are clustered within groups (Duncan, Cuzzort and Duncan, 1961: 64-67). The expression for the "ecological" correlation, $r_{xyb} = p_{\bar{Y}C} + r_{CR}p_{\bar{Y}R}$, is a function of both the net effect of composition implied by the within-group regression and the association of composition with residual factors. Thus the validity of the first type of contextual analysis rests on the identification of the product term with unmeasured variables, processes, or social forces of the investigator's preference. This dangerous procedure ignores what has aptly been described as "the unlimited capability of the human intellect for producing plausible explanations by the carload lot" (Brownlee, 1960:491; see also Blalock, 1961).

In expressions 2.26 and 2.27 it is also clear that the values of the within- and between-group correlations, but not the value of the total correlation, vary with the set of categoric boundaries that are applied to the population. This was demonstrated by the shift in values of the "ecological" correlation in Robinson's color-literacy example as the areal units were changed from states to census divisions. The same problem is created artificially when investigators merge data on social groups which are relatively homogeneous with respect to values on the covariate, as has sometimes been recommended (Davis, Spaeth and Huson, 1961; Riley, 1964)—a procedure which tends not only to reduce the intergroup variation of both the covariate and the dependent variable but also to distort the values of the within- and between-group coefficients of correlation and regression. If a set of social groups forms the units of analysis, then it is obviously useful to preserve in the course of data reduction as much as possible of what is unique to each group. In the analysis of covariance this may be accomplished by treating each observed collectivity as a separate category.

Nonadditive Contextual Effects

The second type of contextual effect is formally identical with the observation of statistical interaction of treatment and covariate. This situation, where the within-group regression lines are not parallel, is depicted in panel D of Figure 2.3. The validity of the covariance adjustment depends on the assumption that the average within-group regression slope,

$$b_w = \frac{C_{xyw}}{C_{xxw}}, \tag{2.28}$$

describes the relationship between x and y in every group. We can also calculate a within-group regression slope for every subgroup,

$$b_j = \frac{C_{xyj}}{C_{xxj}}, \tag{2.29}$$

which may or may not be identical to b_w. Differences among the b_j reduce or eliminate the descriptive validity of the covariance adjustment in the interpretation of group differences. While the preceding exposition has assumed the comparison of adjusted y-means at the grand mean of x, it is clear from panels A, B, and C of Figure 2.3 that the outcome of such a comparison does not vary with respect to the value of x at which the comparison is made. In those cases adjustment to the grand mean of x is simply a convention with particular cogency in the presence of mild interaction. On the other hand, in the situation in panel D, a comparison of means adjusted on observed within-group regression lines obviously depends on the value of x at which the comparison is made, and the average within-group regression line has no descriptive validity.

Before we interpret data like those in panel D as showing the "contextual effect" of group composition, it is useful to satisfy four conditions: (1) statistically significant interaction; (2) substantively significant interaction; (3) inclusion of multiple covariates or transformation of variables; and (4) observation of a definite relationship between group composition and regression slopes. The substantive interpretation of differences in regression coefficients which could be attributed to sampling error is obviously not recommended. Schuessler (1969) describes cases where this stricture was not observed. More important, the presence of statistically significant interactions in large sample studies need not indicate that nonadditivity is of great substantive import. In such cases the magnitude of the interactions should be considered in deciding whether to calculate covariance adjustments. Calculation of covariance adjustments may also be justified by the absence of any obvious basis for interpreting the observed interactions. Interaction in zero order relationships may sometimes be eliminated by mathematical transformation of the data or by the introduction of additional explanatory factors. Again, the advocate of "contextual" analysis must justify on a theoretical basis the inclusion or exclusion of particular variables. Finally, the interpretation of observed interactions as the effects of composition should be justified by *a priori* considerations and by replication. We have found it hard to interpret the interactions in the large body of data used in this study. The apparent cogency of some interpretations of contextual effects may be a function of the limited number of cases to be explained.

III

THE DAVIDSON
COUNTY
DATA

The Davidson County data were obtained from student questionnaires, school records, school officials and U. S. Census reports.   In this chapter their sources and limitations are described in detail.

The Reseach Site

Davidson County, Tennessee is coextensive with the Nashville Standard Metropolitan Statistical Area (SMSA). As often happens in social research, it was chosen as the site of our research as much because an appropriate body of local data was available as because of theoretical objectives. The student survey and school record search were carried out in 1957 by Professor Albert J. Reiss, Jr., and Albert Lewis Rhodes as part of a larger study of conforming and deviating behavior among adolescents (Reiss and Rhodes, 1959). The combination of a rich set of variables with a large number of observations invited secondary analysis. On the other hand, if we had secured data from a national sample or from one of the larger metropolitan areas, we might have been more confident of the general applicability of the study. Should our findings be treated as anything more than illustrations of an analytic method? With some cautions the query can be answered in the affirmative.

Nashville is not one of the leading metropolitan centers of the United States (Duncan *et al.*, 1960:433-437), but for our purpose it is important to think of it as an aggregate of consuming rather than of producing units. While the relationship between a city's economic role and its population structure are well documented (Duncan and Reiss, 1956), it seems likely that metropolitan areas are more heterogeneous in regard to roles in the national division of labor than in the organization of a local service like secondary education. Indeed, the essential homogeneity in the organization of public educational services is amply documented by a recent national inventory (Coleman *et al.*, 1966).

Several illustrative comparisons between the population of the Nashville SMSA and that of the metropolitan United States are presented in Table 3.1. In many respects the two populations are similar. However, residents of the Nashville SMSA rank lower on most socio-economic indexes than the residents of the metropolitan United States—a differential which can in part be attributed to Nashville's higher proportion of Negroes. There is probably greater similarity between the white population of the Nashville SMSA and of the metropolitan United States than between their total populations. The characteristics of the research site do not appear to pose a major obstacle to cautious generalization from the analysis of the schooling process which we will develop in later chapters. Still, as the analysis proceeds, specific empirical findings will be compared with those of national studies wherever possible. We will show that the elimination of certain subpopulations from the analysis probably limits the generality of findings more than does the character of the research site.

The Study Population

In 1957 the Nashville SMSA contained two jurisdictions, the City of Nashville and the remainder of Davidson County, which have since been consolidated in a single metropolitan government. The school survey of nearly all students in grades seven through twelve was conducted in two waves during the year. Students enrolled in city schools were enumerated in April, and those in county schools in October and November. Case records were compared to make sure that students moving from city to county schools between the spring and autumn field operations were not counted twice. Unfortunately the interval between the two enumerations confounded city-county differences with those arising from the stage of the academic year when the data were collected. For example, a twelfth-grade city student was enumerated at the close of his senior year, in the class of 1957, but a twelfth-grade county student was enumerated at the beginning of his senior year, in the class of 1958. In addition to influencing students' responses the time-lag may have produced some irregularities in the data obtained from cumulative school records. Moreover, the questionnaires administered to city and county students were not identical. For our purpose the most important disparity was that aspirations were ascertained only from students in county schools. Consequently, in some analyses city and county

Table 3.1—Characteristics of the population of the Nashville SMSA and of the population of the United States in metropolitan areas, 1960

	Nashville SMSA	All metropolitan areas
Population	399,473	112,885,178
Share of U.S. total	0.2%	62.9%
In central city	42.8%	51.8%
In ring	57.2%	48.2%
Change, 1950-1960	24.2%	26.4%
Central city	—2.0%	10.7%
Ring	55.2%	48.6%
Residence:		
Urban	87.7%	88.2%
Rural farm	1.3%	1.5%
Nonwhite	19.2%	11.7%
Migrant, 1955-1960	16.9%	17.4%
Moved to present house after 1958	30.2%	25.7%
Median age:		
Male	27.5 years	29.2 years
Female	29.5 years	30.9 years
Children ever born per 1000 ever-married women, 35-44	2,433	2,327
Married women, husband present, in labor force	36.2%	31.3%
Unemployment rate	3.5%	5.0%
Employed persons in:		
White-collar occupations	45.9%	45.6%
Manufacturing industries	23.1%	29.0%
Family income:		
Median	$5,332	$6,324
Less than $3,000	23.5%	15.1%
Years of schooling completed:		
Less than 5 years	9.5%	7.0%
Twelve or more years	39.3%	44.2%
Median years	10.3 years	11.1 years
Persons 14-17 years old enrolled in school	87.3%	88.1%

Source: Information from U.S. Bureau of the Census, *City and County Data Book, 1962,* (A Statistical Abstract Supplement), (Washington, D.C.: U.S. Government Printing Office, 1962), Tables 3 and 6; and U.S. Bureau of the Census, *U.S. Census of Population, 1960, Volume I, Characteristics of the Population, Part I, U.S. Summary,* (Washington, D.C.: U.S. Government Printing Office, 1964), Tables 33, 101, 142, 143, 287 and 294.

students were separated. The emphasis of the study was on the process of schooling in the metropolitan area as a whole, and the occasional separate treatment accorded the city and county segments is not intended to suggest any ideal-typical comparisons between the central city and suburban areas.

Social background characteristics and a variety of attitudes were learned from questionnaires administered "anonymously" by homeroom teachers during special 50-minute periods. In a few cases the time limit prevented the completion of data files. The items in each questionnaire included the sex of the student and the month and day of his birth. Completed questionnaires were sealed in separate batches by homeroom section. Using each homeroom teacher's list of students to whom the questionnaire had been given, the appropriate batch of cumulative record folders was obtained and matched within batches by sex and birthdate.

The investigators estimated that about five percent of the population enrolled in cooperating schools was missed because of absences from school on the day the questionnaire was administered. No effort was made to reach those students. It was suggested that the absentees were "more likely to be boys than girls, older than younger, [of] lower than [of] upper occupational status, and deviant (e.g., truant and delinquent) than conforming pupils" (Reiss and Rhodes, 1959:II-21). Loss of school record data through failure to complete the matching process affected only about one-half of one percent of the cases (*ibid.,* p. 12). As will be seen, the absence of information from matched records was a greater problem.

Several sequentially imposed restrictions on the definition of the study population reduced it from the original 21,679 questionnaires which were totally or partially filled out to a final deck of 16,893 cases. The comments in the paragraph above apply to completeness of coverage of the total school population, and it is likely that coverage was better in the study population than in the total school population.

There were 21,444 usable cases in the original analysis decks. All of the cases in three groups of schools were excluded from the analysis. First, in 1957 there were segregated Negro and white school systems in both the city of Nashville and the remainder of Davidson County. The 3,310 students in Negro schools were dropped from the analysis because the data on so many of them were incomplete. The second group was dropped because of possible bias due to selective coverage. It consisted of 507 students from two private schools which had participated in the survey. (An additional seven percent of the population enrolled in secondary school was estimated to attend other private schools.) Finally, we excluded from the analysis 734 students enrolled in courses appropriate to more than one grade in school, in special classes or in ungraded schools. The residually defined study population included 16,893 white students enrolled in regular grades of the public secondary schools in the Nashville metropolitan area.

In order to cover the population we had to assign grades in 972 cases where grade in school was judged to be incorrect. Case record numbers were assigned consecutively within homeroom sections by sex; all of the cases with grade unstated occurred in such clusters. By ordering the card files on case record numbers, we were able to separate students into homeroom sections which could be assumed to be homogeneous with respect to grade, and we could assign each student to a grade on the basis of the modal age in his homeroom. A validation of this method in one large school where all of the grades were ascertained produced 82 percent agreement between assigned and true grades. In two schools none of the cases specified grade; these accounted for 592 of the assignments which we made ourselves in the manner just described. In a third school known to include students in grades seven through nine, no students were coded as eighth graders, and there were roughly twice as many "seventh" as ninth graders. The assignment algorithm was applied to all of the "seventh" grade students in order to create 313 for the "eighth" grade. In a fourth school the procedure was used to assign grade in 67 cases where double punches had occurred in two segments of the card file.

Davidson County students attended 41 schools, of which eleven were in the city and the remainder were in the county ring. Thirty-four schools were represented at grades seven and eight, twenty-one schools at grade nine and seventeen schools at grades ten to twelve. There was no consistent division between upper- and lower-level secondary schools. City schools covered grades seven to nine, seven to twelve and ten to twelve, while county schools covered grade seven only, grade eight only, grades seven and eight, seven to nine, seven to twelve, nine to twelve and ten to twelve.

The Variables

The questionnaire used in the Nashville school survey included a wealth of items relevant to educational outcomes (Reiss and Rhodes, 1959). Because we planned to carry out multivariate analyses on numerous subgroups of the population, we would have produced indigestible quantities of output if we had tried to include every interesting variable in the sociological or social-psychological literature. Hence, we selected variables for the analysis which reflected our concern with the effect of socioeconomic background on educational outcomes. The variables are discussed below under four headings: categoric variables, school characteristics, questionnaire items and school record data.

Categoric Variables

The categoric variables are school attended, grade, sex, place of residence and length of residence at current address. One of our prime concerns was the estimation of school effects, and school attended was used as a categoric variable throughout the analysis. We used grade and sex (with the occasional addition of place of residence) to define subgroups in which basic analyses were replicated. Throughout the analysis the terms "school" or "grade cohort" are used interchangeably to denote the students or the characteristics of the students in a single grade and of the same sex who were attending a given school in 1957. (As used here, the term "school" rarely refers to all of the students at various levels who attended school in a single building.)

There were no missing data on school attended, place of residence or sex, and, as reported above, we assigned grade where it had not been specified. The distribution of students by residence, grade and sex is shown in Table 3.2; roughly two-thirds attended county schools, and one-third attended city schools. The inverse relationship between grade and number of students presumably reflects transfers to private schools, dropouts and the increasing size of birth cohorts during and after World War II. Aspirations were ascertained only from students in county schools, and the county totals are the maximum numbers of observations on which relationships involving those variables are based.

Residual mobility may obscure the degree to which a school affects educational performances, and it may also affect the completeness of school records. Thus, length of residence at current address has been used as a control variable in the examination of the size of between-school variations in students' characteristics and of rates of non-ascertainment of school record

Table 3.2.—Number of white students by residence, grade and sex: public secondary schools, Nashville, Tennessee, 1957

Residence	Grade in school and sex					
	7	8	9	10	11	12
	Males					
Total	1780	1823	1627	1294	918	783
City	591	647	438	432	211	245
County	1189	1176	1189	862	707	538
	Females					
Total	1775	1861	1649	1446	1012	925
City	624	617	491	518	291	288
County	1151	1244	1158	928	721	637

data. No more than four percent of the students in any grade-sex subgroup failed to report length of residence.

Characteristics of the School

At best, school characteristics are gross measures of educational variables. The only value of a school characteristic which can be associated with a student is its value for all of the students in his school. Here, we treat two kinds of school characteristics which have been of special interest to sociologists: the composition of the population of the school and of the neighborhood. Within each grade-sex subgroup the composition of the student body was measured by assigning to each school the arithmetic mean of its students on each variable ascertained from questionnaires or from school records. Neighborhood characteristics were ascertained by approximating school districts with 1960 census tracts and aggregating characteristics of the white population and white-occupied housing units. Some error was introduced at each stage of that process: in ascertaining the boundaries of school districts, in equating school districts with census tracts, in using 1960 census data to characterize 1957 school districts, and in eliminating data on the nonwhite population and nonwhite-occupied housing units.

Because of the governmental consolidation in Davidson County, neither the city nor the county school system still existed in 1967. It was easy to locate each school; it was quite another thing to find the exact boundaries of school districts in 1957. The head of the attendance office of the combined school system sketched a set of boundaries of county school districts for us by drawing upon his records and his recollections. We located the city's district boundaries with greater accuracy, for we found zoning maps for the school year, 1956-57, in a School Board warehouse. Thus, we were able to redraw the boundaries on large-scale census tract base maps. Where school districts varied by grade, as in the case of a junior-senior high school with several junior-high feeder schools, we drew a map for each grade which had a distinct attendance area. Census tracts were fitted to school districts by visual inspection and verified by data on city blocks. Where a tract was completely enclosed in a single school district, it could, of course, be assigned unambiguously to that district. Where a tract was partially enclosed in a school district, and the enclosed area contained a substantial portion of the street grid in the tract, we drew upon the data on city blocks. If the partially enclosed area of the tract contained mainly white-occupied housing units, the tract was assigned to the partially enclosing school district with a weight of one-half. Otherwise, it was dropped from the district.

In aggregating the census tract data we eliminated the characteristics of the nonwhite population and of nonwhite-occupied housing units wherever possible by the device just described. In other cases we subtracted the characteristics of nonwhites in tracts containing 400 or more nonwhites or 100 or more nonwhite-occupied housing units. All of the neighborhood characteristics were in the form of percentages of ratios for which the numerator and denominator were aggregated separately; thus, they were weighted averages of the characteristics of component tracts of a school district.

Several variables were generated from the tract data: percentage of the population over 25 years old with at least a high-school education; percentage of husband-and-wife families with children of school age; percentage of the population over five years old living in the same house in 1955 and 1960; percentage of families with incomes below $3000 in 1959; rate of participation in the labor force of married women living with their husbands; percentage of employed men who were professionals, technicians, managers, officials or proprietors; percentage of housing units occupied by their owners; ratio of sound housing units to all occupied housing units; ratio of housing units in structures built in 1939 or earlier to all occupied housing units; and percentage of occupied housing units with 1.01 or more persons per room. The first two of these indexes proved about as powerful as any plausible combination of two or three of them, and only the first was used in many parts of the analysis.

The definitions of school district boundaries were also used to approximate geographic feeding patterns in the school system. That is, we assumed that the 1957 boundaries were about the same as those in earlier and later years. Under that assumption, the 1957 boundaries indicated where students in the lower grades would attend school in later years. Because school districts were larger in the higher grades, the same assumption was not as dependable in determining where students at higher levels had gone to school in earlier years. Still, we were able to match school data on grade cohorts in the upper and lower grades and the matched data made possible a crude synthetic cohort analysis of organizational change in the schools.

The Student Questionnaires

The student questionnaires provided data on socioeconomic background, membership in school organizations, father's educational aspiration, and educational and occupational aspirations. The socioeconomic background variables were father's occupation (X), father's education (V), number of siblings (S), and intactness of family (F). Father's occupation (X) was ascertained from the questions:

"Does your father have a job?"
"What kind of a title does your father give his job? (Like minister, salesman in a store, barber, plumber's helper, or truck driver)"
"What kind of work does he do on his job? (Like if he's a truck driver, does he drive a gravel truck or a milk truck?)"

Occupations were originally coded into a set of 100 titles, and these were assigned two-digit scores in Duncan's socioeconomic index for occupations (Reiss, Duncan and Hatt, 1961). Where the occupation title included Census titles which differed in socioeconomic status (SES), it was assigned the average of the scores of the Census titles, weighted according to occupational composition in the Nashville SMSA in 1960. Some arbitrary assignments were made where no exact match existed between occupational titles in the original code and in the Census code. Unemployed and retired fathers were assigned the SES code of the last occupation they held, when that information was given. Father's educational attainment (V) was ascertained from the question:

"How far did your father go in school?"

Responses were coded from 1 to 6 in the categories: less than eight years of school; eight years of school; one to three years of high school;

completed high school; one to three years of college; graduated from college. Number of siblings (S) was ascertained from four questions in the form:

"How many (older) (younger) (brothers) (sisters) do you have?"

The question may appear unnecessarily complicated for the present purpose, but it was originally used to determine sibling position as well as the number of siblings. Intact family (F) is a dummy variable which distinguished students living with two real or adoptive parents from all other students. Students were asked, "Whom do you live with now?", and the family was coded non-intact if the student responded "real mother only, real father only, or other."

Rates of response to each of the background items were satisfactory, the lowest rate being 82.3 percent to father's occupation among 7th grade boys. Most of the grade-sex specific response rates were greater than 95 percent. Girls were more likely than boys to provide codifiable responses, and students in higher grades were more likely to provide codifiable responses than those in lower grades. Rates of response by grade and sex were reported by Hauser (1968:64, 72) for all of the student variables (from questionnaires and school records). Rates of response to the background items are comparable to those of younger cohorts in the OCG survey (Blau and Duncan, 1967:472).

Organizational membership (O) was ascertained from the question:

"Do you belong to school organizations, clubs, or activities?"

Students circled the number of groups to which they belonged. Responses were coded from 0 to 7 with an upper open interval coded 8. Organizational membership is interpreted as an index of the integration of the student into school activities outside the classroom. This is not necessarily a good measure of student integration into the society of age-peers since it does include both academic and non-academic activities, and does not include activities not approved by the school. Rates of response to the question on organizational membership were comparable with those to the family background items.

Three items were designed to tap a student's perception of what his parents expected of him as an adult: his father's and mother's hopes for his education and the parents' hopes for his eventual occupation. The first two of these were frequently identical; in entire schools no student reported discrepant parental educational aspirations. This may have resulted from the design of the questionnaire rather than from failure of the students' perception. The rates of response to the question on parents' occupational aspiration were about 60 percent in each grade. For that reason, only father's educational aspiration (Z) was used in the final analysis. It was ascertained from the question:

"What grade in school or year in college have your parents always wanted you to finish before you quit going to school?

Mother .... Father ...."

Nearly all of the responses named the categories, "high school" or "college graduation," but the code retained the original detail. While response rates in grade twelve (82.9 per cent of boys and 90.8 percent of girls) were only slightly lower than those discussed above, the differences by grade and sex were much stronger here. Only 57.6 percent of seventh-grade boys and 72.0 percent of seventh-grade girls reported their fathers' aspirations. Younger students may have a less clear notion of their parents' hopes for them than older students, but the differential may also have been produced by attrition between the seventh and twelfth grades. The fact that grade differentials in response were stronger in the case of father's aspiration than in that of other self-reported items does suggest that the salience of parental aspirations increases as the student progresses through school.

Occupational (T) and educational (J) aspirations were ascertained only from students attending schools in the county ring. The questionnaire items were:

"What grade in school or year in college do you want to finish before you quit going to school?"

and

"What kind of job do you want to have when you quit school? (Like minister, salesman, plumber, or truck driver)"

Educational aspiration (T) was coded in the same way as father's educational aspiration. Occupational aspiration (J) was originally coded in major occupation groups and recoded as a two-digit score of the Duncan index (Rhodes, Reiss and Duncan, 1965:683). The rates of response to the question on educational aspiration ranged from 88.3 percent to 98.6 percent. Even with "housewife" coded as a nonresponse the rates for occupational aspiration were only slightly lower. On occupational aspiration the sex differential nearly disappeared, and the grade differentials were small for both variables.

School Record Data

From cumulative record folders we obtained measures of intelligence (Q), Stanford Mathematics Grade Equivalent (M), Stanford Reading Grade Equivalent (W), arithmetic mark (A), and English mark (E). In most cases intelligence was ascertained from Otis or Kuhlmann-Anderson group-administered tests. In a small number of cases scores were obtained from individually administered tests. In both the city and county school systems intelligence tests were administered in every odd-numbered grade; that is, eleventh-grade scores should have been recorded for eleventh- and twelfth-graders, ninth-grade scores for ninth- and tenth-graders, and seventh-grade scores for seventh and eighth-graders. However, because the data on county students were obtained at the beginning of a school year, this may not always have been the case. That is, in the case of eleventh-grade county students intelligence may have been measured as early as the ninth grade, of ninth-grade students as early as the seventh grade, and of seventh-grade students as early as the fifth grade.

Academic achievement and course marks of students in the eighth grade and above were ostensibly recorded as of the eighth grade and of the younger students as of the seventh grade. Here, again, there was probably some error because of the interval between the two occasions of collecting data. While the decision to record these variables as of the eighth grade for the older students increased their rates of nonascertainment, it was defensible on *a priori* grounds. In the lower grades it could be assumed that students were enrolled in courses for which it would be valid to compare grades. It was also desirable to measure achievement no later than course marks and to avoid a ceiling effect on the achievement test scores. The Stanford Grade Equivalents ranged from grade one to grade eleven on each of the variables.

Marks in arithmetic and English were originally given numerically in the city schools and alphabetically in the county schools, but we equated the two systems thus: A=90+, B=80-89, C—70-79, D=60-69, E=0-59. In the present study marks were simply recoded on a five-point scale. Because of these arbitrary procedures marks in city and county schools were analyzed separately, but few interpretable differences appeared.

The rates of ascertainment of marks in arithmetic and English were close to ninety percent in each grade for both sexes while those of intelligence were about eighty percent and these, too, varied little by sex or grade. On the two measures of academic achievement the rates of ascertainment were substantially lower, and there was a marked tendency for rates of ascertainment to vary inversely with grade. Achievement scores on mathematics and reading were obtained for about 80 percent of the seventh graders, but only about 55 percent of the twelfth graders.

Because of the possibility of bias, an effort was made to find out what produced the low rates of ascertainment of academic achievement (Hauser, 1968:74-78). A more detailed examination of response rates revealed differentials by residence as well as grade in school. Academic achievement was less likely to have been ascertained in the case of county than of city students. Apparently the major factors accounting for the low rates of ascertainment of students in the higher grades and in county schools were residential mobility and the time-lag in data collection. It turned out that students in the city and in lower grades were more likely than others to have moved recently. On the other hand, the interval within which moving could affect the availability of an early achievement test score was greater in older than younger students and in those enumerated at the beginning rather than at the end of the academic year. In addition, one large school's policy of discarding all achievement test scores had the effect of lowering the county rates of ascertainment.

Bivariate Nonresponse

The computing routine used in the analysis of covariance eliminated cases for which data were not available on both members of any pair of individual variates. In such cases the estimators of bivariate relationships were manipulated to perform multivariate analyses. This meant that entries in a correlation matrix were not all based on the same cases. At the risk of algebraic inconsistency, then, we used more of the data than we would have by dropping all cases where any of the data were missing. The procedure is especially important because data were missed for any of several independent reasons. If there were a strong tendency for data to be absent on one variable whenever they were absent on another, it would not matter much which procedure were used. Each estimated relationship would be based on the same cases, and the effective response rate would not be much lower than that of the worst single variable. On the other hand, if data were missed for independent reasons, we would rapidly run out of cases which had data present on several variables at once. In the present instance the causes of loss of data were not the same for items from the questionnaire as from school records, and the use of bivariate estimators in multivariate analyses became important.

Bivariate response rates of twelfth grade boys were examined in detail. In that subgroup rates of response to the self-reported items were high, while the rates of ascertainment of the school record items were quite low. The joint response rates in most of the pairs of self-reported items exceeded 80 percent, but there was some tendency for nonresponse to be correlated. For example, the univariate response rates to X and V were 89.0 and 95.1 percent, respectively, and their joint response rate was 86.7 percent. The maximum joint response rate was 89 percent, and the minimum was $(95.1 - (1-89.0)) = 84.1$ percent. The observed joint response rate was 2.6 percentage points higher than the minimum and 2.1 percentage points higher than the level of $84.6\% = 89.0\% \times 95.1\%$, which would have been observed if nonresponse to the two items were uncorrelated. Still, 8.4 percent of the students reported V but not X, and 2.3 percent reported X but not V. This pattern is typical of the joint response rates among the questionnaire items. The deviations of observed rates from those expected on the hypothesis of independence were all non-negative, ranging from 0 to 3.3 percentage points, with an average value of 1.4 percentage points.

Non-ascertainment of the school record data, on the other hand, was highly intercorrelated. The extreme case was that of M and W, for which 53.9 and 52.6 percent of the cases had known values, and the joint rate was 51.8 percent—only 0.8 percentage points lower than the maximum and 23.4 percentage points higher than expected under conditions of independence. The results for the joint distributions of the other school record data were similar, though less extreme. However, rates of response to the questionnaire and school record items were weakly associated. The deviations of observed values from those expected under conditions of independence were small, and in several cases they were negative.

One consequence of nonresponse was a simple loss of degrees of freedom but that gave us little difficulty because there were so many cases. Biased estimators are a second possible consequence of nonresponse. We have already established that missing data on the school record items were associated with grade, residence and mobility, and there probably was some selection by ability to complete the self-reported items as well. In short, the possibility of nonresponse bias cannot easily be dismissed. The disastrous consequences of ignoring selective nonresponse on univariate statistics are common knowledge; but this study made very little use of univariate estimators. Less is known about the effects of bias in nonresponse on bivariate or multivariate statistics. If the biases are additive and do not greatly reduce variance, their effects need not be large. Indeed, there is some lore to the effect that nonresponse does not affect statistics of relationship—but little research to verify it.

In our study the major reason for concern about nonresponse bias is the low rate of ascertainment of school record data. Some indirect evidence of the possibility of bias was obtained from twelfth-grade boys. The relationships among several variables were compared for students for whom Q, M, and W were known and unknown. We assumed that markedly different relationships between the school record items and the other variables in the two subgroups would be reflected in different relationships among the other variables. Because residential mobility and school system were already known to affect ascertainment of the school record data, we also controlled those variables. We found that the relationships among the questionnaire items were much the same in each category of the ascertainment-residence-mobility classification.

Linearity

The use of covariance analysis and multiple correlation analysis in our study was based on the assumption that relationships among the interval variables are linear. The assumption of linearity requires that interpretations would not be substantially changed if an independent variable were raised to a power other than one. No exhaustive effort was made to test this assumption. There is a long history of use of linear methods in analyses involving the variables treated here; moreover, apparent nonlinearity in bivariate relationships may disappear when additional variables are introduced. Still, we tested for nonlinearity in the relationships between the variables among the twelfth-grade boys attending schools in the county ring. We examined nearly every bivariate relationship treated in the study but found no substantial evidence of nonlinearity. In only 5 of 66 relationships we examined did the departure from linearity achieve significance at the .05 level and the proportions of variance involved in those cases were substantively trivial. Examination of scatter diagrams of those and other relationships provided no evidence that the departure could be eliminated by any simple transformation of the variables.

IV

SCHOOL
EFFECTS

In this chapter we examine the size and persistence of the effects of schools in detail. We repeat that the absence of effects would not imply that "what happens in school" contributed nothing to the preparation of children for adult role performance. In order to understand "what happens in school" we must examine all the variation in educational performance, and most of that variation occurs within schools.

The effects of schools may reveal themselves in two ways: in variation among schools in the educational performance of their students and in the operation of variables which influence educational performance within schools. To use the language of covariance analysis, the first type of effect is a difference among school means, an additive effect which contributes to between-school variance, while the second type is variation in the slopes of within-school regression lines, a nonadditive or interaction effect. Either may be produced by differences in the selection of students, in resources or in day-to-day functioning. In interpreting between-school variance we can examine (a) overall or gross differences in the composition of student bodies; (b) net differences in levels of school performance which remain after other causal factors have been taken into account; and (c) associations of gross and net differences with global characteristics of the school or school district. We have noted (Chapter II) that the use of average within-school slopes in the statistical adjustment of levels of school performance is equivocal if the within-school slopes differ among schools; thus, the interpretation of additive school effects depends on the assumption that there are no large nonadditive effects.

Studies of School Effects

This chapter has two major parts: a review of studies of school effects below the college level and a presentation of preliminary findings in the Nashville SMSA. In both parts we are concerned with the comparability of the Nashville data and with the substantive interpretation of gross and net differences between schools. In the review four topics are considered: (1) the size of gross school differences; (2) the interpretation of gross school differences; (3) the interpretation of net school differences and (4) the size of nonadditive school effects.

Size of Gross School Differences

The gross effect of the school on an educational performance in a population of students can be expressed by the correlation ratio of performance on school attended or by its square, the proportion of variance lying between schools. Although there have been at least three national surveys and numerous smaller studies concerned with school effects, correlation ratios have been reported in few instances. Most of the numerical results reported below are based on our own calculations from published data, the Project Talent and *Equality of Educational Opportunity (EEO)* results being the major exceptions. In a report on the 1960 national survey of Project Talent, Flanagan and his associates (1962: Chapter XI, p. 1) ignore the magnitude of school differences through most of their discussion, but conclude:

> Nearly all of the students in some high schools achieve at a relatively high level, while the opposite is found in other schools . . . . On most achievement tests the standard deviation for school means is about 60 percent as great as the standard deviation for scores of individual students.

The 60 percent figure implies that some 36 percent of the achievement variance lies between schools. Nowhere does the report show that this statement applies to the study population as a whole, which included most students in nearly 1400 U. S. high schools. At one point the requisite data are presented for 10th grade students (*ibid.*, Chapter V, p. 7). Between-school variance ranges from 35 percent among boys on a general information test to 28 percent among all students on English achievement, 25 percent on reading comprehension, 18 percent on creativity, and 19 percent on achievement in mathematics. Apparently, the size of gross school effects depends on the educational performance under investigation. *EEO* (Coleman *et al.,* 1966:292-295) displays percentages of variance lying between schools in verbal and non-verbal components of achievement and ability by ethnic-regional group (averaged over grade) and by grade (averaged over ethnic-regional group). Few of these figures are larger than 20 percent in any large population subgroup. The Project Talent and *EEO* results are not directly comparable; the former pertain to all students in a single grade, and the latter are calculated separately for ethnic-regional groups.

EEO *(ibid.,* p. 296) also presents percentages of variance lying between schools in the verbal component of ability by grade in school and ethnic-regional group. Among whites in the South the between-school variance is 10 percent at grade twelve and 9 percent at grade nine, and the between-school variance is even smaller in the case of northern whites. When only the four major racial-regional groups are considered, the gross school effects on southern Negroes are largest, 23% in grade twelve and 20% in grade nine. While the Project Talent and *EEO* surveys measured educational variables other than ability and achievement, it was not possible to ascertain correlation ratios for those other performances from published tabulations.

In several studies of the effect of the school on aspiration the data have been aggregated for groups of schools with similar values on a socioeconomic index (Michael, 1961; Wilson, 1959, 1963, 1967; Krauss, 1964; Boyle, 1966a; Turner, 1964; McDill and Coleman, 1965; Sewell and Armer, 1966a). Both the aggregation procedure and the use of an index of status to represent the school reduce the amount of variability that might properly be attributed to the schools as units on a gross basis. For example, in his analysis of data from a 1955 survey of 35,000 seniors in 500 U. S. high schools, Michael presents rates of planning to attend college among students in the top quartile on the Scholastic Aptitude Test (SAT) in each of five "high school climates." The "climates" were defined by the proportion of students in each school with high rank on a composite SES measure. Michael (1961:585) concluded, "the amount of college attendance (sic) varies radically from one high school to another." In fact, the high school classification accounts for less than nine percent of the variance in college plans within the high ability subgroup. Michael does not substantiate his argument for students at other ability levels. It was also possible to determine that "high school climate" accounts for about five percent of the variance in SAT scores *(ibid.,* pp. 588-593).

In Wilson's study of senior boys in eight high schools in the San Francisco area (1959:839, 842) less than twelve percent of the variance in educational aspiration and in course marks is accounted for by a three-category classification of schools by socioeconomic context. In Wilson's (1963:221) study of sixth-graders in fourteen schools in three "school strata" in Berkeley, the classification of schools accounts for twenty-two percent of the variance in reading achievement, eight percent of the variance in reading mark, and seven percent of the variance in arithmetic mark. In this population the school classification accounts for less than five percent of the boys' variance in educational aspiration (Wilson, 1963:227). In Turner's (1964:56) study of seniors in ten Los Angeles high schools a three-category socioeconomic classification of schools accounts for eleven percent of the boys' variance and five percent of the girls' variance in the proportion planning to complete at least four years of college. Boyle's (1966a:636) four-category classification of seventy high schools by socioeconomic status and metropolitan location accounts for eleven percent of the variance in college plans in a sample of Canadian girls. If the high school has a marked effect on a student's aspiration, it must be obscured by broad socioeconomic groupings of schools (Dubin, 1969:196-197).

In some studies schools were chosen to represent extremes rather than any actual distribution of levels of performance. Still, gross school effects are not large. For example, Shaycoft retested a panel of 1963 seniors who were in the 1960 Project Talent sample as ninth graders. They were chosen from a "wide variety of schools representing as many different strata in all respects as possible" (Shaycoft, 1967:2-2). On six key mental tests the proportions of variance lying between schools in the ninth grade ranged from 9.8 percent to 22.5 percent, and in the twelfth grade they ranged from 13.2 percent to 18.5 percent (*ibid.,* Table 6-1a, Table 7-2d). In *The Adolescent Society* Coleman studied ten schools in Illinois, which were "selected not for their similarities nor their 'representativeness' but for their differences" (Coleman, 1961a:58). By combining the results of a histogram showing the proportions of boys who reported planning on going to college (p. 114) with numbers of observations on the nine largest schools reported elsewhere in the text (p. 241), we find that less than seven percent of the variance in plans lies between schools.

Duncan, Featherman, and Duncan (1968:218) have reported that twelve percent of the variance in college plans lies between schools in the 1957 cohort of Wisconsin high school seniors studied by Sewell and his associates, and eleven percent lies between schools in the case of the North Carolina senior boys studied by Alexander and Campbell. In short, the available evidence consistently favors the conclusion that overall school differences in achievement, course marks and aspiration are small in comparison with their total variability.

Interpretation of Gross School Differences

Several studies of school effects have fallen into the classical pattern of the "ecological" or "aggregative" fallacy by offering social-psychological interpretations of differentials in aggregate levels of performance by aggregate socioeconomic characteristics of the school. From the preceding evidence and the exposition of method in Chapter II it should be clear that, for one thing, such "explanations" are concerned with a small part of the total variation in performance and, for another, that the straightforward use of social-psychological interpretations to account for the differences is unjustified.

For example, Sexton (1961) joins tables of school resources and levels of performance by average family income with an interpretation which is clearly directed to the differential performance of school children by family income. Herriott and St. John (1966) base their extensive analysis of effects of "school SES composition" on the perception of characteristics of schools and of students ascertained from a national sample of teachers and principals. Schools in four perceived socioeconomic status categories at the elementary, junior high, and high-school levels were compared with respect to reports of stability of the home, parental support, level of student achievement, problems of discipline and characteristics of teachers and principals. While Herriott and St. John were careful to maintain that their data pertained to the perception of social class and other characteristics, the putative level of aggregation of the data did not prevent them from deriving most of their hypotheses about student achievement from earlier studies of individuals.

Burkhead and his associates (1967) equated school differences with differences in schooling subject to public control. They performed multiple regression analyses of dropout rates, reading achievement and IQ level and intention to go to college using between-school correlations. Their predictor variables included median family income and a variety of school resources. Analyses were run on schools in Chicago and Atlanta and on the Project Talent subsample of high schools in smaller communities. They entered median family income first in each regression analysis to "control" the "input" characteristics of student bodies. As did Coleman and his associates, they found that other school input factors added little to the effect of socioeconomic composition.

In one of the Project Talent reports Flanagan and his associates (1962) present massive matrices of between-school correlations among educational resources and performances. The report contains an excellent explication of the algebra of the analysis of covariance (Chapter V) but the authors use it only to argue that school means are reliable and not to interpret school differences. A perfunctory effort to control variations in initial characteristics of students was made by constructing a seventeen-category typology of schools by type of curriculum, region, size of city and housing quality and reporting between-school correlations within each cell of the classification.

Because of the limited variance in educational performance which occurs between schools, studies of between-school correlations can tell us little about educational differentials. When such studies identify school characteristics with student characteristics, they are simply wrong, and they produce no useful findings.

Interpretation of Net School Differences

Duncan, Cuzzort, and Duncan (1961:140-141) remarked that the use of "region" as an explanatory variable is justifiable where the reasons for variation among regions are well understood. Where the reasons are unknown, the allusion to region informs us of the places where the causal conditions in question vary, but not of the nature of these conditions. The same observation applies to the use of the school to explain educational performance. The problem is exacerbated by the use of the socioeconomic composition of student bodies as a surrogate for the school, as we have already noted. Since student bodies of similar socioeconomic composition do vary in performance, the procedure leads to underestimates of the gross effect of the school. Further, the use of socioeconomic school classifications multiplies the possibilities of misinterpreting net school effects. Unlike the gross correlational school studies, these studies do attempt to control the socioeconomic status of individual students in cross-tabulations, or they enter both school and student SES measures in multiple regression analyses. The net covariation of level of performance with the schools' socioeconomic composition is then identified as an effect of a normative climate, atmosphere or context, which is usually associated with the functioning of the adolescent peer group in or outside school.

Since the effect of students' status on performance is presumably controlled, the net effect of student body or neighborhood composition can only be attributed to an association of the schools' SES composition with other school variables. There is no basis for assigning specific content to the unmeasured school variables. They might be effects of the peer group, but they might also be attributable to newer buildings, better teachers or more extra-curricular activities. On the argument of Chapter II it would be quite as easy to assume that composition of the student body is a consequence of some unmeasured aspect of school quality. High-status or ambitious parents of unusually bright children may choose to live in areas where schools are reputed to be of high quality. The direction of causation is equivocal.

Further, there is no justification for the use of one or two inadequate statistical controls as a catalyst for the operationally and causally questionable interpretations advanced in studies of the school context (Hauser, 1970). Studies of net school effects have not offered any rationale for the use of control variables beyond the assumption that they affect the dependent variable. As we show in following chapters, the statistical controls used in studies of school effects are inadequate theories of the differentiation of performances within schools. Insofar as the normative or educational processes supposedly indexed by the school's socioeconomic level actually do vary within schools, contextual analyses understate their importance. Finally, insofar as socioeconomic context is used to index the residual effects of the school attended, without regard to the mechanisms by which that influence takes place, the use of the socioeconomic classification of schools also understates those effects, just as it understates gross school effects. For example, Sewell and Armer (1966a) found that neighborhood status in Milwaukee added only 1.8 percent to the variance in college plans explained by sex, ability and socioeconomic status. In Wilson's 1959 data from San Francisco high schools (Tables 5, 7) controlling father's occupational status reduces the residual variance in educational aspirations attributable to the school classification to 4.7 percent, and controlling mother's education alone reduces the variance to 4.9 percent. Turner (1964:60-61) reports that more than three quarters of the difference in educational ambition between high- and low-status schools is eliminated when student background and intelligence are controlled using the method of expected cases. In Boyle's (1966a) data on Canadian girls controlling a composite family background measure reduces the net effect of a school classification from 10.6 to 4.8 percent of the variance. While these residual school effects are not all trivial, they might well be reduced further by controlling other relevant causal factors.

At best, the identification of residual effects of socioeconomic composition with unmeasured normative processes or educational variables is a definition, while at worst it is a dangerous form of speculation since it sounds so much like explanation. The dangers in question are not merely those of inadequate explanation in the scientific sense. Thanks to *Equality of Educational Opportunity* (1966) and *Racial Isolation in the Public Schools* (U. S. Commission on Civil Rights, 1967) the supposed effect of the socioeconomic context on educational performance has become generally accepted as a fact. Reasoning from the observation that socioeconomic status is associated with residual variation in performance among schools, some analysts appear to have taken the position that students of low status will perform better, *ipso facto,* if they are placed in schools with students of higher status (Coleman, 1967:22; Pettigrew, 1968; Cohen, 1968; Yinger, 1968). Indeed, some argue that segregation in the schools by social class contributes more to inequality of educational opportunity than does racial segregation (Wilson, 1969; Pettigrew, 1969). Other analysts have moved toward specifying the nature and effect of the peer culture as it bears on educational performance (Campbell and Alexander, 1965; Duncan, Haller and Portes, 1968; Sewell, Haller and Portes, 1969). In some studies of the value climates of schools normative attributes are carefully measured, but like the studies using gross correlations of school characteristics, they fail to provide a consistent basis on which to interpret the data (McDill, Meyers and Rigsby, 1967; McDill, Rigsby and Meyers, 1969). In a comprehensive review of the literature on school climates, Brown and House (1967:400) report that "the list of climate correlates seems endless." As long as studies of net school effects persist in using inadequate statistical controls and in measuring social processes by miserably crude aggregate operations, they will produce no more valid findings than do gross correlation studies.

Nonadditive School Effects

The second type of contextual effect, nonadditivity, has also been observed but no strong evidence of such effects has appeared. The possibility was suggested by Rogoff (1961a) in reference to a classification of schools by type of community but no strong interaction was apparent in a second article on the subject (1961b) in which she examined the relationships between "family status quintile" and scholastic standing and college plans by size of community in a national sample of high school seniors. Coleman (1959) has argued that students receiving high marks are relatively more intelligent in schools where academic achievement is valued than where it is not. This suggests that the regression of marks on intelligence should be steeper in some schools than in others. The data Coleman presented were from a small sample of schools in Illinois which was designed to represent extreme variation. The substantive importance of the postulated interaction was never established, and the finding has not been replicated. In a similarly unrepresentative sample of schools in Los Angeles, Turner (1964) found that the correlations between background status and an index of aspiration were generally lower in schools low in status than in schools of higher standing but this may have been a result of differences in the slopes of within-school regression lines or in the variance of the independent variables between school contexts. Using the same data as Rogoff, Michael (1961) found an irregular tendency of the effects of socioeconomic status and scholastic ability to increase directly with socioeconomic level of the high school. Again, the substantive importance of the apparent interactions was questionable. Other evidence of nonadditivity can be found in the context studies cited above, but it is not clear whether the findings are of stable interactions or whether they should be attributed to inadequate controls or to unreliably small numbers of observations.

Differences between Schools in the Nashville SMSA

In the rest of the chapter we present major findings on the size and temporal stability of additive and nonadditive effects of schools in the Nashville SMSA. Our aim in doing so is twofold. First, we are now in a position to compare Nashville findings with those from presumably more heterogeneous populations. Second, we can assess school effects more systematically by measuring them in a single population than by reviewing studies which differ greatly in coverage and method.

Size of Gross School Differences

Educational Performance

Table 4.1 displays the percentage of variance in each measure of educational performance which occurs between schools. They are absolute upper limits on the combined influence of all causal factors associated with the school attended. About one-fifth of the variance in academic achievement, one-ninth of the variance in aspirations and one-sixteenth of the variance in course marks may be attributed to gross school effects. There are some fluctuations in percentages of between-school variance from grade to grade and between the sexes but we see no obvious basis for their interpretation. The small share of between-school variance in course marks relative to that in achievement is not a consequence of the separate calculations for city and county schools. Between-school variance in achievement is larger than that in course marks in both city and county schools (Hauser, 1968:192).

Relative to the null hypothesis of no association, between-school variance is large. Nothing in Table 4.1 suggests that gross school effects in the Nashville SMSA are small relative to those found in other localities or in regional or national studies. At the same time, gross variation in performance among schools is modest, relative to the total variance in educational performance. In no grade-sex subgroup is the between-school variance in a performance measure as large as thirty percent, and in most it is far smaller than that. Variables unrelated to the school attended must account for most of the variance in educational performance.

Could we have neglected some factor which suppresses observable between-school variance? Later, we shall show that this is true to some degree of course marks, which vary less from school to school than do standards

Table 4.1.—Percentages of variance lying between schools in educational performance by sex and grade, white public secondary school students: Nashville SMSA, 1957

Sex and grade	N	M	W	A		E		T	J
		SMSA	SMSA	City	County	City	County	County	County
Males									
12	16	21.7%	10.5%	14.4%	4.6%	5.3%	12.2%	13.7%	9.7%
11	16	29.0	16.6	9.9	5.2	4.4	11.8	14.6	10.7
10	15	15.8	13.0	5.0	7.4	4.7	11.4	14.0	10.5
9	20	19.6	15.3	6.1	5.2	6.6	7.0	9.7	9.3
8	32	21.7	19.7	7.0	9.3	8.7	9.6	14.0	9.1
7	34	12.8	15.5	4.9	3.7	7.2	4.8	9.6	12.8
Females									
12	16	21.8%	21.0%	6.8%	11.5%	4.0%	6.6%	8.1%	6.8%
11	16	28.4	10.9	10.3	4.8	5.3	5.1	12.6	5.7
10	16	14.9	10.2	2.3	3.0	3.9	4.7	7.4	4.2
9	20	18.9	18.3	6.2	4.3	6.4	3.0	10.6	2.6
8	31	19.1	20.3	3.9	8.4	3.8	8.5	12.8	3.4
7	34	15.4	17.0	7.3	5.3	11.2	5.3	11.8	2.8

Note: Item identifications are: N-Number of schools in sex-grade subgroup (9 city schools in grades 7-9 and 6 city schools in grades 10-12); M-Stanford Mathematics Grade Equivalent; W-Stanford Reading Grade Equivalent; A-Arithmetic mark; E-English mark; T-Student's educational aspiration; and J-Student's occupational aspiration.

of performance. Confining our interest here to factors which affect all of the educational performances, two sources of error come to mind. First, the mobility of students among schools may reduce between-school variance; the effect of a school will not be measurable in students who attend it for only a short time. Moreover, if many students transfer among schools with different organizational properties, the "fit" of school type and student performance will not be good; school effects will be understated. Table 4.2 displays percentages of between-school variance in academic achievement and aspiration which were calculated only for students who had not changed residence within four years. The data provide some support for the hypothesis that mobility suppresses school differences. In all but 8 of the 40 possible comparisons between Table 4.1 and Table 4.2 the between-school variance is larger among the non-movers in Table 4.2. However, as defined here mobility is a very strict criterion. Non-movers included about three-quarters of the students in the upper grades and little more than half in the lower grades. Further, the restrictions on inter-school variance due to mobility are not large. Taken at face value, the entries in Table 4.2 do not seem to require any modification of our initial conclusion that factors other than the school account for most of the variance.

Differences in the reliability of measurement could also suppress esti-

Table 4.2.—Percentages of variance lying between schools in academic achievement and aspiration by sex and grade, white public secondary school students not moving within four years: Nashville SMSA, 1957

Sex and grade	M SMSA	W SMSA	T County	J County
Males				
12	25.7%	12.6%	15.5%	13.4%
11	24.9	19.8	16.6	12.5
10	14.6	11.6	13.7	10.7
9	18.3	15.4	20.7	12.7
8	22.5	20.5	nc*	nc
7	15.2	16.2	nc	nc
Females				
12	23.2%	21.9%	7.4%	5.7%
11	28.8	11.2	13.3	7.1
10	15.2	9.5	9.0	5.9
9	21.9	18.5	11.4	2.7
8	24.6	27.3	nc	nc
7	19.1	17.8	nc	nc

Note: Item identifications are: M-Stanford Mathematics Grade Equivalent; W-Stanford Reading Grade Equivalent; T-Student's educational aspiration; and J-Student's occupational aspiration.

* Not computed.

mates of the percentage of variance lying between schools. Suppose school performance was measured reliably and individual performance within schools was not. Then the denominator of the ratio of between-school to total variance would contain a relatively larger component due to error of measurement than would the numerator. The observed ratio of between-school variance to total variance would be smaller than the ratio of reliable between-school variance to reliable total variance. Here, we do not have access to measures of reliability in the strict sense of the term. However, we can assume that the common variance of each pair of indicators of educational performance is more reliable, even though it may not include all of the reliable variance in each separate indicator. Under that assumption the correlation between each pair of indicators represents reliable variance, and it may be partitioned into between- and within-school components using equation 2.26. The between-school components of such decompositions are shown in Table 4.3. As in the case of the mobility hypothesis, the data support the claim that between-school variance has been suppressed. In most, but not all instances the percentage of between-school variance common to a pair of indicators is larger than that in either of the indicators taken separately. Estimates of between-school variance in academic achievement cluster between 20 and 25 percent. For aspiration the estimates increase to about 20 percent for boys and 15 percent for girls but in the case

Table 4.3.—Percentages of common variance lying between schools in academic achievement (M and W), course marks (A and E) and aspiration (T and J) by sex and grade, white public secondary school students: Nashville SMSA, 1957

Sex and grade	Academic achievement	Course marks		Aspiration
		City	County	County
Males				
12	21.8	14.7	8.5	17.6
11	29.7	12.4	7.2	20.6
10	20.6	11.0	13.1	20.4
9	22.8	9.6	7.1	17.1
8	26.7	9.2	10.9	21.8
7	17.7	8.5	4.4	21.5
Females				
12	29.0	1.8	6.9	11.2
11	20.4	5.6	0.1	18.0
10	14.8	16.9	3.7	11.5
9	23.6	7.1	4.8	9.9
8	24.2	3.7	8.7	11.9
7	19.9	13.2	5.4	17.9

Note: Item identifications are: M-Stanford Mathematics Grade Equivalent; W-Stanford Reading Grade Equivalent; A-Arithmetic mark; E-English mark; T-Student's educational aspiration; and J-Student's occupational aspiration.

SCHOOL EFFECTS

Table 4.4.—Percentages of variance lying between schools in student background variables by sex and grade, white public secondary school students: Nashville SMSA, 1957

Sex and grade	X	V	S	Q	Z
Males					
12	22.2%	23.0%	5.1%	15.9%	26.8%
11	28.3	24.2	7.8	14.7	29.6
10	17.4	17.8	7.9	17.8	23.5
9	19.0	22.1	8.7	17.0	26.6
8	25.9	28.4	11.4	22.9	24.5
7	22.8	28.5	10.5	15.4	25.3
Females					
12	25.6%	29.6%	5.9%	13.6%	20.2%
11	24.8	27.9	6.0	10.0	24.7
10	21.9	19.7	8.7	15.1	22.0
9	23.5	27.7	9.7	20.0	23.7
8	35.1	33.6	13.2	19.8	28.9
7	29.3	29.9	11.8	17.8	20.7

Note: Item identifications are: X-Father's occupation; V-Father's education; S-Number of siblings; Q-Intelligence; and Z-Father's educational aspiration.

of course marks they are still quite low. At the same time, even this substantial adjustment of the data casts no doubt on our initial conclusion that variables unrelated to the school attended must account for most of the variance in educational performance.

Student Background Variables

Beginning with Wilson's seminal article (1959), sociologists have accepted without question the assumption that socioeconomic segregation is great enough to warrant the claims made on behalf of socioeconomic context as a variable. Typically, the assumption has been supported by no more data than a well-chosen comparison between slum and suburb. The fact of residential differentiation by socioeconomic status is as well-documented as any in sociology, and there is no quarreling with it. (It is the basis of the calculation of covariance adjustments in later chapters.) On the other hand, just as in the case of educational performance, it is easy to overestimate the extent of differences between schools in socioeconomic composition. Percentages of variance in student background variables lying between schools are shown in Table 4.4. As in the case of educational performance, moderate proportions of variance in student background variables occur between schools: about a quarter of the variance in father's occupation, education and educational aspiration, twenty percent or less of the variance in intelligence, and only a small share of the variance in number of siblings.

The substantial and consistent pattern of socioeconomic segregation found among schools is not strong enough to preclude contact between individuals from widely varying levels of the class structure in any one school (Rhodes, Reiss and Duncan, 1965). More precisely, segregation of the schools by socioeconomic s t a t u s could produce correlations among the background characteristics of randomly chosen classmates as large as the proportions of variance exhibited in Table 4.4; that is, on the order of .20 to .30. While we have no data of our own on this point, there is every reason to believe that there is substantially greater similarity between the characteristics of school chums than is implied by this model of residential segregation. In the light of estimates from other bodies of data, a reasonable estimate would be that no more than half the observed homophily is attributable to segregation (Duncan, Haller and Portes, 1968:120; Duncan, Featherman and Duncan, 1968:215-217). In short, there is substantial socioeconomic heterogeneity within areas large enough to form a school district at the secondary level, and socioeconomic heterogeneity among schools is not sufficient to account for differential association by socioeconomic level.

Persistence of Differences between Schools

Leaving to one side the size of differences between schools relative to individual differences, we may ask whether school effects persist in time. The treatment of characteristics of students who attend different schools as effects of the school suggests they are an enduring property of each cohort that passes through the school system. That is, it would be hard to define as an effect of school a pattern of school differentials in educational performance which varied as a particular cohort of students progressed through the given institutions. The Davidson County data were gathered at a single point in time and it was impossible to trace the changes in any single grade cohort as it passed through the school system. However, as noted in Chapter II, we could treat the students in different grades in the same feeding channel as a synthetic cohort in order to estimate the stability of performance over time.

The use of the synthetic cohort may produce more convincing evidence of school effects than the longitudinal examination of real cohorts, since there are reasons to expect a less than perfect relationship between the characteristics of successive grade cohorts at different stages of schooling. We can assume initially that there are real differences in the make-up of successive grade cohorts. Moreover, the cohort concept is not perfectly applicable in the present instance. Unlike the birth cohort, the potential membership of the grade cohort is not invariant with respect to time. While the idea of a birth cohort entering school at a given age and progressing through the several grades in lock-step is an appealing abstraction, it is inaccurate. A grade cohort is subject to greater attrition (through leaving school) than the birth cohort with which it may nearly have corresponded at the age of entering school. It is possible to move from one grade cohort to another by being rapidly promoted or by failing. When a grade cohort is identified with a particular feeding pattern in its progress through the school system as well as an approximate location in time, geographic as well as "temporal" mobility enters in. A student may change his grade cohort by moving from one school district to another, or a feeding pattern may be modified through changes in district boundaries, the construction of new schools, and the like. Thus, while the cohort concept is strictly applicable to the students who attend a given school in a given grade in a given year, the assumption of annual promotion is no guarantee that the cohort will exist as a social unit for any period of time.

Feeding patterns were assumed to follow geographic nesting of school districts. Where necessary, a grade cohort in a higher grade was paired with more than one feeder in a lower grade and each pair of observed school means was arbitrarily weighted by the number of students in the lower grade. The averages of the correlations of the five adjacent grade cohort pairs, 7-8, 8-9, 9-10, 10-11 and 11-12 are displayed in the first column of Table 4.5. The intercorrelations of student background characteristics (father's occupation and education, and number of siblings) might be characterized as moderate to high, as are those of intelligence, father's educational aspiration, and the student's educational and occupational aspiration; those of achievement test scores, course marks and membership in organizations are lower.

Table 4.5.—Stability of school means, white public secondary schools: Nashville SMSA, 1957 *

Variable	Average inter-grade correlation	Combined inter-sex correlation	Stability from grade 7 to 12	
			Actual	Expected
X	.913	.924	.760	.634
V	.915	.942	.772	.641
S	.786	.821	.508	.300
Q	.749	.848	.619	.236
M	.400	.912	.043	.010
W	.369	.894	.167	.006
A	.428	.742	.164	.014
E	.644	.805	.141	.111
Z	.903	.886	.745	.600
O	.624	.851	.055	.095
T: county	.834	.717	.406	.403
J: county	.707	.375	.191	.177

Note: Item identifications are: X-Father's occupation; V-Father's education; S-Number of siblings; Q-Intelligence; M-Stanford Mathematics Grade Equivalent; W-Stanford Reading Grade Equivalent; A-Arithmetic mark; E-English mark; Z-Father's educational aspiration; O-Organizational membership; T-Student's educational aspiration; and J-Student's occupational aspiration.

* See text for explanation.

In the former case the inter-cohort correlations may be low because of an error in the data. Some indication of the size of the true inter-cohort correlations of achievement test scores can be obtained by comparing the first and second columns of Table 4.5. The second column contains intercorrelations of school means of boys and girls attending the same school in the same grade, calculated over all schools and grades. These are generally larger than the inter-cohort correlations. The single notable exception is occupational aspiration, for which the Duncan SES scores into which occupations were coded may not have had the same validity for boys as for girls. The inter-sex correlations of achievement test scores are of about the same size as the inter-sex and inter-cohort correlations of intelligence. Examination of the full inter-cohort correlation matrices of achievement test scores suggests that the irregularity in school means of those two variables is probably greatest in the eight or ninth grade. (This irregularity complicates our later efforts to interpret differences between schools in academic achievement.)

If inter-cohort change in students' characteristics could be described by a simple causal chain, the intercorrelations between school means from one grade to another would be equal to the product of the inter-cohort correlations of the intervening grades. This allows for substantial changes in intracohort differentials between schools over moderate periods of time. For example, a correlation of .90 of adjacent cohorts implies a grade seven to grade twelve inter-cohort correlation of only .59 under the causal chain hypothesis. However, there can be greater persistence in schools' characteristics over long periods of time than would be expected from a simple causal chain.

It is hard to test this hypothesis because the inter-cohort correlations are based on small numbers of schools, and there is only one inter-cohort correlation of each variable from grade seven to grade twelve. Those intercorrelations are shown in the third column of Table 4.5, and intercorrelations expected from a causal chain hypothesis are shown in the fourth column. The latter figures are simply the fifth power of the entries in the first column; these smoothed figures yield higher expected values than would be obtained from the actual products of inter-cohort correlations. The causal chain model provides a close fit only for membership in organizations, students' aspirations and achievement in mathematics. In every other instance the observed seventh to twelfth grade intercorrelations are larger than the (artificially inflated) expected values. Because the conclusion holds true of students' background characteristics as well as of educational performance, we have elsewhere considered the hypothesis that the persistence of levels of performance results from the schools' attractiveness to similar students rather than from any property of their internal organization (Hauser, 1969:609).

Nonadditivity of School Effects

If relationships among variables differed from school to school, the unique effect of each school could not be expressed by an additive effect, as is re-

Table 4.6.—Nonadditivity of selected school effects, public secondary schools: Nashville SMSA, 1957

Relationship	Within-school variance explained by		Average correlation of slopes	
	Average regression	Added by interaction	Inter-cohort	Inter-sex
W on V	2.79%	3.10%	.008	.108
W on Q	31.67	2.84	−.103	.071
E on V	2.95	1.76	−.004	.133
E on Q	19.51	2.49	.055	.185
T on V (county)	6.33	1.81	.167	−.021
T on Q (county)	5.20	2.62	.070	−.065

Note: Item identifications are: W-Stanford Reading Grade Equivalent; E-English mark; T-Student's educational aspiration; V-Father's education; and Q-Intelligence.

quired for covariance adjustment. Examination of the appropriate variance ratios of a large number of the relationships dealt with in the present study has indicated that there is little statistically significant interaction or nonadditivity in school effects, despite our large numbers of cases. However, the data probably do not meet the distributional requirements for strict interpretation of tests of significance, and we tried to assess the substantive import of the observed interactions.

Some relevant analyses are summarized in Table 4.6. These analyses required considerable hand computation and were performed only for six bivariate relationships. The relationships were chosen on the basis of their varying strength and their pertinence to each of the three classes of educational performance which we examined. The first column of Table 4.6 shows the percentage of within-school variance in each dependent variable which is explained by the predetermined variable under the assumption that there is a common slope of the within-school regression for the students of each sex in each grade. The second column shows the additional percentage of within-school variance explained by estimating a within-school slope for the students of each sex in each school in each grade. The assumption that each school has a unique relationship adds about two to three percentage points to the within-school variance explained by the average within-school regression lines. The size of the interaction effect does not appear to vary with the size of the average relationship. The interaction effect is larger than the main effect in one case where the main effect is very small, and it is less than a tenth the size of the main effect in one case where the main effect is large.

We might be satisfied with these results as the basis of the assumption that the effects of schools are additive. The major part of the analysis is based on multivariate interpretations, where the problem of interaction is presumably less than that experienced here. However, the size of the interactions, like the magnitude of the other relationships we treated, is not as important as the extent to which they can be interpreted. The most convincing evidence of additivity is provided by the inter-cohort and inter-sex correlations of within-school regression slopes which are shown in the last two columns of Table 4.6. These results give no support to the assumption of temporal stability or inter-sex consistency of separate within-school regression slopes. In the absence of such persistence there is little point in interpreting departures from a common slope or in rejecting a model which requires the assumption of one.

V

ACADEMIC
ACHIEVEMENT

Variation in educational performance among schools can be interpreted only in the context of assumptions about what happens in school. Further, most variation in students' backgrounds and in educational performance occurs within schools. Thus, the next step of our inquiry is to analyze the sources and implications of differential educational performance within schools.

In this and the next two chapters we describe parallel analyses of three kinds of educational performance measured in the Davidson County survey —academic achievement, course marks and aspiration—oriented by our interest in evaluating socioeconomic theories of educational performance. The initial criterion is complete explanation; we wish to learn to what extent socioeconomic background variables can account for variance in performance. When background variables fail to satisfy this criterion, we turn to a second, less stringent criterion, namely, the capacity of background variables to account for the common variance in similarly determined measures of educational performance. We are able to use this second criterion because there are two indicators of each kind of performance: achievement in mathematics and reading, marks in arithmetic and English, and educational and occupational aspiration. This procedure is similar to the explanation of "spurious" relationships in cross-tabular analysis popularized by Lazarsfeld (1955) and his students. When socioeconomic theories also fail this test, we modify the theories by adding intervening variables, by adjusting to allow for error in measurement or by altering our causal assumptions.

After looking at differences in performance *within* schools, we return to the interpretation of differences *among* them. Levels of school performance are adjusted using the method described in Chapter II in order to take account of the differences among student bodies in terms of variables found to influence performance within schools. The process of adjustment yields components of between-school variance which may be attributed to direct effects of composition and of other student and school variables, as well as to joint effects of composition and other variables. In general, the adjustments are based on within-school models of performance which do not satisfy the criteria of explanatory adequacy which we developed earlier. Thus, the process of adjustment yields interpretations of differences between schools which uniformly understate the important role of differences in the composition of the student body. Finally, we examine the effect of neighborhood characteristics on the composition of the student body and on the other factors which influence school performance.

Standardized and Metric Measures of Effect

Throughout the following discussion, statistical measures of effect are presented in standardized rather than metric form. (Standardized measures of effect are expressed in ratios of standard deviations, variances or covariances, while metric measures are expressed in ratios of raw units of measurement.) In view of recent criticism of standardized measures (Blalock, 1967a; Wiley and Wiley, 1970; Cain and Watts, 1970) some defense of our tactic is required. Critics rightly maintain that standardized measures can be interpreted as indicators of degree or closeness of association. They are affected by the variability of a population, so they may differ in populations in which the corresponding metric coefficients are the same. Further, it is easier to comprehend the meaning of changes in policy when they are expressed in the raw units of policy variables. When such observations are accompanied by the contention that metric coefficients describe "the laws of science" (Blalock, 1961a:51) a preference for metric coefficients is easily rationalized.

A case for standardized measures can also be made. The fact that standardized measures may change from one population to another does not mean they must change. Standardized measures of effect may remain constant when the heterogeneity of the population changes, and they may remain constant when metric coefficients change. Indeed, our discipline's preoccupation with interaction effects suggests that sociologists in general do not believe that metric measures of effect are invariant across populations. Like changes in metric measures of effect, changes in heterogeneity from one population to another ought to be documented rather than postulated. The strength of a relationship between variables in a social system may be as interesting and important sociologically as the exact function describing the relationship. Finally, the utility of metric coefficients in sociology is limited because we so rarely replicate direct measurements and because we impute great theoretical importance to unobservable constructs whose metric is indeterminate (Costner, 1969; Blalock, 1969, 1970).

Our choice of measures was not based on a dogmatic stand on the merits of metric or of standardized coefficients. We used metric coefficients extensively in our statistical analyses, but we found standardized measures appropriate and convenient in inquiring whether alternative causal models could account for actual process of social differentiation in a population and also in interpreting the role of various causal factors in those processes. That is, we used causal models primarily for purposes of analysis and description rather than synthesis and projection. For our purposes, metric coefficients could be used only at the cost of greater algebraic complexity. Had our goal been to project the consequences of change in one or more parameters of a particular causal model, metric coefficients would have been more useful.

Our analysis is not thereby devoid of implications for policy. If a theory or model is to be useful in projecting the consequences of social change, it ought also to produce valid accounts of past events. The present analysis can provide information relevant to educational policy by helping us make judgments about the validity of contemporary theories of educational performance.

Interactions by Grade

Major portions of the within-school analyses were replicated in sex and grade subgroups (Hauser, 1968:117-347, 375-410). Interactions by grade were rather difficult to interpret, and for the most part they were not large or interesting enough to warrant detailed presentation and discussion of the findings.

For example, both standardized and unstandardized regression coefficients tended to vary inversely in absolute magnitude with grade in school. It is hard to choose among the several explanations of the tendency which can be offered in the case of academic achievement. Academic achievement was ostensibly measured in the eighth grade in the case of students in grades eight to twelve and in the sixth grade in the case of students in the seventh grade, but the scores for some eighth-grade students may have been obtained earlier (Chapter II). The results in even the four upper grades cannot be interpreted strictly as replications. First, and more important, students in the higher grades are not as representative of any birth cohorts as students in the lower grades because their distribution on variables related to ability, socioeconomic status, or school performances was presumably skewed or truncated by dropping out, by failing one or more grades, and by transferring to private schools. Second, the measures of family background pertained to the time when student questionnaires were administered, rather than to the administration of achievement tests. Thus, the temporal ordering of the measurements of academic achievement and family background was the reverse of the causal ordering assumed below, and the length of time between the two measurements increased with grade. Both elements of noncomparability may be expected to attenuate relationships observed among students in the higher grades. Consequently, relationships which became weaker with increasing grade in school could not be interpreted as "depending" on grade in any substantive sense. Interactions in which relationships grew stronger in higher grades could be interpreted substantively, but that pattern was almost never followed. Although the possibility that attrition would attenuate relationships is generally recognized in studies of the effect of social background on achievement beyond high school (Sewell and Shah, 1967:17; Lavin, 1965:125-127), its application at the high school level appears to have been overlooked in *Equality of Educational Opportunity* (Coleman *et al.,* 1966:300).

Rather than belabor the reader with small or ambiguous differences among our subgroups, we relied heavily on the analysis of simple unweighted means of their within-school correlation coefficients. It would have made more sense to weight the correlations, to take weighted averages of Z transforms, or to use true within-grade within-school correlation and regression coefficients. Unfortunately, we did not think of these alternatives when we made the decision to ignore grade interactions. On the other hand, while there is no formal rationale for the procedure used here, the results were so uniform across grades that reweighting would have made little difference, and the procedure did yield a stable set of data which could be used efficiently in the construction and comparison of alternative explanations.

Determination of Academic Achievement Within Schools

We chose as our dependent variables two standard measures of academic achievement: the Stanford Mathematics Grade Equivalent (M) and Stanford Reading Grade Equivalent (W). The choice of academic achievement to indicate educational performance requires little defense; the prevailing view has been stated by Bloom (1963:379):

> While it may or may not be true that the most important changes in the learner are those which may be described as cognitive, i.e., knowledge, problem-solving, higher mental processes, etc., it is true that these are the types of changes in students which most teachers do seek to bring about. These are the changes in learners which most teachers attempt to gauge in their own tests of progress and in their own final examinations. These, also, are the changes in the learners which are emphasized in the materials of instruction, in the interaction between teachers and learners, and in the reward system which the teachers and the schools employ.

We need only add the assumption that academic achievement also influences opportunities for social achievement outside the educational system.

We treated four family characteristics as predetermined with respect to academic achievement: father's occupational status (X), father's educational attainment (V), number of siblings (S), and whether family was intact (F).

No causal ordering was assumed among the four background variables. That is, we assumed that they could all influence achievement by way of any number of mechanisms, but for two reasons we did not attempt to analyze or interpret their intercorrelations. First, analysis of the relations among the four background variables would have added no substance to the analysis because our primary interest was in their combined influence on achievement. Second, intuitively plausible orderings of the variables would have been of doubtful validity and interest because the variables describe statuses of origin in a population of students, not those of a population of families.

Throughout most of the analysis we treated the measured intelligence of the student (Q) as a predetermined variable with the same causal priority as family background. Social scientists so persistently assume that socioeconomic background directly affects intelligence that the matter deserves some attention and comment. (For example, *Equality of Educational Opportunity* (Coleman *et al.*, 1966:298-325) made a verbal component of intelligence the major dependent variable in its controversial analysis of the effect of school and student factors on academic achievement.) The reason we did not assume a direct causal link between socioeconomic background and intelligence in the present context was that the status of the family and intelligence of the student have unmeasured common causes. That is, the parental abilities, attitudes and practices which facilitate the development of children's intelligence also contribute to the attainment of parental status, so the link between socioeconomic background and intelligence is partly spurious. This view is consistent with both positions in the recently revitalized nature-nurture controversy because hereditary or environmental variables may produce relevant parental differences. Moreover, the assumption that intelligence is exogenous with respect to achievement in secondary school is consistent with the generally accepted proposition that intelligence is most susceptible to environmental influence in the early years of life. Still, at several points in the analysis it was useful to assume that family background does affect intelligence because of the heuristic value of that assumption in clarifying the role of intelligence testing in the process of achievement. Finally, we should note that the ordering of the two factors, socioeconomic background and intelligence, has absolutely no effect on estimates of the direct influence of either on subsequent variables.

Averages of within-school correlations among the background variables and indicators of academic achievement are shown in Table 5.1. Because there were no interesting interactions by sex in the determination of achievement, the within-school correlations were averaged over both sex and grade. Of course, the correlations are generally lower than those one would expect to find in a total population because the slopes and variances are not confounded with school differences.

The correlations involving intactness of family are particularly weak (Table 5.1). This finding is consistent with Beverly Duncan's observation (1967:366-368) of a downward trend in the association of intactness of

Table 5.1.—Average over grades of within-school correlations among student background factors and academic achievement, white public secondary school students: Nashville SMSA, 1957

	V	S	F	Q	M	W
X	.471	−.127	.032	.200	.149	.189
V		−.187	.006	.207	.164	.209
S			−.015	−.146	−.123	−.169
F				.051	.042	.031
Q					.556	.570
M						.640

Note: Item identifications are: X-Father's occupation; V-Father's education; S-Number of siblings; F-Intact family; Q-Intelligence; M-Stanford Mathematics Grade Equivalent; and W-Stanford Reading Grade Equivalent.

family with father's occupation and education and size of family in cohorts completing their schooling in recent years. However, there is one pertinent source of error in the Davidson County data: Students whose fathers did not live with them may have failed to report X and V. Since X and V represent only father's education and occupation and not characteristics of the heads of father-absent households, the low level of association of F with those factors could be an artifact of differential response rates on X and V by family stability. At the same time, there is no reason to believe that correlations of F with other variables are affected by the same kind of error. Thus, the use of artifactually low correlations between F and paternal status could lead to overestimates of the effect of F on achievement, net of X and V.

Aside from the meager size of the correlations involving intactness of family, there are no surprises in the correlation matrix. As one would expect, all the correlations are positive except those involving number of siblings, which are all negative. The correlations of intelligence with family background are weaker than one might guess in the light of the popular argument that intelligence testing is no more than an administrative mechanism bringing about socioeconomic discrimination. The generally larger correlations of background with W than with M are consistent with numerous observations that verbal skill and behavior are more sensitive to social background than non-verbal skills. It would be easy to engage in further speculation about the causal processes underlying the observed correlations, but it would serve no useful purpose to do so. Here, the task is neither to replicate well-known relationships in still another student population, nor to add to the mass of verbiage produced to describe them, but to try to combine those relationships in explicit and internally consistent quantitative interpretations.

Socioeconomic Background and Academic Achievement

The path diagram in Figure 5.1 depicts the determination of achievement by socioeconomic background. Analyses which purport to exhaust the ex-

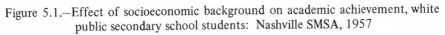

Figure 5.1.—Effect of socioeconomic background on academic achievement, white public secondary school students: Nashville SMSA, 1957

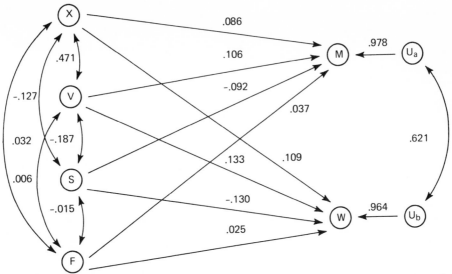

Note: Item identifications are: X-Father's occupation; V-Father's education; S-Number of siblings; F-Intact family; M-Stanford Mathematics Grade Equivalent; W-Stanford Reading Grade Equivalent; U_a-Unmeasured determinants of M; and U_b-Unmeasured determinants of W.

planatory power of a particular cluster of variables are always subject to the criticism that one or another indicator was too important to have been left out. Actually, three or four good indicators are usually more than sufficient to represent an explanatory construct, and beyond that number little more is achieved than a splitting of effects among predetermined variables (Blau and Duncan, 1967:188-194,203; Gordon, 1968; Sewell and Shah, 1968a). We assume that X, V, S and F are sufficiently important and reliable indicators of background to represent most of its effects on achievement. In that sense the diagram in Figure 5.1 depicts a complete, if preliminary model of the determination of academic achievement.

The uses of path analysis in sociology are discussed in several recent articles (Duncan, 1966; Land, 1969; Heise, 1969), and numerous applications of it have appeared. However, the present discussion is an attempt at a more or less self-contained introduction to the topic. The curved, two-headed paths in Figure 5.1 symbolize unanalyzed relationships, and the numbers beside them are correlation coefficients. In the case of the relations among X, V, S and F the coefficients are zero-order correlations taken directly from Table 5.1, while the coefficient on the path connecting U_a and U_b is derived from the other results shown in the diagram. The straight, unidirectional paths symbolize direct causal influence. That is, the diagram specifies that X, V, S and F act directly on M and on W, while there are no direct links between the two indicators of achievement. In order to obtain a numerical solution of the model we assume that M and W are determined completely by the combined effects of the measured variables (X, V, S and F) and by those of other, residually defined variables (U_a and U_b), which are uncorrelated with the measured variables. Hence, we also show direct effects of U_a on M and of U_b on W, but there are no links, either direct or indirect, between U_a or U_b and any of the measured predetermined variables. These assumptions define an ordinary least-squares solution, that is, one which minimizes the explanatory importance of the residual variables. Further, we assume that the causal relationships in the model are linear and additive, that is, that the effect of each variable can be described adequately by a straight line of constant slope over the observed range of all variables in the model. The residual variables or disturbances represent the combined effects of errors of measurement, of violations of the assumptions of linearity and additivity, and of the substantive variables not related to those in the model.

While the path diagram describes the model accurately, greater understanding of the derivation and interpretation of the coefficients may be obtained by the equivalent expression of the model as a system of linear equations. We denote the direct effect of variable k on variable j by p_{jk} and express each variable in standard form, as the ratio of a deviation from its mean to its standard deviation. The equations for the model in Figure 5.1 can be written as follows:

$$M = p_{MX}X + p_{MV}V + p_{MS}S + p_{MF}F + p_{Ma}U_a \qquad (5.1)$$

and
$$W = p_{WX}X + p_{WV}V + p_{WS}S + p_{WF}F + p_{Wb}U_b, \qquad (5.2)$$

where $r_{aX} = r_{aV} = r_{aS} = r_{aF} = r_{bX} = r_{bV} = r_{bS} = r_{bF} = 0$. Suppose we multiply equation 5.1 by X, sum over all observations, and divide by the total number of observations. If N is the number of cases, the resulting expression is

$$\frac{\sum XM}{N} = p_{MX}\frac{\sum XX}{N} + p_{MV}\frac{\sum VX}{N} + p_{MS}\frac{\sum SX}{N}$$
$$+ p_{MF}\frac{\sum FX}{N} + p_{Ma}\frac{\sum U_aX}{N}. \qquad (5.3)$$

Each sum of products in equation 5.3 is just the definition of a zero order Pearsonian correlation coefficient. Hence, we can rewrite 5.3 as

$$r_{XM} = p_{MX} + p_{MV}r_{VX} + p_{MS}r_{SX} + p_{MF}r_{FX}, \qquad (5.4)$$

dropping the path coefficient of U_a because $r_{ax}=0$ by assumption. This is a straightforward application of the basic theorem of path analysis, namely that

$$r_{ij} = \sum_k p_{jk}r_{ki}, \qquad (5.5)$$

where i and j are any two variables in the system and k runs over all variables in the system from which direct paths lead to variable j.

ACADEMIC ACHIEVEMENT

Equation 5.4 may also be reproduced directly from the path diagram following a simple visual algorithm. Start with the variable of interest that comes last in the system (M). Then take the sum of the products of coefficients along each direct or indirect path leading to the second variable of interest. Thus, in writing an expression for r_{MX}, we include in the sum the direct path, p_{MX}, and the indirect paths, $p_{MV}r_{VX}$, $p_{MS}r_{SX}$, and $p_{MF}r_{FX}$. However, indirect paths are not allowed if they contain more than one unanalyzed correlation or if they involve more than one change of direction from forward to backward or *vice versa*. Thus, the algorithm excludes complex indirect paths like $p_{MS}r_{SV}r_{VX}$ or $p_{MV}r_{VS}p_{MS}p_{MX}$. The ismorphism of diagram and system of equations makes path analysis easily accessible as a means of estimation and interpretation of multivariate systems.

Repeated application of the basic theorem yields expressions for r_{MV}, r_{MS}, and r_{MF}:

$$r_{MV} = p_{MX}r_{XV} + p_{MV} + p_{MS}r_{SV} + p_{MF}r_{FV}, \tag{5.6}$$

$$r_{MS} = p_{MX}r_{XS} + p_{MV}r_{VS} + p_{MS} + p_{MF}r_{FS} \tag{5.7}$$

and $$r_{MF} = p_{MX}r_{XF} + p_{MV}r_{VF} + p_{MS}r_{SF} + p_{MF} \tag{5.8}$$

Equations 5.4, 5.6, 5.7, and 5.8 are four linear equations in the four unknown path coefficients which each of them contains, and they can readily be solved for those coefficients. The reader may already have recognized that these four equations are simply the normal equations of a multiple correlation analysis of M on X, V, S and F, and the direct path coefficients are beta coefficients or regression coefficients in standard form. The use of this unconventional notation for conventional calculations will be justified by later applications of path analysis which have no analogue in correlation analysis. Application of the basic theorem to the correlation of M with itself yields

$$r_{MM} = 1 = p_{MX}r_{XM} + p_{MV}r_{VM} + p_{MS}r_{SM} + p_{MF}r_{FM} + p_{Ma}r_{aM}, \tag{5.9}$$

and

$$r_{Ma} = p_{MX}r_{Xa} + p_{MV}r_{Va} + p_{MS}r_{Sa} + p_{MF}r_{Fa} + p_{Ma} = p_{Ma}, \tag{5.10}$$

so $$p_{Ma}^2 = 1 - (p_{MX}r_{XM} + p_{MV}r_{VM} + p_{MS}r_{SM} + p_{MF}r_{FM}). \tag{5.11}$$

Substitution of known path and correlation coefficients in equation 5.11 yields a conventionally positive value for p_{Ma}, which is in this case an ordinary coefficient of alienation, and completes the derivation of coefficients involving M directly. The sum in parentheses in equation 5.11 is the proportion of variance in M "explained" by the four background variables, but its four components should not be interpreted as "unique" contributions of the background variables because the corrrelation coefficients may be decomposed further, using equations 5.4, 5.6, 5.7, and 5.8 (Hauser, 1969a). Analogous applications of the basic theorem to the determination of W by equation 5.2 yield estimates for p_{WX}, p_{WV}, p_{WS}, p_{WF} and p_{Wb}.

The path coefficients in Figure 5.1 are regression coefficients in standard form. That is, they state the direction and size of net change in the dependent variable produced by a one-standard-deviation change in a predetermined variable in terms of standard deviations of the dependent variable. For example, a one-standard-deviation change in father's occupation produces a 0.086 standard deviation change in mathematics achievement, net of the association of father's occupation with father's education, number of siblings and intactness of family. With nearly seventeen thousand degrees of freedom the standard errors of the path coefficients are very small, in the neighborhood of 0.01, and all of the direct effects shown in Figure 5.1 are undoubtedly statistically significant. At the same time, all of the effects are small. A one-standard-deviation change in father's education or occupation produces a change of about a tenth of a standard deviation in either measure of achievement. The equally large direct effects of number of siblings suggest that size of family is more than a redundant measure of social standing. If the "socioeconomic resources" of the student's family find "absolute" measure in father's occupation and education, then each additional child is a separate drain on those resources.

The effects of the intactness of the family on achievement are small relative to the social importance sometimes attributed to that variable (Office of Policy Planning and Research, 1965:36 and references cited therein), but the finding here is consistent with other recent studies (Coleman *et al.*, 1966:301-302; Wilson, 1969:20-24). The minor impact of intactness of family is all the more striking in view of our earlier observation that its influence may have been overestimated; neither its limited variance in the Davidson County population nor our use of standardized coefficients is responsible for that variable's negligible importance. The net difference in achievement between youths in broken and intact families was on the order of 0.16 grade equivalents, or less than a tenth of the within-school standard deviation of achievement in almost every grade. Of course, in evaluating this finding the reader should keep in mind that the data pertain to a white population in secondary school for which the intactness of the family was measured contemporaneously with or subsequent to academic achievement. Because of its meager impact on achievement (and other dependent variables), intact family was dropped from the analysis.

How good is the explanation of achievement in Figure 5.1? The residual path coefficients, $p_{Ma} = .978$ and $p_{Wb} = .964$, make it abundantly clear that variables unrelated to socioeconomic background must account for virtually all of the variance in achievement within schools. The socioeconomic variables account for only 4.3 percent of the variance in mathematics achievement and 7.1 percent of the variance in reading achievement. Clearly, the model does not satisfy our first criterion of adequacy of explanation, accounting for variance in achievement.

The second explanatory criterion is that the model account for the correlation between two indicators of the same kind of performance. That is, if there are no direct causal links between two indicators of performance, an adequate model will contain the common causes which produce the observed covariation between the indicators. The model in Figure 5.1 provides a direct test of the hypothesis that the second criterion is met. The correlation between the two measures of achievement, $r_{MW} = .640$, was not used in calculating the direct effect of background on M and W. However, an expression for that correlation coefficient can be obtained on repeated application of the basic theorem. Working back from M, we have

$$r_{MW} = p_{MX}r_{XW} + p_{MV}r_{VW} + p_{MS}r_{SW} + p_{MF}r_{FW} + p_{Ma}r_{aW}, \quad (5.12)$$

but
$$r_{aW} = p_{WX}r_{Xa} + p_{WV}r_{Va} + p_{WS}r_{Sa} + p_{WF}r_{Fa} + p_{Wb}r_{ba}$$
$$= p_{Wb}r_{ba}, \quad (5.13)$$

so
$$r_{MW} = p_{MX}r_{XW} + p_{MV}r_{VW} + p_{MS}r_{SW} + p_{MF}r_{FW} + p_{Ma}r_{ab}p_{Wb}. \quad (5.14)$$

The sum of the first four terms on the right-hand side of equation 5.14 is the value of the correlation between M and W implicit in their mutual causation by X, V, S and F. The model implies that the remainder of the correlation is accounted for by $p_{Ma}r_{ab}p_{Wb}$, the joint effect of variables unrelated to X, V, S or F. That is, a failure of the measured common causes of M and W to account for their intercorrelation requires us to postulate a correlation between their residual causes. The error correlation, r_{ab}, is the fourth-order partial correlation between M and W with X, V, S and F controlled; the model of Figure 5.1 makes explicit the rationale for calculating such a coefficient. Without the assumption of correlated error it may not be possible to render the model consistent with all of the available data.

As in the case of equation 5.11, equation 5.14 is not a complete or unique interpretation of the correlation of interest, except in regard to the division between "explained" and "unexplained" components of variation. For example, had we begun our effort to express r_{MW} with W, we would have obtained

$$r_{MW} = p_{WX}r_{XM} + p_{WV}r_{VM} + p_{WS}r_{SM} + p_{WF}r_{FM} + p_{Wb}r_{ba}p_{Ma}. \quad (5.15)$$

The problem is that neither 5.14 nor 5.15 decomposes the part of r_{MW} explained by background variables into their direct and joint effects. The complete and correct decomposition may be obtained by substitution of the appropriate expansions of the observed correlations on the right-hand side of either equation 5.14 or equation 5.15.

In Figure 5.1 the failure of the socioeconomic variables to account for the correlation between M and W forces us to assume a correlation between the residual variables, $r_{ab} = .621$, which is nearly as large as the zero-order correlation between the two indicators of achievement. The value of r_{MW} implied by the socioeconomic variables alone is .055, which is only 8.6 percent of the observed value of the correlation. While the socioeconomic model of academic achievement appears slightly better when judged by our second criterion, it is still miserably inadequate. While it is of great sociological interest to document and interpret the effect of social origin on academic achievement, that effect is in no sense an adequate theory of achievement. Hence, socioeconomic variables alone are inadequate controls in studies of the net effect of the school on achievement; their use may lead to unwarranted inferences about the latter's importance.

Intelligence, Socioeconomic Background, and Achievement

In Figure 5.2 the set of predetermined variables in the preliminary model has been modified by the removal of intact family and the addition of measured intelligence. The path coefficients were derived from the correlations in Table 5.1 in exactly the same way as the coefficients in Figure 5.1. In terms of either of our explanatory criteria this second model is a substantial improvement over the first. With the addition of Q the model accounts for 31.3 percent of the variance in M and 34.0 percent of the variance in W. Further, the value of r_{MW} implied by the measured predetermined variables is .325, implying $r_{ab} = .469$. That is, the combined effect of

Figure 5.2.—Effect of socioeconomic background and intelligence on academic achievement, white public secondary school students: Nashville SMSA, 1957

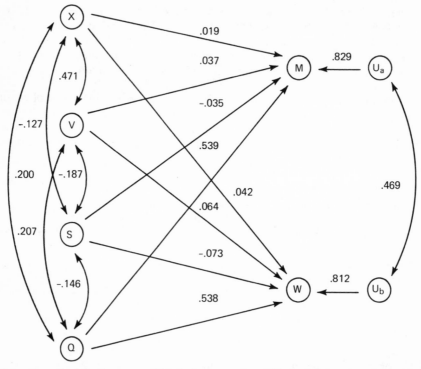

Note: Item identifications are: X-Father's occupation; V-Father's education; S-Number of siblings; Q-Intelligence; M-Stanford Mathematics Grade Equivalent; W-Stanford Reading Grade Equivalent; U_a-Unmeasured determinants of M; and U_b-Unmeasured determinants of W.

socioeconomic background and intelligence accounts for (.325/.640) x 100 = 50.8 percent of the correlation between the two indicators of achievement. At the same time, half an explanation is not a satisfactory explanation, and our earlier caution about the use of socioeconomic variables as controls in studies of the effect of the school applies with almost equal force to this revised model.

The outstanding feature of the path model in Figure 5.2 is the powerful influence of intelligence, which practically washes out the direct effects of the other variables. With one exception, each of the direct effects of the socioeconomic variables is at least twice as large in Figure 5.1 as in Figure 5.2. That is, the model suggests that the association of socioeconomic background with achievement is primarily a function of its association with intelligence and only secondarily a function of its influence on achievement by other mechanisms. This impression can be quantified using the estimating equations to interpret relevant correlations. For example, we can express r_{VW} as

$$r_{VW} = p_{WX}r_{XV} + p_{WV} + p_{WS}r_{SV} + p_{WQ}r_{QV} \qquad (5.16)$$

The sum of the first three terms on the right-hand side of 5.16 includes the direct effect of V and its association with W by way of its correlation with the other two socioeconomic variables, and the fourth component represents association of V with W by way of its correlation with Q. Here, the socioeconomic effects sum to .098, and the component involving Q is .111.

Table 5.2.—Direct and indirect components of the association of socioeconomic background and intelligence with academic achievement, white public secondary school students: Nashville SMSA, 1957

Correlation	Effect via X, V and S	Effect via Q	Total
r_{XM}	27.6%	72.4%	100.0%
r_{VM}	31.9	68.1	100.0
r_{SM}	36.0	64.0	100.0
r_{QM}	3.0	97.0	100.0
r_{XW}	43.1	56.9	100.0
r_{VW}	46.8	53.2	100.0
r_{SW}	53.6	46.4	100.0
r_{QW}	5.7	94.3	100.0

Note: Item identifications are: X-Father's occupation; V-Father's education; S-Number of siblings; Q-Intelligence; M-Stanford Mathematics Grade Equivalent; and W-Stanford Reading Grade Equivalent.

Expressed in relative terms, $(.111/.209) \times 100 = 53.2$ percent of the correlation between father's education and reading achievement is attributable to the association of father's education with the intelligence of his child.

Similar decompositions of the other correlations between background variables and indicators of achievement are displayed in Table 5.2. Intelligence is responsible for about half the correlation between each socioeconomic indicator and achievement in reading, and it is responsible for about two-thirds of the association of each socioeconomic indicator with achievement in mathematics. Obversely, socioeconomic background plays only a minor role in accounting for the correlations between intelligence and the two indicators of achievement. Only 5.7 percent of the correlation between Q and W and 3.0 percent of the correlation between Q and M are attributable to the association of Q with the socioeconomic variables.

One other calculation may be useful in our efforts to assess the relative importance of socioeconomic background and intelligence in the determination of academic achievement. We may write the correlation between achievement in reading and mathematics implied by the model as

$$r'_{MW} = p_{MX}r_{XW} + p_{MV}r_{VW} + p_{MS}r_{SW} + p_{MQ}r_{QW}, \tag{5.17}$$

where the prime ($'$) is used to distinguish the implied and observed correlation coefficients. Substituting the interpretations of the four observed correlations on the right hand side of 5.17, we have

$$
\begin{aligned}
r'_{MW} = {} & p_{MX}(p_{WX} + p_{WV}r_{VX} + p_{WS}r_{SX} + p_{WQ}r_{QX}) \\
& + p_{MV}(p_{WX}r_{XV} + p_{WV} + p_{WS}r_{SV} + p_{WQ}r_{QV}) \\
& + p_{MS}(p_{WX}r_{XS} + p_{WV}r_{VS} + p_{WS} + p_{WQ}r_{QS}) \\
& + p_{MQ}(p_{WX}r_{XQ} + p_{WV}r_{VQ} + p_{WS}r_{SQ} + p_{WQ}). \tag{5.18}
\end{aligned}
$$

Multiplying through and rearranging terms, we can express the implied correlation as

$$r'_{MW} = A + B + C, \tag{5.19}$$

where

$$
\begin{aligned}
A = {} & p_{MX}p_{WX} + p_{MV}p_{WV} + p_{MS}p_{WS} + p_{MX}r_{XV}p_{WV} + p_{MX}r_{XS}p_{WS} \\
& + p_{MV}r_{VX}p_{WX} + p_{MV}r_{VS}p_{WS} + p_{MS}r_{SX}p_{WX} + p_{MS}r_{SV}p_{WV} \tag{5.20}
\end{aligned}
$$

includes the direct and joint effects of the socioeconomic background variables;

$$
\begin{aligned}
B = {} & p_{MX}r_{XQ}p_{WQ} + p_{MV}r_{VQ}p_{WQ} + p_{MS}r_{SQ}p_{WQ} + p_{MQ}r_{QX}p_{WX} \\
& + p_{MQ}r_{QV}p_{WV} + p_{MQ}r_{QS}p_{WS} \tag{5.21}
\end{aligned}
$$

includes the joint effects of the socioeconomic variables and intelligence; and

$$C = p_{MQ}p_{WQ} \tag{5.22}$$

is the direct effect of intelligence. Here, we find $A = .008$, $B = .026$ and $C = .290$. That is, intelligence alone accounts for 89.3 percent of the implied value of r_{MW}; the socioeconomic variables account for 2.6 percent of the implied value; and joint effects of intelligence and the background variables account for the remaining 8.1 percent of the implied correlation. Clearly, intelligence plays a crucial role in mediating the effect of social origins on academic achievement, and it adds substantially to the explanation of achievement by socioeconomic background alone. At the same time, the addition of intelligence to the model does not provide a complete explanation of achievement.

Intelligence Testing and Socioeconomic Discrimination

In one widely accepted explanation of the high correlation between measured intelligence and academic achievement intelligence testing is seen as a discriminatory administrative mechanism. The theory has been expressed with particular force by Sexton (1961:51-52):

> One very destructive function of the IQ score is that it serves as a kind of cement which fixes students into the social classes of their birth. . . . Typically, the lower-income child comes to school and sooner or later he learns that he cannot compete with upper-income students. . . . For these reasons he does poorly on IQ tests. The teacher learns that he has a low IQ rating and puts him into a slow-moving group where he is not expected to do much or given much attention. . . . Intellectually he is lost.

Stated in a more general way, the explanation is that there is an element of socioeconomic discrimination in intelligence tests; students with middle- and upper-class backgrounds outperform their less privileged peers who are equal or better in the abilities purportedly measured by the tests. Further, tests are used by schools in a variety of ways to increase the educational opportunities of students who do well on them and to reduce the opportunities of students who do poorly (Goslin, 1963:153-191). Consequently, as an administrative mechanism, intelligence testing has the character of a self-fulfilling prophecy (Rosenthal and Jacobson, 1968), whose major function is to restrict the educational opportunities of the poor.

The socioeconomic theory of intelligence testing can be dealt with by a simple rearrangement and reinterpretation of our data. In the path model in Figure 5.3 this is done by depicting intelligence test score as the sole intervening variable mediating the effects of the socioeconomic variables on achievement. Figure 5.3 differs from Figure 5.2 in that the paths from X, V and S to M and to W have been deleted, and direct paths have been drawn from X, V and S to Q. That is, socioeconomic background influences intelligence, and intelligence influences achievement, but there are no direct effects of background on achievement. We now think of Q as representing a biased set of test scores, rather than the true trait values. We interpret the effects of X, V and S on Q as the extent of socioeconomic bias in the test scores and the effect of Q on M and W as consequences of differential treatment based on performance on tests.

Figure 5.3.—Intelligence as an intervening variable in the determination of academic achievement, white public secondary school students: Nashville SMSA, 1957

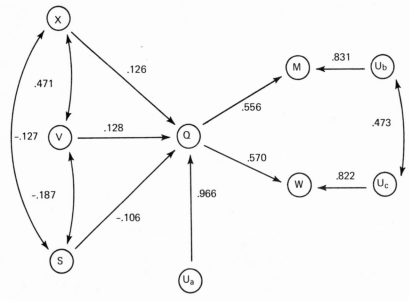

Note: Item identifications are: X-Father's occupation; V-Father's education; S-Number of siblings; M-Stanford Mathematics Grade Equivalent; W-Stanford Reading Grade Equivalent; U_a-Unmeasured determinants of Q; U_b-Unmeasured determinants of M; and U_c-Unmeasured determinants of W.

The coefficients shown in Figure 5.3 were obtained simply by regressing Q on X, V and S and regressing M and W on Q. The deletion of direct paths from socioeconomic background to achievement added six more correlation coefficients (r_{MX}, r_{MV}, r_{MS}, r_{WX}, r_{WV}, and r_{WS}) to the one (r_{MW}) not used in obtaining path coefficients in the earlier models. Consequently, our confidence in the descriptive validity of the model depends in part on its ability to reproduce those seven zero-order correlation coefficients. With respect to the explanation of r_{MW} this model is very little worse than that of Figure 5.2. As we already had reason to suspect, intelligence alone accounts for about half the correlation between the two indicators of achievement. The implied correlations between the achievement indicators and background variables are obtained from expressions like

$$r'_{MX} = p_{MQ}r_{QX},\qquad(5.23)$$

under the assumption that the background variables are uncorrelated with the residual causes of achievement (i.e. $r_{bX} = r_{bV} = r_{bS} = r_{cX} = r_{cV} = r_{cS} = 0$). Using equation 5.23, we find $r'_{MX} = .111$, while $r_{MX} = .149$, so the model understates the observed correlation by .038 or about a quarter of its value. The other five correlation coefficients are not reproduced so closely by the model. For example, $r'_{SW} = p_{WQ}r_{QS} = -.083$, which is less than half the observed value, $r_{SW} = -.169$.

Despite this less than perfect fit of model and data, the model does hold some substantive interest. First, the data are consistent with the conclusion that intelligence testing plays a major role in the determination of achievement. It is possible to conclude that half to three-fourths of the effect of socioeconomic background on academic achievement is mediated by the testing process and its consequences. It should be understood this is a maximum estimate of the role of the testing process in the determination of achievement. That is, we have exaggerated the role of intelligence testing as a stratifying mechanism to the extent that variables other than test-related bias produce the correlation between background and measured intelligence, and variables other than administrative manipulation produce the correlations between intelligence and achievement. Second, the treatment of measured intelligence as a dependent variable emphasizes the fact that it is not very strongly related to the socioeconomic background variables. This fact is expressed most succinctly by the large coefficient for the residual path leading to Q, $p_{Qa} = .966$. In terms of its effects on achievement, our conclusion is that most of the influence of measured intelligence is the indirect expression of factors unrelated to socioeconomic background. The assertion that intelligence testing functions to "cement" the relationship between social origin and academic achievement is incomplete and misleading without the qualification that testing also introduces a large component of variance in achievement that is independent of social origin.

Under certain conditions the failure of a measured intervening variable to mediate all of the influence of a set of antecedent variables on a set of dependent variables may be explained away by an assumption about measurement error in the intervening variable. Empirically, this is very nearly so in the case of the socioeconomic theory of intelligence testing. A much improved fit of data and model is obtained if we merely postulate a coefficient of attenuation of .704 for Q (Hauser, 1968:162-166). In the present theoretical context this is not a satisfactory solution. When we think of intelligence as a true individual trait, it is reasonable to think our measures of that trait are subject to attenuation. Here we think of Q as an administrative datum with direct consequences upon the treatment of individual students. Whatever the true value of a student's intelligence, schools can base decisions only on its measured value.

There is one other procedure which would improve the fit of data and model while retaining the substance of the socioeconomic theory of intelligence testing; in it discrimination in the quality of teaching appears as an explicit hypothetical construct. The actual extent of discriminatory teaching practice and its relation to social origins, intelligence and achievement are, of course, unknown, but we can consider a range of possibilities compatible with the data. We begin with the assumption that quality of teaching, denoted by K, is the missing variable accounting for that portion of the common content of M and W not explained by intelligence.

We assume that the relationships of X, V, S, and Q with M and W are identical in order to simplify the computations. We use the values $r_{QM} = r_{QW} = .560$; $r_{XM} = r_{XW} = .169$; $r_{VM} = r_{VW} = .186$; and $r_{SM} = r_{SW} = -.146$. We also assume that K, like the background variables, has identical gross relationships with M and W, that is $r_{KM} = r_{KW}$. In the two interpretations shown in Figure 5.4 socioeconomic background is presumed to influence intelligence and quality of teaching, and the latter variables act directly on achievement, completely accounting for $r_{MW} = .640$ with $r_{ab} = 0$. The conceptual distinctions among

Figure 5.4.—Two hypothetical models of the achievement process within schools, white public secondary school students: Nashville SMSA, 1957

A. Equal Access

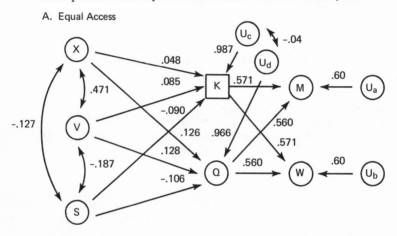

B. Elite Selection

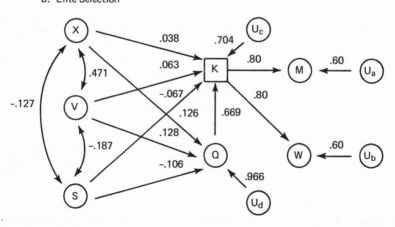

Note: Item identifications are: X-Father's occupation; V-Father's education; S-Number of siblings; K-Effects of teaching; M-Stanford Mathematics Grade Equivalent; W-Stanford Reading Grade Equivalent; Q-Intelligence; U_a-Unmeasured determinants of M; U_b-Unmeasured determinants of W; U_c-Unmeasured determinants of K; and U_d-Unmeasured determinants of Q.

ACADEMIC ACHIEVEMENT

Q, K, and M and W are now rather fine; Q is what the student *can learn*, K is what the student is *taught*, M and W are what the student *has learned*.

In the top model in Figure 5.4 it is assumed that there is no causal relationship and no covariation between Q and K. Because measured intelligence is ignored by teachers, the model can be described as one of equal access to educational facilities. The path coefficients and correlations involving M may be obtained from the equation

$$r_{MW} = p_{MK}r_{KW} + p_{MQ}r_{QW}. \tag{5.24}$$

Because it has been assumed that $r_{KW} = r_{KM}$ and $r_{QW} = r_{QM}$, equation 5.24 can be rewritten as

$$r_{MW} = p_{MK}r_{KM} + p_{MQ}r_{QM}. \tag{5.25}$$

Because $r_{KQ} = r_{Ka} = r_{Qa} = 0$, it can be shown that $r_{KM} = p_{MK}$ and $r_{QM} = p_{MQ}$. Thus, equation 5.25 can be rewritten as

$$r_{MW} = r_{KM}^{2} + r_{QM}^{2}, \text{ or}$$
$$r_{KM}^{2} = 0.64 - (0.56)^2 = 0.326 \tag{5.26}$$

Taking the positive root, we find $r_{KM} = p_{MK} = .571$. Because the right side of equation 5.25 is also an expression for the proportion of variance in M explained by K and Q, the residual path can be found as $p_{Ma} = \sqrt{1 - r_{MW}} = .60$. The solutions for the path coefficients and correlations involving W are analogous.

Given the assumed values of the correlations of X, V, and S with the indicators of academic achievement and the assumption that the background factors are uncorrelated with U_a and U_b, values of the correlations of X, V, and S with M and W are implied by the equations

$$r_{MX} = r_{WX} = p_{MK}r_{KX} + p_{MQ}r_{QX}, \tag{5.27}$$

$$r_{MV} = r_{WV} = p_{MK}r_{KV} + p_{MQ}r_{QV}, \tag{5.28}$$

and $\quad r_{MS} = r_{WS} = p_{MK}r_{KS} + p_{MQ}r_{QS}. \tag{5.29}$

By substitution of known path coefficients and correlations, we find $r_{KX} = .099$, $r_{KV} = .124$, and $r_{KS} = -.112$; the values of the path coefficients of the socioeconomic background variables can be found in the usual fashion.

Under these assumptions the implied correlations between background variables and quality of teaching are two-thirds to three-fourths as large as the original correlations between background and achievement. While background does have an effect on teaching, that effect need not be large to account for the relation between background and academic achievement; nearly all of the variation in quality of teaching must be explained by variables unrelated to background.

The solution just obtained depends on the assumption that quality of teaching is unrelated to intelligence, but we do not know whether this was the case. We can test the conclusion by adopting an extreme alternative assumption: that measured intelligence as well as background affects teaching, while the latter alone accounts for the common content of the measures of achievement. We again allow the background variables to influence directly both K and Q, but not M or W. This second set of assumptions seems more congruent than the first with the suggestion offered by critics of intelligence testing that it functions to select an educational elite from the higher strata of origin.

The elite model is shown in the lower panel of Figure 5.4. The application of the algorithm just described yields the values, $r_{KM} = p_{MK} = r_{KW} = p_{WK} = .80$; $p_{Ma} = p_{Wb} = .60$; $r_{KQ} = .70$; $r_{KX} = .211$; $r_{KV} = .233$; and $r_{KS} = -.182$. The implied correlations between socioeconomic background and teaching are now 25 percent larger than the original correlations between background and achievement. This greater gross "discrimination" by socioeconomic background follows from the assumption that more intelligent students are taught more. Larger correlations between socioeconomic background and quality of teaching could be generated only by assuming that intelligence has a negative direct effect on academic achievement. In this sense, the elite-selection model provides a maximum reasonable estimate of the influence of background on teaching. The elite model is formally consistent with the assumption that intelligence-testing is a mechanism which discriminates against the poor, but the data suggest the mechanism is not very effective. While half the variance in quality of teaching is "explained" in the elite model, most of the explanation is attributable to intelligence, and the direct effect of socioeconomic background on quality of teaching is smaller in the elite model than in the equal-access model. Obversely, even in the elite model, half the variance in teaching quality is independent of social background and measured intelligence. In neither interpretation does background account for much of the variation in intelligence. Again, the latter variable introduces a large component of variation in achievement which is independent of social origin.

The value of these conclusions depends, of course, on the validity of prior assumptions. We want to emphasize most strongly that the preceding discussion is a quantitative speculation, not an exercise in statistical estimation. Quality of teaching was not measured directly; it is simply a plausible label for the unobservable variable K under stated conditions. In particular, it is worthwhile to reconsider the assumption of both models that K accounts for that portion of the common content of M and W not explained by intelligence. It is possible that quality of teaching has little of the influence we imputed to it. In that case, background must have a large effect on teaching if it is to mediate the effects of background on achievement. As long as intelligence and quality of teaching are assumed to account for the influence of background on achievement, the data are consistent with either the assumption that quality of teaching has a powerful influence on achievement or that background has a powerful influence on teaching quality, but those two assumptions are mutually inconsistent. If we started with the latter assumption, of more status discrimination, we would estimate the effect of discrimination on achievement to be smaller. Then, no longer being able to account for the correlation between the indicators of achievement, we would be forced to look for new and powerful influences on achievement which were unrelated to background.

Reciprocal Causation of Academic Achievement

Our rejection of socioeconomic theories of achievement and speculations on alternative models of the process of achievement have all been based on the assumptions (1) that an adequate model will account for the observed correlation between achievement in reading and in mathematics and (2) that there are no direct causal links between achievement in the two fields of learning. At this point we question the second assumption. The proposition that achievement stimulates achievement seems almost self-evident; it underlies most curriculum design and most sequences of grades and courses, and the assumed transferability of basic intellectual skills is a major *raison d'etre* of "general" education at every level of schooling.

Still, we did not begin with the assumption of direct causal links between achievement in the two fields. We wanted to examine the merits of explanations of individual variation in achievement which have been used to rationalize statistical controls in studies of the effect of schools, and with a single exception (Shaycoft, 1967) recent levels of achievement have not been used as statistical controls in studies of the effects of secondary schools. Further, as long as we retain a recursive framework, either the assumption that achievement in reading causes achievement in mathematics, or the reverse, would exhaust the data. That is, either assumption would be sufficient to account for the correlation between achievement in reading and in mathematics and we could not make both assumptions at the same time. On *a priori* grounds it is difficult to decide which kind of achievement should be given causal priority. Reading skills may be as necessary for understanding mathematics texts and tests as they are for comprehending history or literature. On the other hand, skill in the manipulation of numbers and other abstract concepts may improve one's ability to organize and retain non-mathematical information.

In sociology it has become traditional to treat the problem of reciprocal causation by specifying arbitrarily that causation flows only in one direction, by collecting panel data, or by ignoring it. Actually, models incorporating instantaneous reciprocal causation are not intractable if requisite assumptions have been met. Although there has been only one published application of such a model in sociology (Duncan, Haller and Portes, 1968), they are conventional in economics under the rubric of simultaneous equation models (Johnston, 1963:231-274; Goldberger, 1964:288-388).

The path model in Figure 5.5 depicts achievement in reading and in mathematics as simultaneously determined by each other and, as well, by intelligence and socioeconomic background. Unlike our earlier constructions, this path model is just-identified; that is, it makes use of all the information in the correlation matrix and reproduces each correlation coefficient exactly. There is no "test" of the model beyond the plausibility of the numerical solu-

Figure 5.5.—Simultaneous determination of reading and mathematics achievement, white public secondary school students: Nashville SMSA, 1957

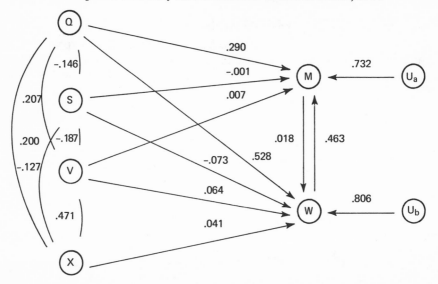

Note: Item identifications are: X-Father's occupation; V-Father's education; S-Number of siblings; M-Stanford Mathematics Grade Equivalent; W-Stanford Reading Grade Equivalent; Q-Intelligence; U_a-Unmeasured determinants of M; U_b-Unmeasured determinants of W.

tion and the causal assumptions underlying it. The crucial substantive feature of the model which permits us to estimate both of the mutual effects of achievement in reading and in mathematics is the assumption that father's occupational status affects achievement in mathematics only indirectly. That is, X affects M by virtue of its correlations with V, S and Q, which affect M directly, and also by virtue of its indirect influence on M via W, but there is no direct path from X to M. In the present case the numerical solution is not very sensitive to which of the paths from the background variables to achievement in mathematics is dropped, but the deletion of p_{MX} seems most plausible.

Because of the introduction of reciprocal effects, the path diagram no longer provides accurate guidance in writing equations, and greater reliance must be placed on application of the basic theorem. As a reminder, the arrows have been deleted from the paths depicting unanalyzed correlations. The structural equations of the model are

$$M = p_{MQ}Q + p_{MS}S + p_{MV}V + p_{MW}W + p_{Ma}U_a \qquad (5.30)$$

and $\qquad W = p_{wQ}Q + p_{wS}S + p_{wV}V + p_{wX}X + p_{wM}M + p_{wb}U_b, \qquad (5.31)$

and we assume further that $r_{aQ} = r_{aS} = r_{aV} = r_{aX} = r_{bQ} = r_{bS} = r_{bV} = r_{bX} = r_{ab} = 0$. At this point it is useful to distinguish the exogenous variables (X, V, S and Q), which never appear as dependent variables in the system,

ACADEMIC ACHIEVEMENT

from the endogenous variables (M and W) which appear so at least once. Applying the basic theorem to equation 5.30, we can write expressions for the correlations of M with the exogenous variables:

$$r_{MQ} = p_{MQ} + p_{MS}r_{SQ} + p_{MV}r_{VQ} + p_{MW}r_{WQ}, \qquad (5.32)$$

$$r_{MS} = p_{MQ}r_{QS} + p_{MS} + p_{MV}r_{VS} + p_{MW}r_{WS}, \qquad (5.33)$$

$$r_{MV} = p_{MQ}r_{QV} + p_{MS}r_{SV} + p_{MV} + p_{MW}r_{WV}, \qquad (5.34)$$

and $\qquad r_{MX} = p_{MQ}r_{QX} + p_{MS}r_{SX} + p_{MV}r_{VX} + p_{MW}r_{WX}. \qquad (5.35)$

These are not the symmetric normal equations of multiple regression analysis, but they may readily be solved for p_{MQ}, p_{MS}, p_{MV} and p_{MW}. Applying the theorem again to equation 5.30, we find

$$r_{MW} = p_{MQ}r_{QW} + p_{MS}r_{SW} + p_{MV}r_{VW} + p_{MW} + p_{Ma}r_{aW}, \qquad (5.36)$$

while $\qquad r_{aW} = p_{WM}r_{Ma} \qquad (5.37)$

from equation 5.31, so

$$r_{MW} = p_{MQ}r_{QW} + p_{MS}r_{SW} + p_{MV}r_{VW} + p_{MW} + p_{Ma}p_{WM}r_{Ma}. \qquad (5.38)$$

Also, we find that

$$r_{MM} = 1 = p_{MQ}r_{QM} + p_{MS}r_{SM} + p_{MV}r_{VM} + p_{MW}r_{WM} + p_{Ma}r_{aM}. \qquad (5.39)$$

Rearranging equations 5.38 and 5.39, we can solve for

$$p_{WM} = \frac{r_{MW} - (p_{MQ}r_{QW} + p_{MS}r_{SW} + p_{MV}r_{VW} + p_{MW})}{1 - (p_{MQ}r_{QM} + p_{MS}r_{SM} + p_{MV}r_{VM} + p_{MW}r_{WM})}. \qquad (5.40)$$

Applying the basic theorem to equation 5.31 to express the correlations of W with the exogenous variables and shifting terms in p_{WM} to the left-hand side, we find

$$r_{WQ} - p_{WM}r_{MQ} = p_{WQ} + p_{WS}r_{SQ} + p_{WV}r_{VQ} + p_{WX}r_{XQ}, \qquad (5.41)$$

$$r_{WS} - p_{WM}r_{MS} = p_{WQ}r_{QS} + p_{WS} + p_{WV}r_{VS} + p_{WX}r_{XS}, \qquad (5.42)$$

$$r_{WV} - p_{WM}r_{MV} = p_{WQ}r_{QV} + p_{WS}r_{SV} + p_{WV} + p_{WX}r_{XV}, \qquad (5.43)$$

and $\qquad r_{WX} - p_{WM}r_{MX} = p_{WQ}r_{QX} + p_{WS}r_{SX} + p_{WV}r_{VX} + p_{WX}. \qquad (5.44)$

Since p_{WM} and all of the correlation coefficients are known, equations 5.41 to 5.44 may be solved for p_{WQ}, p_{WS}, p_{WV} and p_{WX}. By substitution we can solve equation 5.39 for $p_{Ma}r_{aM}$ and equation 5.36 for $p_{Ma}r_{aM}$. Applying the basic theorem to equation 5.30, we find that

$$r_{aM} = p_{Ma} + p_{MW}r_{Wa}, \qquad (5.45)$$

so $\qquad p_{Ma}^2 = p_{Ma}r_{aM} - p_{MW}p_{Ma}r_{aW}, \qquad (5.46)$

which may be solved by substitution for a conventionally positive value of p_{Ma}. Values for r_{aM} and r_{aW} may be obtained by back substitution. Finally, an analogous application of the basic theorem to equation 5.31 yields expressions for r_{MW}, r_{WW}, r_{bW}, which may be manipulated to yield values for p_{Wb}, r_{bW} and r_{bM}.

The remarkable fact about the numerical solution to the model in Figure 5.5 is that the results are almost identical with those we would have obtained by ordinary regression of W on X, V, S and Q and of M on X, V, S, Q and W. That is, while we have allowed for the possibility that M affects W directly, we find a negligible coefficient ($p_{WM} = .018$) for that path and a large coefficient for the effect of W on M ($p_{MW} = .463$). Each of the socio-economic background variables has a modest direct effect on achievement in reading and a negligible direct effect on achievement in mathematics. (Of course, $p_{MX} = 0$ by assumption.) Intelligence again plays a key role in this model since it exerts a large direct effect on achievement in reading, and on achievement in mathematics its indirect effect, via achievement in reading, is almost as large as its direct effect.

The fact that the model in Figure 5.5 is just-identified means we cannot evaluate it by trying to reproduce the correlation between the indicators of achievement. Of course, one may wish to propose other criteria of explanatory adequacy, but we have satisfied the second of our initial criteria by assumption. If one believes the initial assumptions of this model, achievement in reading ought to be used as a statistical control in studies of school effects on achievement in mathematics.

Net School Differences in Achievement

Because most of the variation in academic achievement occurs within schools, we have given close attention to alternative interpretations of the role played in within-school variation in achievement by background, intelligence and other variables. Our major finding has been that it cannot be accounted for by socioeconomic variables, even when supplemented by measured intelligence. At this point we turn to the implications of our findings about within-school variation for the explanation of between-school variation in academic achievement. Despite the inadequacies of socioeconomic theories of achievement, the fact is that students with different backgrounds do differ systematically in academic achievement. Further, we have seen (Chapter IV) that schools differ in the background characteristics and intelligence of their student bodies. We can now ask how much between-school variation in achievement can be explained by these two facts.

Components of between-school variance in academic achievement explained by the socioeconomic variables, intelligence, and school variables are displayed in Table 5.3 by grade and sex. These partitions of variance are derived from covariance adjustments based on within-school regressions of M and W on X, V, S and Q. Following the model already described (Chapter II, equation 2.22), there are three components in the allocation of variance in each subgroup: composition, joint and residual. Composition represents the combined net effects of intelligence and the background variables, i.e., the extent to which school differences can be explained "mechanically" by the fact that student bodies differ in composition on variables that affect academic achievement. Joint variance exists because variables in the composition of student bodies which affect achievement covary with other aggregate characteristics of schools which also influence achievement. Residual variance represents the influence of other aggregate characteristics of the school, net of the composition of the student body. While we could make a finer decomposition of between-school variance if we would assume that composition affected the other school variables, or *vice versa* (Duncan, Cuz-

Table 5.3.—Allocation of variance in between-school model of determination of academic achievement by composition on family background characteristics, intelligence, and residual factors by sex and grade, white public secondary school students: Nashville SMSA, 1957

Sex and grade	Determination of M				Determination of W			
	Composition	Joint	Residual	Total	Composition	Joint	Residual	Total
Males								
12	6.0%	24.0%	70.0%	100.0%	11.1%	24.7%	64.2%	100.0%
11	11.5	28.9	59.6	100.0	24.3	35.0	40.6	100.0
10	25.4	31.8	42.9	100.0	35.9	28.8	35.4	100.0
9	24.0	− 8.2	84.2	100.0	43.9	−21.8	78.0	100.0
8	38.7	−38.4	99.7	100.0	41.7	−23.5	81.8	100.0
7	39.0	−23.5	84.6	100.0	38.7	4.6	56.7	100.0
Females								
12	10.5%	− 1.4%	91.0%	100.0%	8.5%	14.4%	77.1%	100.0%
11	5.7	7.3	87.0	100.0	22.7	2.2	75.2	100.0
10	28.3	28.1	43.6	100.0	53.8	25.0	21.2	100.0
9	30.0	−14.5	84.6	100.0	36.9	− 2.2	65.3	100.0
8	35.2	−19.6	84.3	100.0	44.6	−17.6	73.0	100.0
7	54.4	−10.6	56.2	100.0	56.0	4.8	39.2	100.0

Note: Family background characteristics are: X-Father's occupation; V-Father's education; and S-Number of siblings. Academic achievement measures are: M-Stanford Mathematics Grade Equivalent; and W-Stanford Reading Grade Equivalent. Components may not add to 100 percent because of independent rounding.

zort and Duncan, 1961:120-128; Taeuber and Taeuber, 1965:86-95), we were unwilling to do so because the "other school factors" are defined only residually. In the present context our most specific label for "other school factors" would be "school quality." In a school system where school attended is determined primarily by residence there is no reason to prefer the hypothesis that good schools attract high-status families with bright youngsters to its opposite, that bright youngsters from families of high status make schools good.

It should be kept in mind that the allocations of variance in Table 5.3 refer only to between-school variance in achievement. The explanation achieved in the between-school segment of the covariance model is discounted to the extent that school achievement fails to correlate perfectly with individual students' achievements. For example, in the case of seventh-grade girls, composition on X, V, S and Q accounts directly for 56 percent of the between-school variance in reading achievement. Since between-school variance in reading achievement is only 17 percent of the total in that subgroup (see Table 4.1), the net contribution of composition on X, V, S and Q to the total variance is (56%) (17%) = 9.5 percent. Also, X, V, S and Q account for 38 percent of the within-school variance in reading achievement of seventh-grade girls (Hauser, 1968:139), and 83 percent of the total variance occurs within schools. Thus, the contribution of the socio-economic variables and intelligence to the explanation of reading achievement via the within-school segment of the model is (38%) (83%) = 31.5 percent of the total variance. In all X, V, S and Q account directly for 9.5 + 31.5 = 41.0 percent of the variance in reading achievement of seventh-grade girls, largely because of their effect on achievement within schools.

The apparent instability of the results over subgroups does not preclude an overall impression that composition accounts for moderate proportions of the variance in achievement among schools, in spite of the inadequacies of the models used to adjust for composition. In the twelve grade-sex subgroups composition explains from 6 percent to 56 percent of the variance in achievement between schools. Residual components of variance range from about 20 percent to near unity, while those of joint variance fluctuate wildly and in several cases are negative. The instability of these and other between-school analyses is in part a function of the number of observations at hand. In the within-school analyses there were thousands of cases, but here the number of schools in each subgroup is small. No more than thirty-four schools were represented at grade seven, and because one school did not retain achievement test scores there were as few as sixteen schools at grade twelve.

The direct effect of composition is generally larger in the lower grades than in the higher, larger on girls than on boys and larger on achievement in reading than in mathematics. These differentials are consistent with detailed findings from within-school regressions for the subgroups. The smaller contributions of composition in the higher grades may be a result of dropping out of school rather than of a real increase in differences in the socializing effect of the school. The negative joint components are probably not trustworthy or meaningful because of the previously noted problem with students in the lower grades whose test scores were reported for the wrong levels of schooling. However, such negative components are what one would expect to find if there were compensatory allocation of educational resources to schools with unfavorable composition. That is, positive joint effects mean that schools with favorable composition reach higher levels of achievement than one would expect from their composition alone, while schools with unfavorable composition reach levels which are lower than expected. Negative joint effects mean the opposite; schools with favorable composition will perform worse than expected from composition, and *vice versa*.

The large residual components of between-school variance are in part a reflection of the inadequacy of the within-school regression models on which the adjustments for composition have been based. The size of those components is also of interest substantively, since they represent the effect of school net of family background and intelligence. That is, within the modest role of differences between schools in the determination of academic achievement there is considerable room for the operation of causal factors unrelated to intelligence and family background. If there is some consistency between composition of the student body and other aspects of the school's quality, it is far from perfect, and attending a school with bright peers, high in status, is no guarantee of educational excellence.

Neighborhood Composition and Academic Achievement

To interpret the joint school effects one may use neighborhood variables to explain the composition of the student body and the quality of school, the latter being defined for the purpose as the residual component of school achievement. The literature on the effect of the school on achievement rather uniformly argues that the correlation between the composition of the student body and other aspects of school quality is both large and positive (Coleman *et al.*, 1966:302-325; Sexton, 1961; Herriott and St. John, 1966; Conant, 1961). Indeed, positive overlap of these factors is the empirical basis of the operational definition of "school contexts" using aggregate socioeconomic characteristics. The argument is sometimes based on the idea that the local community served by the school determines the composition of the student body and the effective demand for educational resources in the school. Leaving to one side the fact that the analysis of the preceding section lends only partial support to the claim that joint effects are large and positive, we may ask whether neighborhoods account for the composition of the student body and the quality of the school.

The two components of school levels of achievement in reading and in mathematics were each regressed on two neighborhood variables: the proportion of males over 25 with at least a high-school education and the proportion of owner-occupancy in white-occupied housing units. We interpret the former as an index of the socioeconomic status of the school district's population and the latter as an index of the stability of the area and the proportion of residents likely to be concerned with school expenditures. The regressions were not intended to account for student body composition in any formal demographic sense nor to express the effect of interaction among students outside of the school proper. With census tract data, the first effort would be futile, since the school survey and the census were conducted three years apart, and households represented in the census might have several or no offspring enrolled in school. The second interpretation would be equally pointless, since the effect of interaction in the neighborhood would have to be represented in the within-school segment of the model. Here, we are only attempting to indicate the connection between urban residential differentiation and achievement in school.

Each pair of regressions could be replicated 24 times, once for each measure of achievement in each combination of sex and grade. The two neighborhood characteristics accounted in most subgroups for from sixty to eighty percent of the variance in the composition of the student body and from twenty to fifty percent of the variance in school quality. The latter finding implies that from fifty to eighty percent of the variance in school quality is not explained by the neighborhood variables, which is to say that quality is not primarily a function of the socioeconomic status of school districts (Hauser, 1968:179-180).

The joint effects of the student body's composition and school quality are not accounted for by our finding that each component of school achievement depends on neighborhood characteristics in the expected fashion. Just as we tested the ability of earlier models to account for the relationship between achievement in mathematics and in reading, we now tested the degree to which the mutual dependence of student body composition and school quality on neighborhood variables accounted for their intercorrelation. While the results were again rather unstable, the neighborhood variables accounted fairly well for the intercorrelations of composition and quality (*ibid.,* p. 182). Over the 24 replications the mean value of the observed correlation between composition and quality was .112, while the mean value of the correlation implied by the neighborhood variables was .131. That is, the model tended to predict slightly larger correlations than were actually observed. A scatter plot of the 24 expected and observed correlation coefficients suggested the relation between the two was nearly linear, and the zero-order correlation between the two sets of coefficients was .91. In short, while the dependence of school quality on the socioeconomic level of the neighborhood was not especially strong, the mutual dependence of the composition of the student body and the quality of the school on neighborhood status was large enough to explain the observed correlations between those variables without recourse to the assumption that composition influenced levels of school achievement except by virtue of the effects of socioeconomic background and intelligence at the level of the individual.

VI

ALLOCATION OF
COURSE MARKS

Performance on objective tests of academic achievement is the measure by which professional educators commonly judge the quality of a school or school system and the progress of an individual student. For the student the significant measure of performance and progress is the course mark. A course mark is an immediate return, both official and permanent, on a student's investment in a course. A record of good marks opens the way to other rewards in the school while a succession of failing marks can lead to failing an entire grade. Marks are a manifest basis of selection in the educational system, as students and teachers know. Both may attempt to make course marks reflect facts other than the learning accomplished, and this makes marks more than imperfect but redundant measures of academic achievement. Sanctions other than course marks may be at the disposal of teachers, but it is not difficult to assume that they are dispensed largely to correspond with course marks. While performance on objective tests may measure what schooling has done for the student, course marks are probably a better measure of the message which he has actually received about his performance.

In this chapter we examine the effects of family background, ability and academic achievement on course marks. The analysis has three objectives: (1) to assess the role of the student's background in the assignment of course marks; (2) to assess the role of ability and academic achievement in the assignment of course marks; and (3) to interpret differences in marking among schools.

The predetermined variables are those treated in the discussion of academic achievement: X, V, S, Q, M, and W. The dependent variables are two course marks, A = mark in arithmetic and E = mark in English. Like the two achievement test scores, the two course marks were measured in the eighth grade in the case of students in the higher grades and in the seventh or eighth grade in the case of those in the two lower grades. As in the case of academic achievement, the treatment of family background characteristics as determinants of course marks of students in the upper grades reverses their temporal priority. It is doubtful, however, that any attenuation of relationships resulting from failure to measure the background variables contemporaneously with the course marks is large in comparison with differences in relationships between students in the lowest and the highest grades which are the result of dropping out of school or other changes.

There is some difficulty in combining data on course marks from the City of Nashville and the Davidson County ring. In one category of residence the marks were reported in letters (A, B, C, D, E), and in the other they were reported on a scale running from 0 to 100. In recoding them for the present analysis, we arbitrarily equated marks on a five-point scale. This procedure failed to eliminate two problems: (1) comparison of marking in the city and county schools and (2) comparison of relationships between marks and other variables in city and county schools.

It was not possible to combine city and county data to determine the amount of variance in marks lying between schools in the metropolitan area as a whole because the procedure outlined above provided no clear basis for comparing marking in the city and county. It was assumed initially that there would be significant differences between the city and county schools in the slopes of regressions involving course marks, but no evidence of such interaction appeared in several tests of that assumption. Results of the between-school analyses were also the same whether the residence groups were treated separately or combined, and only the combined results are reported here.

Within-School Variation in Marks

In the within-school model for the determination of course marks the deviations of students' marks from the average for the school in their grade-sex subgroup are regressed on the deviations from the group averages on predetermined variables. There are two explanatory objectives: (1) to account for the variance in A and in E and (2) to account for the relationship between A and E. As noted earlier, these two objectives are separable, and the latter is of greater interest than the former.

Within-School Correlations

The averages over all of the grade-sex-residence subgroups of the average within-school correlations among the variables are shown in Table 6.1. (The

ALLOCATION OF COURSE MARKS

Table 6.1.—"Average" of within-school correlations among student background factors, measures of academic achievement, and course marks, white public secondary school students: Nashville SMSA, 1957

	V	S	Q	M	W	A	E
X	.471	−.127	.200	.149	.189	.105	.134
V		−.187	.207	.164	.209	.119	.151
S			−.146	−.123	−.169	−.116	−.141
Q				.560	.574	.361	.416
M					.644	.487	.486
W						.368	.463
A							.569

Note: Item identifications are: X-Father's occupation; V-Father's education; S-Number of siblings; Q-Intelligence; M-Stanford Mathematics Grade Equivalent; W-Stanford Reading Grade Equivalent; A-Arithmetic mark; and E-English mark.

upper left-hand portion of the matrix was discussed in Chapter V.) The absolute magnitudes of the correlations of the background variables with course marks are lower than their correlations with the corresponding measures of academic achievement. This suggests that the influence of family background on marks may be mediated by academic achievement. Similarly, ability is less highly related to marks than to academic achievement. In congruence with the previous finding that background is more closely related to achievement in reading than in mathematics, the background variables and ability are more highly correlated with mark in English than with mark in arithmetic.

There is an important asymmetry in the relationships between academic achievement and course marks. Achievement in mathematics has nearly identical relationships with marks in English and in arithmetic. Achievement in reading, however, is less highly correlated with arithmetic mark than with English mark and achievement in mathematics is more highly related to English mark than is achievement in reading. The correlation between A and E, which is the major matter to be explained, is slightly less than the intercorrelation of the two test scores on achievement.

Except for the occasional anomalies to be expected in relationships based on small numbers of observations, the pattern just described also holds for the individual subgroups. In general, the coefficients vary in size inversely with grade in school and are larger for girls than for boys and larger in the county ring than in the city. While these interactions undoubtedly reflect real differences in the organization of city and county schools, they are not very strong. The average correlations for sex-residence subgroups do not often depart more than .05 from the average correlations in Table 6.1. Hence, for summary purposes we shall make extensive use of this average matrix.

Net Effect of Family Background on Marks

There is nothing novel in the finding that students with favorable family background achieve high marks in secondary school (Havighurst and Neugarten, 1957; Abrahamson, 1952a, 1952b; Hollingshead, 1949; Coleman, 1961a; Wilson, 1959, 1963; Gottlieb, 1964; Lavin, 1965; Sexton, 1961). Such findings are sometimes interpreted as a result of conscious or unconscious discrimination on the part of middle-class teachers against lower- and working-class children and in favor of middle- and upper-middle class children (Abrahamson, 1952a, 1952b; Hollingshead, 1949; Wilson, 1959, 1963; Sexton, 1961). However, it is already clear from Table 6.1 that gross within-school relationships between family background and course marks are not large, and they are smaller than the relationships between family background and academic achievement. Further, we have already found that there is little evidence of discriminatory treatment in the determination of academic achievement.

One way to analyze discrimination in the assignment of marks is to ask whether family background adds anything to an explanation of course marks based on ability and academic achievement. That is, we assume that ability and achievement are more proximate determinants of course marks than is family background, and we ask whether the latter adds anything to the explanation of marks in terms of the former. For the averages of the within-school correlations, the coefficients of determination (or proportions of variance explained) in the regressions of A and E on M, Q, and W are .250 and .288, respectively. When X, V, and S are added to the regression equations, the coefficients of determination are raised only to .252 and .291. Hence we conclude that family background adds virtually nothing to the explanation of course marks based on ability and achievement alone (Also see Sewell, Haller and Portes, 1969).

Indirect Effect of Background on Marks

If there is "discrimination" within schools in the assignment of course marks in our Nashville sample, it operates through the differential ability and achievement of students who vary in family background and not through overt discrimination in marking. This interpretation is shown on the path diagram in Figure 6.1, where X, V, and S influence M, Q, and W directly; Q influences M and W directly; and M, Q, and W influence A and E directly, while there are no direct paths from X, V, and S to A or E. The path coefficients shown in Figure 6.1 were estimated by ordinary least squares from the average intercorrelations in Table 6.1.

The effects of X, V and S on Q and of X, V, S and Q on M and W were discussed in Chapter V, so that part of the model requires no further interpretation here. One striking feature of the model, which we have already treated in summary fashion, is its ability to reproduce the correlations of the course marks with each of the background variables. As shown in the last column of Table 6.2, the worst aspect of the fit of data and model is the error of $-.052$ in reproducing r_{ES}, the correlation between mark in English and number of siblings. If one is content to treat errors no larger than that as trivial, it is not necessary to modify the model by drawing a direct path from any of the background variables to course marks.

The model permits us to decompose these background-mark correlations

Figure 6.1.–Family background in the determination of course marks, white public secondary school students: Nashville SMSA, 1957

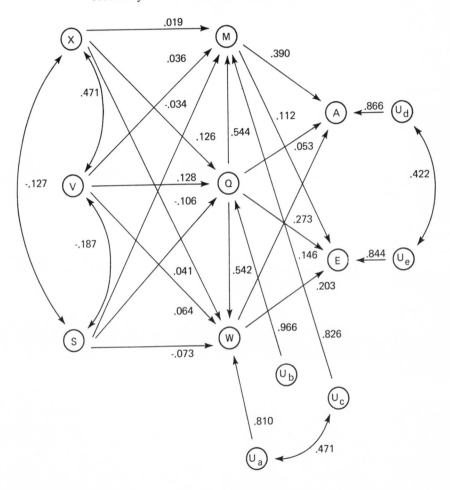

Note: Item identifications are: X-Father's occupation; V-Father's education; S-Number of siblings; M-Stanford Mathematics Grade Equivalent; Q-Intelligence; W-Stanford Reading Grade Equivalent; A-Arithmetic grade; E-English grade; U_a-Unmeasured determinants of W; U_b-Unmeasured determinants of Q; U_c-Unmeasured determinants of M; U_d-Unmeasured determinants of A; and U_e-Unmeasured determinants of E.

Table 6.2.–Interpretation of calculated values of correlations of background variables with course marks, white public secondary school students: Nashville SMSA, 1957

Correlation	Interpretation	Observed value	Effects of background via			
			M	Q	W	Error
r_{AX}	1	.105	.058	.022	.010	.015
	2	.105	.016	.070	.004	.015
r_{AV}	1	.119	.064	.023	.011	.021
	2	.119	.020	.073	.005	.021
r_{AS}	1	−.116	−.048	−.016	−.009	−.043
	2	−.116	−.017	−.051	−.005	−.043
r_{EX}	1	.134	.041	.029	.038	.026
	2	.134	.011	.081	.016	.026
r_{EV}	1	.151	.045	.030	.042	.033
	2	.151	.014	.085	.019	.033
r_{ES}	1	−.141	−.034	−.021	−.034	−.052
	2	−.141	−.012	−.059	−.018	−.052

Note: Item identifications are: X-Father's occupation; V-Father's education; S-Number of siblings; Q-Intelligence; M-Stanford Mathematics Grade Equivalent; W-Stanford Reading Grade Equivalent; A-Arithmetic mark; and E-English mark. Source: Table 6.1 and Figure 6.1. See text for explanation of decompositions.

into effects mediated by each of the proximate causes of course marks. To continue our examination of r_{SE}, we may write it as

$$r_{SE} = p_{EM}r_{MS} + p_{EQ}r_{QS} + p_{EW}r_{WS} + p_{Ee}r_{eS} \qquad (6.1)$$

(gross)　　(via M)　　(via Q)　　(via W)　　(via unmeasured variables)

$$-.141 = .273(-.123) + .146(-.146) + .204(-.169) + .844(-.062)$$

or

$$-.141 = \quad -.034 \qquad -.021 \qquad -.034 \qquad -.052$$

Despite the minimal contribution of the family background variables to the explanation of course marks, net of their indirect influence through ability and achievement, the relationship between number of siblings and the un-measured determinants of mark in English is the largest single component of the relationship between S and E. The effects of size of family on mark in

English by way of mathematics and achievement in reading are equal in size, and each is about fifty percent larger than the effect mediated directly by intelligence. As shown in the rows labelled "interpretation 1" in Table 6.2, much the same pattern holds for the interpretations of r_{EX} and r_{EV}. That is, most of the influence of background on mark in English is ultimately mediated by achievement in mathematics and in reading, and by each to about the same extent. This pattern shifts when the background correlations with mark in arithmetic are decomposed. Hardly any of the effects are mediated by achievement in reading, but the fact remains that academic achievement ultimately mediates most of the effects of background on course marks.

This is not to say that intelligence plays a less important role in the mediation of effects of background on grades than on achievement. While interpretation 1 is correct, it does not express the extent to which effects of background on academic achievement are mediated by intelligence. To describe the crucial role of intelligence in the model we must decompose the correlations of M and W with the background variables. To return to our interpretation of r_{ES}, we need

$$r_{MS} = p_{MS} + p_{MV}r_{VS} + p_{MX}r_{XS} + p_{MQ}r_{QS} \qquad (6.2)$$

and

$$r_{WS} = p_{WS} + p_{WV}r_{VS} + p_{WX}r_{XS} + p_{WQ}r_{QS} \qquad (6.3)$$

Substituting 6.2 and 6.3 for r_{MS} and r_{WS} in 6.1 and combining the effects involving Q, we obtain

$$
\begin{aligned}
r_{ES} = \; & p_{EM}\,(p_{MS} + p_{MV}r_{VS} + p_{MX}r_{XS}) \\
& \text{(effects via M and family background)} \\
& + p_{EM}p_{MQ}r_{QS} + p_{EQ}r_{QS} + p_{EW}p_{WQ}r_{QS} \\
& \text{(effects via Q and family background)} \\
& + p_{EW}\,(p_{WS} + p_{WV}r_{VS} + p_{WX}r_{XS}) \\
& \text{(effects via W and family background)} \\
& + p_{Ee}r_{eS} \qquad\qquad\qquad\qquad\qquad\qquad (6.4) \\
& \text{(effects via unmeasured variables),}
\end{aligned}
$$

or

$$
\begin{array}{ccccc}
-.141 = & -.012 & -.059 & -.018 & -.052. \\
& \text{(via M)} & \text{(via Q)} & \text{(via W)} & \text{(via residual)}
\end{array}
$$

Under the interpretation of equation 6.4 the effects of S transmitted through Q become the largest component of the relationship between S and E, despite the fact that Q has the least direct influence on E of its three measured determinants. The rows labelled "interpretation 2" in Table 6.2 present decompositions of each correlation of a background variable with a course mark analogous to those of equation 6.4. In each case the assumption that intelligence influences achievement directly makes intelligence the most important variable transmitting the effects of background to course marks. Indeed, the residual effects of the background variables are large in comparison with the effects transmitted through M and W. The components of each correlation attributable to Q are about three times as large in interpretation 2 as in interpretation 1. That is, the indirect effects of background on marks via Q and M or W are about twice as large as those mediated by Q alone. Clearly, ability plays a key role in bringing about the relationships between background and course marks, mainly by virtue of its indirect influence on marks through achievement.

Intelligence, Achievement, and Course Marks

It is clear from the direct path coefficients for the residual determinants of A and E in Figure 6.2 and from the correlation between the residuals that academic achievement and intelligence do not explain marks in arithmetic and English. The correlation between A and E implied by the model under the assumption that $r_{de} = 0$ is

$$r'_{AE} = p_{AM}r_{ME} + p_{AQ}r_{QE} + p_{AW}r_{WE} = .261. \qquad (6.5)$$

The model accounts for less than one half of the observed correlation, $r_{AE} = .569$. Apparently there are powerful determinants of course marks which operate net of family background, intelligence, and academic achievement. For example, if a single factor, K, accounted for the remainder of the correlation between A and E, had equal net effects on these two variables, and was unrelated to M, Q and W, we would find for the data of Table 6.1 that

$$r_{AE} = .569 = .261 + p_{EK}p_{AK} \qquad (6.6)$$

or

$$p_{AK} = p_{EK} = .556.$$

This result implies path coefficients for the residual variables of

$$p'_{Ad} = \sqrt{p^2_{Ad} - p^2_{AK}} = \sqrt{(.866)^2 - (.556)^2} = .665$$

and

$$p'_{Ee} = \sqrt{p^2_{Ee} - p^2_{EK}} = \sqrt{(.844)^2 - (.556)^2} = .636.$$

It would take the addition of a factor whose net effects on course marks were of the same magnitude as the gross effects of ability and achievement to account for the relationship between the two course marks. In the following paragraphs the effects of ability and achievement on course marks are discussed in more detail in an effort to interpret the relationship between the course marks in a more satisfactory way.

Differential Influence of Mathematics and Reading Achievement

Suppose the test of achievement in mathematics isolated all the special skills required for success in the arithmetic course, and the test of achievement in reading isolated all the special skills required for success in the English course. Then the direct effects of M on A and of W on E would be large, and the direct effects of M on E and of W on A would be small. In the light of this interpretation the direct effects of intelligence on the two course marks could be large or small, but we might expect them to be nearly equal. It is clear from the earlier discussion of the correlations of M, Q, and W with A and E that the direct effects of M, Q, and W on A and E do not exhibit this neat and symmetric pattern. In Figure 6.1, where M, Q, and W are each allowed to influence both A and E directly, the direct effect of achievement in reading on mark in arithmetic is small and the direct effects of intelligence on marks in arithmetic and English are not too dissimilar. Both of these findings are congruent with the interpretation just advanced, but achievement in mathematics has the largest single direct effect on marks both in arithmetic and in English.

We might conclude that intelligence and achievement in mathematics adequately represent the reading skills required in the arithmetic course, but intelligence and achievement in reading do not incorporate all the analytical skills required in the English course. There is some precedent in previous research for these asymmetric results. Lavin (1965:56) cites two studies which provide comparable correlations of numeric and verbal components of batteries of ability or achievement tests with marks in arithmetic and English courses. Wolking (1955) administered the Differential Aptitude Test battery (DAT) and the Primary Mental Abilities test (PMA) to 139 girls and 138 boys in the eleventh grade of a La Crosse, Wisconsin, high school and computed the correlations of numerical and verbal components of each test with previously earned marks in several courses. Jacobs (1959) obtained scores from the DAT battery and Arithmetic and Reading Proficiency tests which were administered in the eighth grade to students in three Cincinnati high schools, "whose marking practices were sufficiently consistent in relation to ability to justify pooling of the senior populations" (p. 334). These scores were correlated with average marks achieved later in several subjects.

Pertinent results of the Wolking and Jacobs studies are compared with those of the present study in Table 6.3. In all of the cases except the PMA in the Wisconsin population and for both sexes the correlations of the numerical or arithmetic tests with both marks are higher than those of the verbal or reading components. In several instances the correlation of the numeric or arithmetic component with mark in English is higher than its correlation with mark in arithmetic, while the correlation of the verbal or reading component with mark in arithmetic is in every instance lower than its correlation with mark in English.

Of course, this evidence is imperfect, since our primary concern is the effect of each achievement variable net of ability. Our multiple correlation analyses could not be replicated on the Wolking or Jacobs data because the correlations among their predictors were not published. Moreover, only one of the comparisons in Table 6.3 involves correlations of nominal achievement tests with marks, since the DAT and PMA batteries are nominally tests of aptitude or ability. Both authors make note of the differential effects of performance in arithmetic and in reading. Wolking (1955:118) states, "The tests do not generally predict best in the subject usually assumed to be measured by that test," and Jacobs (1955:339) notes that grade point averages are "apparently based to a larger extent on quantitative abilities." We conclude that the pattern of differential effects on achievement in mathematics and in reading on marks in English and arithmetic is not a peculiarity of the Nashville students.

Reciprocal Influence of Marks

Having greater confidence in the generality of this asymmetric pattern, we tried to alter the assumptions of Figure 6.1 so as to explain the correla-

Table 6.3.—Correlations of components of ability and achievement with arithmetic and English marks by sex, white public secondary school students: Nashville SMSA, 1957

Study	Predictor	Males		Females	
		Arithmetic	English	Arithmetic	English
Nashville (average of grades 7-12)	Stanford Arithmetic Achievement	.456	.448	.518	.523
	Stanford Reading Achievement	.330	.416	.407	.510
La Crosse (11th grade)	PMA: Numerical	.31	.47	.34	.44
	Verbal	.42	.49	.46	.55
	DAT: Numerical	.58	.55	.63	.58
	Verbal	.54	.45	.48	.54
Cincinnati (8th grade ability and achievement, high school grades)	DAT: Numerical	.495	.499	.654	.661
	Verbal	.379	.496	.566	.568
	Arithmetic Proficiency	.610	.520	.671	.690
	English Proficiency	.408	.514	.617	.647

Note: See text for reference to sources. PMA is Primary Mental Abilities Test. DAT is Differential Aptitude Test Battery. For the La Crosse study correlations with "arithmetic" mark are average of reported correlations with algebra and geometry marks.

tion between the two marks. After some experimentation, we arrived at the following interpretation: Assume that mark in arithmetic is influenced by achievement in mathematics, intelligence, mark in English and unmeasured variables, and that mark in English is influenced by achievement in mathematics and reading, intelligence, arithmetic mark and unmeasured variables. These assumptions are portrayed by the path diagram in Figure 6.2. The path coefficients were estimated from Table 6.1 in the same way as those in Figure 5.5. Like that model, the model in Figure 6.2 is just-identified. It yields no excess predictions and must be evaluated in terms of its face validity.

There is ample justification for the assumption that marks influence one another directly, net of achievement and intelligence. Lavin (1965:52) for example, states, "While it has been conventional to use the high school grade as an ability measure for predicting college performance, it should be noted that ability is not the only factor determining the high school record. Numerous personality and social factors are involved." Such influences may include the student's reputation, creativity, motivation, self-concept, cheating and study habits. Whatever the specific mechanisms, they cannot represent to any

Figure 6.2.—Simultaneous determination of course marks, white public secondary school students: Nashville SMSA, 1957

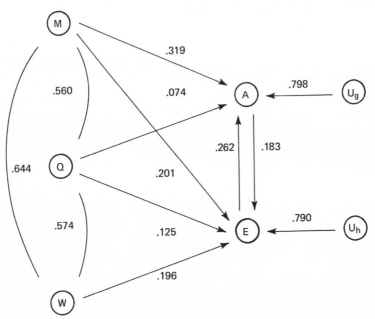

Note: Item identifications are: M-Stanford Mathematics Grade Equivalent; Q-Intelligence; W-Stanford Reading Grade Equivalent; A-Arithmetic mark; E-English mark; U_g-Unmeasured determinants of A; and U_h-Unmeasured determinants of E.

large extent the effect of his background, and they must operate net of intelligence and achievement, which are represented explicitly in the system.

The coefficients obtained for Figure 6.2 provide a seemingly plausible interpretation of how course marks are determined. Each mark has a modrate effect on the other, and the two reciprocal effects are roughly equal in size. Achievement in mathematics has substantially larger direct effects on mark in arithmetic than does intelligence, and intelligence has a smaller direct effect on A than on E, despite the fact that W has not been allowed to influence A directly. These results provide additional evidence of the greater complexity of skills or abilities underlying the achievement of marks in English; that is, not only is it necessary to allow all of the predetermined variables to influence English marks, but only one of the predetermined variables has substantial direct influence on arithmetic marks. Lest the reader be misled, we note that the model is equivocal with regard to the importance of achievement in reading in the determination of marks; that is, the role of W is not clear unless we interpret the correlations among M, Q, and W. For example, if we believe the interpretation of Figure 5.5, the effects of M in Figure 6.2 are to a large degree a manifestation of the influence of reading skill.

Finally, the findings up to this point carry the usual implications for studying effects of the school. In the absence of a substantive rationale for the large and positive value of r_{de} in Figure 6.1 the statistical controls implicit in that model must be judged inadequate for the measurement of net school effects. If one believes some alternative scheme, like that in Figure 6.2, that model ought to be used in the measurement of school effects, but no study has made use of statistical controls based on such a model.

A Hypothetical Variable in the Determination of Course Marks

We have argued that the effect of family background on course marks is largely transmitted through intelligence and academic achievement, although the latter variables alone do not adequately explain course marks. While the model of Figure 6.2 formally satisfies the requirement that r_{AE} be accounted for, it does no better than that of Figure 6.1 at reproducing the background-mark correlations. An alternative modification of Figure 6.1 carries much the same substantive import as Figure 6.2 with respect to the proximate causes of marks, but also allows us to reproduce the background-mark correlations more closely. Suppose that a variable, K, is unrelated to M, Q, and W and accounts for that part of the correlation r_{AE} which is unexplained in the regression of A and E on M, Q and W. We cannot identify any particular content with K, although it includes the effects identified with the reciprocal influence of A and E in the last section. We have already shown in equation 6.6 that for such a variable, $p_{AK}p_{EK} = .261$, and we stated that each path coefficient would be .556 if they were equal. We can obtain separate estimates of these paths and of the relationship of family background to determinants of marks other than intelligence and achievement if we assume that the remaining influences of family background are transmitted through K instead of the uncorrelated residual determinants of A and E. These assumptions are portrayed in the path diagram in Figure 6.3. The assumption of a particular value for each of the correlations r_{KX}, r_{KV}, and r_{KS} implies provisional values for the paths p_{AK} and p_{EK}. In the case of r_{KX}, for example,

$$r_{XA} = p_{AM}r_{MX} + p_{AQ}r_{QX} + p_{AW}r_{WX} + p_{AK}r_{KX}, \qquad (6.7)$$

or $\qquad .105 = .090 + p_{AK}r_{KX},$

and $\qquad p_{AK}r_{KX} = .015.$

Also,

$$r_{XE} = p_{EM}r_{MX} + p_{EQ}r_{QX} + p_{EW}r_{WX} + p_{EK}r_{KX}, \qquad (6.8)$$

Figure 6.3—Path diagram of the determination of course marks by family background, intelligence, achievement, and an hypothetical variable

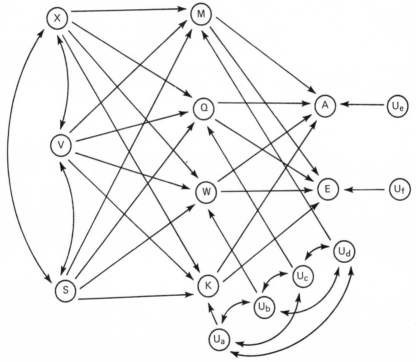

Note: Item identifications are: X-Father's occupation; V-Father's education; S-Number of siblings; M-Stanford Mathematics Grade Equivalent; Q-Intelligence; W-Stanford Reading Grade Equivalent; K-Hypothetical variable; A-Arithmetic mark; E-English mark; U_a-Unmeasured determinants of K; U_b-Unmeasured determinants of W; U_c-Unmeasured determinants of Q; U_d-Unmeasured determinants of M; U_e-Unmeasured determinants of A; and U_f-Unmeasured determinants of E. See text for explanation of assumptions underlying use of hypothetical variable.

or $\qquad$ $.134 = .108 + p_{EK}r_{KX},$

and $\qquad$ $p_{EK}r_{KX} = .026.$

Thus, multiplying the right side of equation 6.7 by the right side of equation 6.8 and the left side of equation 6.7 by the left side of equation 6.8, we obtain:

$$p_{EK}p_{AK}r_{KX}^2 = (.015)(.026) = .000390,$$

or $\qquad$ $r_{KX}^2 = .00039/.261 = .001494,$

and $\qquad$ $r_{KX} = .03865.$

Substituting this result in equations 6.7 and 6.8, we find $p_{AK} = .388$ and $p_{EK} = .673$. Similarly, the equations for r_{VA} and r_{VE} imply $p_{AK} = .408$ and $p_{EK} = .640$, and those for r_{SA} and r_{SE} imply $p_{AK} = .464$ and $p_{EK} = . 562$. In the absence of any better procedure for handling these inconsistencies, we assume

$$\frac{p_{AK}}{p_{EK}} = \frac{.388 + .408 + .464}{.673 + .640 + .562} = \frac{1.260}{1.875} = .672. \qquad (6.9)$$

By substitution in equation 6.6 this assumption yields values of $p_{AK} = .419$ and $p_{EK} = .623$. It has already been shown that mark in English represents a more diverse set of abilities than mark in arithmetic. It is apparent from these results that English mark is also more responsive to family background, net of ability and achievement.

Substitution of these last results in equations 6.7 and 6.8 yields estimates for r_{KX} of .036 and .042. Similar treatment of the other family background variables yields values for r_{KV} of .050 and .053 and for r_{KS} of −.103 and -.083. The revised model is an improvement, but it does not completely explain the effects of the background variables on marks in arithmetic and English. This is undoubtedly a statistically inefficient solution in the sense that other averages of the alternative estimates would have smaller sampling errors (Hauser and Goldberger, 1970). On the other hand, it is easy to compute, and with a sample so large the substantive virtues and deficiencies of the model are readily apparent. In any case the small values of r_{KX}, r_{KV}, and r_{KS} lead inescapably to the conclusion that background adds little to the explanation of course marks beyond its influence on intelligence and academic achievement.

School Differences in Marks

Family background, intelligence, and academic achievement affect the assignment of course marks within schools. This implies that the net influence of composition with respect to background, intelligence, and achievement on the average marks assigned in a school is positive. However, this does not mean that the overall relationship between the student body's composition with respect to the determinants of marks and the average marks assigned in a school is positive. Indeed, it has been found in several populations that inter-school differentials in marks bear a complex relationship to the composition of student bodies.

For example, Wilson (1959, 1963) has twice found a positive gross relationship between the average marks assigned in schools and the socioeconomic composition of their student bodies. In reporting on the educational aspirations of seniors in eight high schools in San Francisco-Oakland, he states (1959:842-843):

> A much higher proportion of students in the middle-class schools obtain "A's" and "B's" than do those in the working-class schools. In addition to the influence of the family and school norms upon achievement . . . there is the possibility that teachers grade more liberally at the middle-class schools—either for entirely extraneous reasons, or, more plausibly, because the parent's expectations and the student's aspirations place pressure on them to raise the grading curve.

> If the latter interpretation is sound, then the students who are high achievers at the (low SES) schools will be higher achievers on an absolute basis, than those at the (high SES) schools. But holding grades constant . . . we see that even under these conditions more students receiving the same grade in the middle-class schools want to go to college.

This last finding implies nothing about devaluation of standards; it implies only that variables other than marks influence desire to attend college. Moreover, Wilson presents no data in support of his suggestion that marking is devalued in relation to achievement in the high SES schools. His Table 11 (p. 843) permits the inference that the proportion of students with intelligence quotients of 110 or more ranges from 64 percent in high SES schools to 31 percent in low SES schools. There is at least a possibility that the average marks may not differ "for entirely extraneous reasons, or . . . because the parents' expectations and students' aspirations place pressure on (teachers) to raise the grading curve." However, in this article Wilson leaves the reader with the impression that a devaluation of achievement in low SES schools tends to reduce the aspirations of low SES students below what should be expected from their academic achievement.

Wilson (1963) was more careful in discussing the determination of marks in a study of sixth-grade students in Berkeley, California. While students in the study population were not actually marked by teachers, he assumed that marks would be indicative of other sanctions applied by teachers, and he asked teachers to rate students as if they were being marked. He found that the socioeconomic status of the student and of the school were positively correlated with the hypothetical marks. However, the socioeconomic status of the school had a small negative net effect on marks when race, sex, and father's occupation were entered in a multiple classification analysis, and it had a large negative net effect when achievement and intelligence were also entered in the analysis (pp. 228-232). In this instance Wilson concluded that divergent grading standards mislead and frustrate lower SES students by encouraging the formation of unrealistically high aspirations (p. 234). Hence, there is at least an historical basis for the conclusion that lower SES students suffer, no matter what the direction of divergence in habits of marking among schools (whose role in the determination of aspirations is discussed in Chapter VII). Here, we consider only the relationship of family background, intelligence, and achievement with the school's average marks. While our interpretations diverge, our empirical findings are much like those reported in Wilson's 1963 paper.

In this part of the analysis the problem of interpreting relationships involving correlated error in the between-school segment of the analysis of covariance model arises again. In Chapter V it did not seem plausible to identify the correlated error term with any specific concept. Here it seems reasonable to refer to the error term as the school's marking standard. This should not be misleading, provided it is kept in mind (1) that the reference is definitional; (2) that it refers to the effects on average school marks of all uncontrolled variables; and (3) that no assumption is made with respect to the direction or mechanism of causation leading to the correlated error. The terms, school marking standard, residual term, unmeasured determinants, and error term, are used interchangeably below. These are not the same as the average marks assigned in a school or the between-school component of course marks. The former terms refer to the net or adjusted differences among schools in course marks, while the latter two refer to gross differences.

It should be kept in mind that little of the variance in course marks lies between schools. Indeed, the explanation of the negative association between the school composition and marking standard reported below is essentially that student's performance varies objectively from school to school, while in every school the average mark is a C. Of course, this is similar to the "frog-pond" phenomenon found at the college level by Davis (1966) and Spaeth (1968). Ultimately, differences in marking among schools have little influence on the marks of individual students.

Family Background, Academic Achievement and Marking Standards

The school means of each sex-grade-residence subgroup were adjusted for the effects of the composition of the student body on individual variates. To generate a stable set of results, the covariance adjustments and residuals were pooled over grades within sex-residence categories, and the schools' average marks were regressed on their two components. Two sets of decompositions were run. In the first, covariance adjustments were made for the effects of family background, and in the second, for intelligence and academic achievement. The allocations of variance for these two decompositions are displayed in the upper and lower panels, respectively, of Table 6.4.

As one would expect from the low within-school correlations between background variables and course marks, background composition does not account for much variance in marks for either sex or residence grouping. The direct effects of the residually defined school marking standards ac-

Table 6.4.—Allocation of variance in between-school model of determination of course marks by composition and residual factors by sex and residence, white public secondary school students: Nashville SMSA, 1957

Sex and Residence	Determination of A				Determination of E			
	Composition	Joint	Residual	Total	Composition	Joint	Residual	Total
Controlling family background:								
All students	7.1%	− 3.5%	96.5%	100.0%	5.6%	− 2.0%	96.4%	100.0%
Males	8.4%	− 4.3%	95.9%	100.0%	7.9%	− 1.7%	93.8%	100.0%
Females	8.4	− 6.6	98.2	100.0	11.1	− 5.5	94.4	100.0
City students	6.3%	− 8.7%	102.4%	100.0%	3.6%	− 3.7%	100.1%	100.0%
County students	7.5	− 0.6	93.1	100.0	6.9	− 0.7	93.8	100.0
Controlling intelligence and academic achievement:								
All students	31.1%	−44.7%	113.6%	100.0%	19.9%	−23.2%	103.3%	100.0%
Males	38.1%	−53.8%	115.7%	100.0%	27.4%	−31.8%	104.4%	100.0%
Females	36.0	−54.8	118.8	100.0	39.5	−49.9	110.4	100.0
City students	18.8%	−28.7%	109.9%	100.0%	11.9%	−13.2%	101.3%	100.0%
County students	37.3	−52.7	115.5	100.0	24.9	−29.3	104.4	100.0

Note: Family background characteristics are: X-Father's occupation; V-Father's education; and S-Number of siblings. Course grades are: A-Arithmetic mark; and E-English mark. Q-Intelligence. Academic achievement measures are: M-Stanford Mathematics Grade Equivalent; and W-Stanford Reading Grade Equivalent. Components may not add to 100 percent because of independent rounding.

count for most of the between-school variation in average school marks. In all of the groups there is negative overlap between the compositional and residual determinants of course marks. That is, average marks are generally lower than would be expected from composition on family background in schools where it was favorable and higher than would be expected in schools where it was unfavorable. To state the matter in a slightly different way, the negative overlap means that the net differences among average school marks are larger than the gross differences. This is congruent with Wilson's finding in the Berkeley elementary schools. However, the substantive importance of the devaluation of marking standards in the low SES schools remains open to question. Indeed, the results approach the ideal experimental situation where the effects of composition are orthogonal to those of the unmeasured variables.

The zero-order correlations among the terms in the decomposition of marking standards on family background are shown in the upper panel of Table 6.5. While the net effect of composition upon marks must always

Table 6.5.—Correlations in the between-school model of the determination of course marks by composition and residual factors by sex and residence, white public secondary school students: Nashville SMSA, 1957

Sex and residence	Determination of A			Determination of E		
	r_{CA}	r_{CR}	r_{RA}	r_{CE}	r_{CR}	r_{RE}
Controlling family background:						
All students	.200	−.068	.964	.195	−.044	.971
Males	.218	−.074	.957	.251	−.032	.960
Females	.174	−.117	.958	.251	−.086	.943
City students	.078	−.171	.969	.092	−.097	.982
County students	.262	−.013	.962	.249	−.015	.965
Controlling intelligence and academic achievement:						
All students	.157	−.376	.856	.186	−.256	.902
Males	.182	−.405	.825	.221	−.297	.866
Females	.144	−.419	.838	.232	−.378	.813
City students	.103	−.316	.911	.154	−.191	.940
County students	.182	−.404	.826	.206	−.287	.878

Note: Course grades are: A-Arithmetic mark; and E-English mark. Q-Intelligence. Family background characteristics are: X-Father's occupation; V-Father's education; and S-Number of siblings. Academic achievement measures are: M-Stanford Mathematic Grade Equivalent; and W-Stanford Reading Grade Equivalent; C-Composition; and R-Other school factors.

be positive, the corresponding gross relationship can be positive or negative, depending on the amount of negative overlap between the compositional and residual components. The evidence here provides a rather weak replication of Wilson's findings of a positive overall relationship between family background and average marks. In the combined subgroups there is a small positive gross relationship between family background and average marks and a small negative overlap between the compositional and residual terms, but reversals occurred in several of the grade-sex subgroups (Hauser, 1968:242).

The interpretation of the decomposition of school levels of academic achievement on student background factors in Chapter V was complicated by the confounding of systematic differences in results by grade with possible discrepancies in ascertainment of the mean levels of achievement in the schools in the lower grades. The same problem affects the examination of average school marks in relation to school levels of intelligence and achievement and marking standards, but here the results were so consistent across grades that there is little ambiguity.

The allocations of variance in the determination of average marks by composition on intelligence and academic achievement are shown in the lower panel of Table 6.4. In every group there is negative overlap between the compositional and residual determinants of average school marks. While the direct positive effects of composition are substantial, the negative joint effects are larger in most instances. Average marks are lower than would be expected from achievement and intelligence in schools placed favorably with respect to those variables, and they are higher than expected in unfavorably placed schools. The net effects of school marking standards are larger than the gross school differences in marks in every group. However, the remarks in the preceding section are again applicable because the gross school differences in marks are so small. While the variation in marks, net of ability and achievement, may be of some substantive interest it is of little substantive importance.

The correlations among the terms in these decompositions are shown in the lower panel of Table 6.5. Although the signs of r_{CA} and r_{CE} are positive for each of the combined subgroups, there is considerable instability in the signs for the grade-sex subgroups (Hauser, 1968:246). In this population there is at most a weak positive relationship between the level of ability and academic achievement of the students in a school and its average marks. This finding and the corresponding results of the background decompositions confirm the hypothesis that marking is done to make any school's average mark a C. That is, rather than consciously raising or lowering absolute standards, teachers grade students relative to their peers. Standardization of the distribution of marks has the effect of making it harder to achieve high marks where one's peers are well endowed than where they are not.

Figure 6.4.—Determination of average school marks by student body composition on intelligence, academic achievement, socioeconomic status and the school marking standard

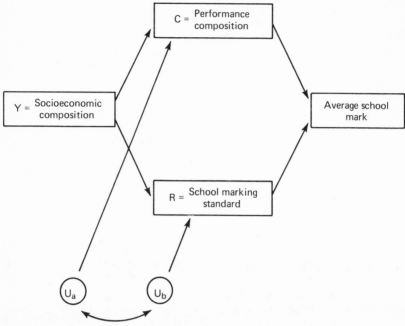

Note: Item identifications are: U_a-Unmeasured determinants of C; and U_b-Unmeasured determinants of R.

Family Background and the Devaluation of Marking Standards

An alternative interpretation is that the negative relationship between composition on intelligence and achievement and marking standards is a consequence of the socioeconomic level of the school's students. This interpretation is shown in the path diagram in Figure 6.4. As noted in the preceding section, the average school mark is completely determined by the performance (intelligence and achievement) composition of the student body (C) and a correlated residual term (R), the school's marking standard. The socioeconomic composition of the student body influences both C and R, and those two variables are also affected by unmeasured factors, denoted by U_a and U_b. The correlation r_{ab} is zero when the socioeconomic composition of the student body accounts for the relationship between R and C.

The interpretation of Figure 6.4 rests on the tenuous supposition that the school's socioeconomic composition influences the unmeasured determinants of the average mark. The assumption is weak because it is impossible to identify the marking standard, R, with any specific content or mechanism. It is certainly possible to imagine contents for R which would justify the casual pattern of Figure 6.4. For example, we could say that teachers' expectations increase with the socioeconomic level of the school, but the contention that R represents "teachers' expectations of perform- ance" can only be supported by a residual definition of that variable (Blalock: 1961b), which could be (but has not been) represented in the within-school segment of the model. The arrangement does seem congruent with Wilson's (1963) contention that school socioeconomic status accounts for the devaluation of course marks relative to intelligence and achieve- ment in schools with students of low intelligence and achievement.

Observed and implied correlations between the residual and performance composition are shown in Table 6.6. Using the notation of Figure 6.4, we can write the expected correlations as

$$r'_{CR} = p_{CY}p_{RY} = r_{CY}r_{RY}, \qquad (6.10)$$

where Y is the background composition term used earlier. That is, socio- economic level has been operationalized as the weighted combination of X, V, and S which best predicts marks within schools. The data provide little support for the hypothesis that differences in socioeconomic status account for the relationship between the school's composition on intelligence and achievement and the residual determinants of average school marks. Only seven of the twenty-four results for grade-sex subgroups support the hypothesis (Hauser, 1968:250) and it is not supported by any of the re- sults for the combined subgroups.

Table 6.6.—Explanation of the correlation between composition on intelligence and academic achievement and school marking standards by socioeconomic composition by sex and residence, white public secondary school students: Nashville SMSA, 1957

Sex and residence	Arithmetic grade		English grade	
	Observed	Implied	Observed	Implied
All students	−.376	−.071	−.256	−.065
Males	−.405	−.067	−.297	−.058
Females	−.419	−.111	−.378	−.108
City students	−.316	−.130	−.191	−.135
County students	−.404	−.046	−.287	−.038

VII

**EDUCATIONAL AND
OCCUPATIONAL
ASPIRATIONS**

Despite the recent emphasis on ability and achievement as indicators of inequality in education and the importance sometimes attached to selection into or out of a college preparatory curriculum early in secondary schooling, sociologists have also given a great deal of attention to the selective processes operating at the end of high school and in the first years of college (Coleman *et al.,* 1966; Turner, 1961, 1964; Folger and Nam, 1967; Clark, 1961; Sewell and Shah, 1967). Much of the latter emphasis has probably been motivated by the failure of substantial proportions of the most able youths in each cohort to attend college (Wolfle, 1961; Michael, 1961; Folger and Nam, 1967). For example, in 1960 roughly 60 percent of males and females between the ages of 25 and 29 had at least completed high school, but in the same year only 46 percent of boys and 38 percent of girls who had graduated from high school in the previous year were enrolled in college and this included only two-thirds of those in the top quartiles in ability and in scholastic standing (Folger and Nam, 1967:59, 61, 143). This substantial attrition at the juncture of secondary and higher education has drawn sociologists' attention to factors other than ability which influence the decision to enter college (*ibid.*, pp. 62-63).

Interest in educational selection has had the wider effect of stimulating

106

investigations into more general indicators of aspiration, ambition, and life-goals. Recent investigations of educational selection after high school have been undertaken with this broader orientation (Duncan, Haller and Portes, 1968; Turner, 1964; Alexander and Campbell, 1964; Bordua, 1960; Boyle, 1966a, 1966b; Cohen, 1965; Coombs and Davies, 1965; Haller and Butterworth, 1960; Hauser, 1969b; Herriott, 1963; Kahl, 1953; Krauss, 1964; Layton, 1954; Michael, 1961; McDill and Coleman, 1963, 1965; McDill, Meyers and Rigsby, 1967; McDill, Rigsby and Meyers, 1969; Rehberg, 1967; Rehberg and Schafer, 1968; Rehberg and Westby, 1967; Rehberg, Schafer and Sinclair, 1970; Sewell and Shah, 1967, 1968a, 1968b; Sewell, 1964; Sewell and Armer, 1966a; Sewell, Haller and Straus, 1957; Sewell and Orenstein, 1965; Sewell, Haller and Portes, 1969; Wilson, 1959). In the greater portion of each birth cohort which reaches secondary school such indicators have a relevance to later achievement which is harder to establish in the case of course marks and academic achievement. The well-documented relationship between high-school and college marks, for example, reveals nothing about the consequences of high-school performance for the adult achievement of students who do not go on to college, and it is not clear whether high-school performance brings any reward unless it is translated into higher educational attainment. Finally, the plans of high-school seniors have been shown to be moderately strong predictors of college enrollment and subsequent educational attainment (Folger and Nam, 1967:59; Sewell and Shah, 1967; Folger, Astin and Bayer, 1970:153-158), and it is commonly held that motivation to attend college has the advantage of being easier to manipulate than other cognitive and social influences on higher education.

The analysis in this chapter has two objectives: (1) to interpret the role of the student's background, paternal aspirations, and performance in school in the determination of his aspirations; and (2) to interpret differences between schools in levels of aspiration. The dependent variables are educational aspiration (T) and occupational aspiration (J). These two variables were not ascertained from students attending schools in the City of Nashville and the present analysis pertains only to students in the twelve grade-sex subgroups in the Davidson County ring. The ring includes roughly two-thirds of the metropolitan population and is almost as heterogeneous as the total SMSA. Two other variables are introduced: number of school-connected organizations to which the student belongs (O) and perceived father's educational aspiration (Z). Mark in English is chosen as a single index of academic performance in light of our earlier evidence of the factorial complexity of that variable.

As in preceding chapters, X, V, S and Q are used as indicators of the student's background. Father's educational aspiration, organizational membership and mark in English are interpreted as variables intervening between background and aspirations. Following the pattern of the earlier chapters, the analysis is intended largely to explain the relationship between the two measures of aspiration. Although there are differences between T and J arising from their specific relevance to education and occupation, respectively, we interpret them here as indexes of ambition.

Grade and sex differences in most of the variables are not very large. However, the differentials in level of aspiration are of some interest: boys' educational aspirations increase with grade in school, while those of girls remain the same, or they decline. While the aspirations of boys and of girls are equal in the seventh grade, the differential increases to more than a full year of schooling among students in the twelfth grade. Both boys and girls perceive their fathers' educational aspirations to be as high or higher than their own in every grade. Differentials in occupational aspiration by sex and grade are much like those in educational aspiration. The occupational aspirations of girls remain at about the same level or possibly decline with increases in grade, while those of boys show a nearly perfect monotonic increase with grade. In consequence, the status of occupations desired by boys is lower than in the case of girls from the seventh to ninth grades, and higher from the tenth to twelfth grades.

It is not clear, of course, that the Duncan index of occupational status provides an appropriate metric for girls' occupational choices. That is, (1) the socioeconomic status of occupations may not be as relevant for girls as for boys to professed occupational choice; and (2) the Duncan index is based on the level of education and income of male occupational incumbents only, and this may differ from the socioeconomic level of female incumbents of occupations with the same title.

An indication of lack of realism in occupational aspiration may be found in a comparison of the boys' average levels of X and J. The socioeconomic status of fathers' occupations is from 13 to 22 points lower than the status of the occupations to which their sons aspire. Among non-Negro men with nonfarm background, aged 25-34 in 1962, the mean of father's occupational status was 34.6, and the mean of son's (i.e., respondent's) current occupational status was 43.3. The difference between father's and son's occupational status was little more than a third the standard deviation (22.4) of the former (Duncan, Featherman and Duncan, 1968:51). The mean of father's occupation of seventh-grade boys in the county ring was 40.6, and the mean of son's occupational aspiration was 53.4 The difference between the latter means is equal to nearly two-thirds the standard deviation (21.5) of the former. It is hard to account for the increase of nearly ten points in mean occupational aspirations of boys from the seventh to twelfth grades. One might guess that the possible effect of an increasingly realistic judgment is outweighed by the effect of low-aspiring boys leaving school.

These differentials by sex and grade may arise from a variety of causes. It would be tempting to conclude that all of the former are attributable to differentiation of sex roles and all of the latter to differentiation of occupational roles, factors which are certainly implicated in the pattern of observed differences. However, it should be kept in mind that students in the various grades represent differentially the birth cohorts from which their membership is drawn; that the pattern of differential representation probably differs by sex; and that real variations may exist among the cohorts other than their differential progress through the school system.

Within-School Variation in Aspiration

In the within-school model of the determination of aspirations the deviations of students' aspirations from the mean of the school and grade-sex subgroup are regressed on similarly defined deviations of pre-determined variables. The analysis has two objectives: (1) to account for the within-school variance in T and J; and (2) to account for the relationship between T and J. Because of the lack of variability in levels of aspiration among schools (cf. Table 4.1), the within-school analysis could account for most of the variation in aspirations, and it has substantial implications for the interpretation of school differences.

Within-School Correlations

The averages over grade subgroups of the average within-school correlations are shown separately by sex in Table 7.1. The correlations involving Z, T, J and O are of special interest, since they were not discussed earlier. The most obvious sex differential is that in the case of girls J is less strongly related to all the other variables than in the case of boys. Some reasons for this were mentioned earlier.

None of the variables is very strongly related to T or J in either sex with the single exception of r_{TZ}, which is equal to .642 for boys and .633 for girls. This relationship cannot be interpreted unambiguously. It could indicate a powerful effect of father's educational aspiration on respondent's educational aspiration. There is some evidence of the validity of Z in its gross relationships with X, V and S, which are stronger than those of T and J with X, V and S. That is, perceived paternal aspiration is more highly correlated with origin statuses than are the student's own aspirations. On the other hand, T and J are students' reports and it is likely that students' reports of their fathers' educational aspirations would be influenced to some degree by their own aspirations. In this connection it is of interest that the correlations of Z with J are considerably lower than those of Z with T. Is, then, Z contaminated by T? Or, an alternative explanation, is the content of paternal educational expectations highly education-specific?

Some tabulations made for twelfth-grade boys and girls did include mother's educational aspiration and parental occupational aspiration. For reasons of economy these variables were not included in the main analysis. The correlations of "mother's" with "father's" educational aspirations were .918 for boys and .821 for girls, and there were no substantial differences in their correlations with other variables. There may be theoretical reasons

Table 7.1.—Average of within-school correlations by sex, white public secondary school students: Davidson County ring, 1957

	X	V	S	Q	M	W	A	E	Z	T	J	O
X	—	.491	−.148	.209	.146	.210	.126	.167	.246	.195	.210	.136
V	.485	—	−.193	.215	.172	.226	.152	.179	.299	.254	.213	.170
S	−.141	−.194	—	−.134	−.112	−.171	−.082	−.125	−.189	−.177	−.173	−.034
Q	.213	.218	−.162	—	.529	.530	.400	.432	.212	.235	.282	.174
M	.178	.175	−.126	.561	—	.613	.502	.483	.233	.268	.252	.169
W	.209	.220	−.165	.573	.660	—	.386	.458	.283	.267	.276	.183
A	.121	.122	−.126	.396	.522	.433	—	.630	.180	.202	.238	.138
E	.162	.169	−.171	.460	.538	.534	.624	—	.219	.272	.292	.153
Z	.223	.288	−.204	.205	.194	.231	.132	.184	—	.642	.342	.184
T	.192	.233	−.143	.189	.201	.231	.146	.196	.633	—	.456	.215
J	.122	.137	−.036	.084	.099	.143	.083	.104	.237	.329	—	.185
O	.151	.200	−.147	.224	.217	.242	.124	.189	.208	.203	.115	—

Note: Entries above diagonal are for males. Entries below diagonal are for females. Item identifications are: X-Father's occupation; V-Father's education; S-Number of siblings; Q-Intelligence; M-Stanford Mathematics Grade Equivalent; W-Stanford Reading Grade Equivalent; A-Arithmetic mark; E-English mark; Z-Father's educational aspiration; T-Student's educational aspiration; J-Student's occupational aspiration; and O-Organizational membership.

for emphasizing mothers' encouragement in the interpretation of children's aspirations but there is apparently little difference between maternal and paternal aspirations as reported by students.

The primary reason why parental occupational aspiration was deleted from the analysis was an extremely low response rate. Among twelfth-grade boys and girls responding to the item, its correlations with occupational aspiration were .646 and .613, respectively, and its correlations with educational aspiration were .352 and .438. Thus, parental occupational aspiration bears about the same relationships to occupational and educational aspirations, in that order, as mothers' and fathers' educational expectations bear to educational and occupational aspirations. Again, this is consistent with occupation-specific and education-specific content in the variables or with an hypothesis of contamination by students' aspirations.

The choice of E as an indicator of boys' performance in school on *a priori* grounds is validated by the observation that it is more strongly related to T and J than are M, W and A. However, for girls W is more highly related to T and J than are the other measures of performance. In any case the use of a single indicator entails some loss in the power to explain. While E accounts for 7.4 percent and 8.5 percent of the boys' within-school variance in T and J, respectively, and 3.8 percent and 1.1 percent of the girls', the corresponding figures for the combination of M, W, A and E are 10.7, 11.5, 6.2 and 2.2 percent. Hence models using E. alone will understate the importance of academic performance.

Background and Aspirations

In these analyses intelligence has been grouped with father's education, father's occupation, and number of siblings an an indicator of background. The direct effects of the four background variables on the educational and occupational aspirations of boys and girls are displayed on the path diagram in Figure 7.1. It is obvious from the path coefficients of the residual variables (U_a and U_b) that background accounts for little of the within-school variation in educational and occupational aspirations. Also background accounts for little of the relationship between the two kinds of aspiration. Using the equation

$$r_{TJ} = p_{TX}r_{XJ} + p_{TV}r_{VJ} + p_{TS}r_{SJ} + p_{TQ}r_{QJ} + p_{Ta}r_{ab}p_{Jb}, \tag{7.1}$$

we find that the correlations between T and J implied (assuming $r_{ab} = 0$) by their determination by X, V, S and Q are $r_{TJ} = .116$ for boys and $r_{TJ} = .086$ for girls; the observed correlations are .456 and .329, respectively. To return to a basic theme, it is clear that socioecomonic background and intelligence do not explain aspiration. Hence, no very strong claims may be offered for school effects which appear when only those variables have been controlled. This result supports the stand taken by Sewell and Armer (1966a, 1966b) against their critics (Turner, 1966; Michael, 1966; Boyle, 1966b).

Figure 7.1.–Influence of background (X,V,S,Q) on aspirations (T,J) by sex, based on average of within-school correlations, white public secondary school students; Davidson County ring, 1957

Males

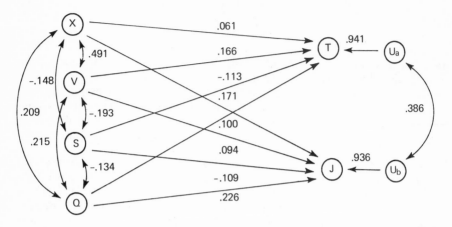

Females

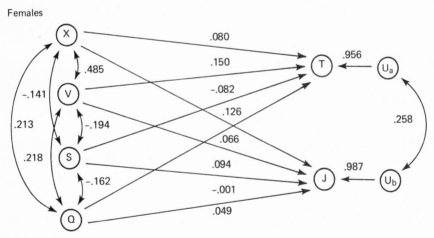

Note: Item identifications are: X-Father's occupation; V-Father's education; S-Number of siblings; Q-Intelligence; T-Student's educational aspiration; J-Student's occupational aspiration; U_a-Unmeasured determinants of T; and U_b-Unmeasured determinants of J.

The results of Figure 7.1 also support the argument that intelligence is more important relative to family status in the determination of boys' aspirations than of girls' (Sewell and Shah, 1967). In the determination of boys' educational and occupational aspirations, Q has a larger direct effect than any of the family status variables. Among girls the direct effect of V is larger than that of Q in the determination of T, and the direct effects of V and X are larger than those of Q in the determination of J. If we disregard the paths involving the disturbance terms and express the correlations in equation 7.1 in terms of known path coefficients and correlations among the predetermined variables, we obtain

$$r'_{TJ} = (p_{TX}p_{JX} + p_{TX}p_{JV}r_{VX} + p_{TX}p_{JS}r_{SX} + p_{TV}p_{JV} + p_{TV}p_{JX}r_{XV}$$
$$+ p_{TV}p_{JS}r_{SV} + p_{TS}p_{JS} + p_{TS}p_{JX}r_{XS} + p_{TS}p_{JV}r_{VS})$$
$$+ (p_{TX}p_{JQ}r_{QX} + p_{TV}p_{JQ}r_{QV} + p_{TS}p_{JQ}r_{QS} + p_{TQ}p_{JX}r_{XQ}$$
$$+ p_{TQ}p_{JV}r_{VQ} + p_{TQ}p_{JS}r_{SQ}) + (p_{TQ}p_{JQ}). \qquad (7.2)$$

The nine terms inside the first parenthesis in equation 7.2 involve only the direct and joint contributions of family status variables to the implied value of r_{TJ}. The six terms inside the second parenthesis are joint contributions of family status and intelligence, and the last term is the net contribution of intelligence. Applying this equation to the results of Figure 7.1, we find for boys that

$$r'_{TJ} = .116 = \underset{\text{(family)}}{.053} + \underset{\text{(joint)}}{.024} + \underset{\text{(intelligence)}}{.039}$$

and for girls that

$$r'_{TJ} = .086 = \underset{\text{(family)}}{.059} + \underset{\text{(joint)}}{.021} + \underset{\text{(intelligence)}}{.006.}$$

Although the implied correlation between T and J is larger among boys than among girls, the combined contribution of the family status variables is larger among girls than among boys. Still, in either sex, the combined variables of family status are more important than intelligence and the greater importance of boys' intelligence in accounting for r_{TJ} is only relative.

Student's Background and Ambition

Larger estimates of the impact of background on prospective achievement are obtained if we postulate that the educational and occupational aspirations which a student expresses are imperfect reflections of an underlying level of ambition. Estimates based on this assumption and the data of Table 7.1 are shown on the path diagrams in Figure 7.2. Ambition, denoted by the letter H, is postulated to account for the relationship between educational and occupational aspirations and to mediate the effects of X, V, S and Q on T and J. The relationships of H with measured variables are derived from these assumptions and the relationships among the measured variables.

The set of equations represented by the path diagrams in Figure 7.2 is:

$$T = p_{TH}H + p_{Ta}U_a, \qquad (7.3)$$
$$J = p_{JH}H + p_{Jb}U_b, \qquad (7.4)$$

and

$$H = p_{HX}X + p_{HV}V + p_{HS}S + p_{HQ}Q + p_{Hc}U_c, \qquad (7.5)$$

where all of the variables are expressed in standard form. It is assumed, also, that the disturbance terms, U_a, U_b and U_c, are not correlated with

Figure 7.2.–Student background (X,V,S,Q), "ambition," and educational and occupational aspirations by sex, white public secondary school students: Davidson County ring, 1957

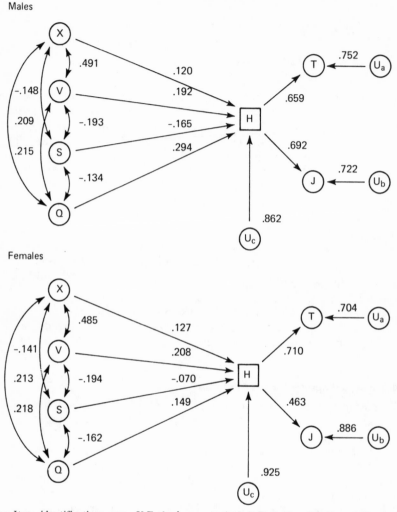

Males

Females

Note: Item identifications are: X-Father's occupation; V-Father's education; S-Number of siblings; Q-Intelligence; T-Student's educational aspiration; J-Student's occupational aspiration; H-Ambition; U_a-Unmeasured determinants of T; U_b-Unmeasured determinants of J; and U_c-Unmeasured determinants of H.

one another or with X, V, S or Q, and that U_a and U_b are not correlated with H. Since we have assumed $r_{ab} = 0$, we can write

$$r_{TJ} = p_{TH}p_{JH} = r_{TH}r_{JH}. \qquad (7.6)$$

Multiplying equations 7.3 and 7.4 through by each of the predetermined

EDUCATIONAL AND OCCUPATIONAL ASPIRATIONS

variables in turn and summing over observations, we obtain four pairs of equations:

$$r_{TX} = p_{TH}r_{HX} \text{ and } r_{JX} = p_{JH}r_{HX}, \tag{7.7}$$

$$r_{TV} = p_{TH}r_{HV} \text{ and } r_{JV} = p_{JH}r_{HV}, \tag{7.8}$$

$$r_{TS} = p_{TH}r_{HS} \text{ and } r_{JS} = p_{JH}r_{HS}, \tag{7.9}$$

and

$$r_{TQ} = p_{TH}r_{HQ} \text{ and } r_{JQ} = p_{JH}r_{HQ}. \tag{7.10}$$

The ratio of these pairs of equations implies a pair of values for p_{TH} and p_{JH} which would perfectly satisfy equation 7.6. For example, from 7.7,

$$\frac{p_{TH}}{p_{JH}} = \frac{r_{TX}}{r_{JX}}, \tag{7.11}$$

which can be solved by substitution in equation 7.6, but we also have

$$\frac{p_{TH}}{p_{JH}} = \frac{r_{TV}}{r_{JV}}, \tag{7.12}$$

$$\frac{p_{TH}}{p_{JH}} = \frac{r_{TS}}{r_{JS}}, \tag{7.13}$$

and

$$\frac{p_{TH}}{p_{JH}} = \frac{r_{TQ}}{r_{JQ}} \tag{7.14}$$

from the remaining expressions. If the ratios of known correlations in equations 7.11 to 7.14 differed greatly, we would be unable to defend the conclusion that background affects aspiration through the common factor H. In the absence of marked variations, we assume

$$\frac{p_{TH}}{p_{JH}} = \frac{r_{TX} + r_{TV} + r_{TS} + r_{TQ}}{r_{JX} + r_{JV} + r_{JS} + r_{JQ}} \tag{7.15}$$

and substitute the result in equation 7.6 to obtain values for p_{TH} and p_{JH}. The system is still overidentified since each of the expressions 7.7 through 7.10 implies two values for one of the correlations of H with a predetermined variable. We again use average values:

$$r_{HX} = \frac{r_{TX} + r_{JX}}{p_{TH} + p_{JH}}, \tag{7.16}$$

$$r_{HV} = \frac{r_{TV} + r_{JV}}{p_{TH} + p_{JH}}, \tag{7.17}$$

$$r_{HS} = \frac{r_{TS} + r_{JS}}{p_{TH} + p_{JH}}, \tag{7.18}$$

and

$$r_{HQ} = \frac{r_{TQ} + r_{JQ}}{p_{TH} + p_{JH}}. \tag{7.19}$$

The calculated values of p_{TH}, p_{JH}, r_{HX}, r_{HV}, r_{HS} and r_{HQ} can be substituted back in equations 7.7 through 7.10 to determine the deviations of calculated from observed values of the correlations of background variables with educational and occupational aspirations. As in the case of the overidentified models in Chapter V and Chapter VI, this estimating procedure is not statistically efficient, but neither is it likely to mislead with so large a sample.

The results of these calculations are displayed in Table 7.2 Among boys the correlations of "ambitions" with educational and occupational aspirations are nearly equal, while educational aspiration is a much better indicator of "ambition" than is occupational aspiration among girls. Ambition accounts for no more than half the variance of the aspiration measures, but background has little influence on aspirations beyond that mediated by ambition. That is, the deviations of observed from calculated correlation coefficients are not large. The boys' deviations for r_{TX}, r_{TV}, r_{JX} and r_{JV} are of the sign to be expected if there were a net influence of father's occupation on son's occupational aspiration and of father's education on son's educational aspiration. However, the deviations are so small that such an interpretation has little substantive importance. These findings challenge our earlier evidence that perceived parental aspirations may have high occupation-specific and education-specific content. The contrast in the findings is puzzling, since one would expect that if parental aspirations were specific they would reflect distinctions in achieved statuses.

The correlations of each of the background variables with "ambition" are larger for boys than for girls, and there is again consistent evidence that ability is more important in the case of boys than of girls. For boys, r_{HQ} is the largest of the correlations of H with X, V, S and Q, while for girls it is only larger in absolute value than r_{HS}. The path coefficients shown in Figure 7.2 were obtained from the implied correlations of H with the background variables. The path coefficient p_{HQ} in Figure 7.2 is nearly twice as large for boys as for girls and is the largest of the direct effects on boy's ambitions. Decomposing the variance in H, we find for boys

$$R^2_{H.XVSQ} = .258 = \underset{\text{(family)}}{.119} + \underset{\text{(joint)}}{.052} + \underset{\text{(intelligence)}}{.087} ,$$

and for girls

$$R^2_{H.XVSQ} = .145 = \underset{\text{(family)}}{.098} + \underset{\text{(joint)}}{.025} + \underset{\text{(intelligence)}}{.022} .$$

Again, while intelligence is relatively more important in the boys' case than in the girls', family status is more important than intelligence in determining the prospective achievement of either sex. Further, the modest values of the coefficients of determination, .258 and .145, make it abundantly clear that even under the common factor interpretation factors other than background play the most important role in the determination of ambition.

Table 7.2.—Calculated and observed correlations for model of student background (X,V,S,Q) determining ambition by sex, white public secondary school students: Davidson County ring, 1957

Correlation	Males			Females		
	Observed	Calculated	Observed-Calculated	Observed	Calculated	Observed-Calculated
r_{TX}	.195	.198	-.003	.192	.191	.001
r_{TV}	.254	.228	.026	.233	.224	.009
r_{TS}	-.177	-.171	-.006	-.143	-.108	-.035
r_{TQ}	.235	.252	-.017	.189	.165	.024
r_{JX}	.210	.207	.003	.122	.125	-.003
r_{JV}	.213	.239	-.026	.137	.146	-.009
r_{JS}	-.173	-.179	.006	-.036	-.071	.035
r_{JQ}	.282	.265	.017	.084	.108	-.024
$p_{TH} - r_{TH}$	—	.659	—	—	.710	—
$p_{JH} - r_{JH}$	—	.692	—	—	.463	—
r_{HX}	—	.300	—	—	.269	—
r_{HV}	—	.346	—	—	.315	—
r_{HS}	—	-.259	—	—	-.152	—
r_{HQ}	—	.383	—	—	.233	—

Note: Item identifications are: T-Student's educational aspiration; J-Student's occupational aspiration; X-Father's occupation; V-Father's education; S-Number of siblings; Q-Intelligence; and H-Ambition.

Intervening Variables

So far we have treated a reduced form of the interpretation outlined at the beginning of this chapter; that is, we have allowed background to influence aspiration or ambition directly. This interpretation is theoretically correct, if one accepts the temporal ordering of the variables, but is is incomplete. In the following sections we examine the role of three intervening variables—father's educational aspiration, academic performance and membership in organizations—which mediate the effects of background on ambition and aspiration.

In a recent article Sewell and Shah (1968b) interpreted "parental encouragement" as a variable intervening between students' ability and socioeconomic status and their college plans. Although parental encouragement had a large direct effect on college plans, in their Wisconsin data it was necessary to assume that socioeconomic status and ability influenced college plans directly as well as via parental encouragement in order to reproduce the overall relationship between background and college plans. Ability and socioeconomic status jointly made a large contribution to the variance in the college plans of boys (10.8%) and girls (8.2%) beyond that of parental encouragement.

A similar analysis can be performed on the Nashville data. Temporarily disregarding the net effect of each variable, we ask whether background adds anything to an explanation of educational aspiration based on father's educational aspiration alone. For the averaged data of Table 7.1, Z alone accounts for 41.2 percent of the boys' variance in T, while X, V, S, Q and Z account for 42.6 percent. Among girls, the comparable figures are 40.1 percent and 40.7 percent. Background adds only 1.4 percent among boys and 0.6 percent among girls to the within-school variance in educational aspiration explained by perception of father's educational aspiration.

The contrast between these findings and those of Sewell and Shah is large enough to deserve attention. For several reasons the two studies are not comparable: (1) We are analyzing within-school correlations in one metropolitan area while Sewell and Shah were dealing with an entire state. (2) While socioeconomic background is represented here by the combined effects of father's occupation, father's education and number of siblings, Sewell and Shah used a composite index of socioeconomic status which also included three direct measures of the ability of the family to finance a college education. (3) Sewell and Shah's measure of "college plans" was based on definite intent "to enroll in a degree-granting college or university," while our definition of educational aspiration is in terms of desired level of educational attainment. (4) While "parental encouragement" and "father's educational aspiration" were each ascertained from replies to a single question, differences in the questions and in questionaire design may have produced differences between the two variables. "Parental encouragement" was ascertained separately from "college plans," which, in fact, was a variable constructed of several discrete items. On the other hand, "educational aspiration" and "father's educational aspiration" were ascertained from consecutive questions with parallel wording.

The effects described under points (1), (2) and (3) above should tend to reduce correlations in the Nashville data relative to those in the Wisconsin data. Hence, we have a rather powerful confirmation of the effect suggested under point (4) in the finding that in the Nashville data the correlations between father's expectation and educational aspiration (.642 for boys and .633 for girls) are larger than those found by Sewell and Shah between parental encouragement and college plans (.51 for boys and .57 for girls). This suggests that the Nashville students' reports of fathers' aspirations were highly affected by the students' own educational aspirations. We now have four pieces of evidence that educational aspirations contaminate perceptions of father's educational aspiration in the Nashville data: (1) the asymmetric pattern of correlations between perceived parental aspirations and educational and occupational aspirations; (2) the nearly symmetric pattern of correlations between educational and occupational aspirations and father's education and occupation; (3) the design of the items from which student aspirations and parental expectations were ascertained; and (4) the differences in correlations between the Nashville and Wisconsin data sets.

Before attempting to exploit these observations, we turn briefly to the treatment of academic performance and membership in organizations as intervening variables. As with Z, we first examine the extent to which O and E can be said to mediate the effect of student background on educational aspiration. For the average data of Table 7.1, E and O alone account for 10.5 percent of the boys' variance in T and 6.7 percent of the girls', compared with 15.9 percent and 11.0 percent, respectively, for the combination of X, V, S, Q, E and O. Less of the variance in T is explained by E and O than by Z, and the background variables have a larger net effect when E and O are controlled than when Z is controlled. However, the comparison of these findings with our results for Z is inconclusive because of the questionable validity of father's aspiration. For example, if our findings about O and E were compared with those of Sewell and Shah we might conclude that performance carries more of the effect of background than does parental encouragement.

Finally, we may ask whether X, V, S and Q add anything to the within-school variance in T explained by Z, O and E. In the average data Z, O and E account for 43.7 percent of the boys' variance in T and 41.1 percent of the girls', while the combination of intermediate and background variables accounts for 44.1 percent of the boys' variance in T and 41.3 percent of the girls'. When Z, O and E are treated as intermediate variables, the net contributions of the background variables are reduced to 0.4 percent and 0.2 percent for boys and girls, respectively.

While we might conclude at this point that the effect of background on aspiration is mediated entirely by school performance, membership in organizations and perception of father's educational aspiration, we still have to contend with the evidence that the latter is contaminated by the student's own educational aspiration.

For that reason it is instructive to compare the findings on educational aspiration with similar calculations concerning occupational aspiration. For the average data of Table 7.1 the intermediate variables account for 17.6 and 6.3 percent of the variance in J of boys and girls, respectively, while the combination of background and intermediate variables accounts for 20.5 and 6.9 percent of the variance in J. At least the net contribution of boys' background is not negligible. We may conclude conservatively that background makes a small contribution to aspiration, net of parental expectation, performance in school and membership in organizations but that it is possible to interpret those intervening variables as transmitting most of the effect of background.

A Two-Stage Model

The discussion above led us to interpret the determination of aspirations as a two-stage process in which the background variables (X, V, S and Q) influence intermediate variables (Z, O and E) which cause aspirations directly. The interpretation is displayed in the path diagrams in Figure 7.3 and Figure 7.4 where the path coefficients are based on the boys' and girls' averages of Table 7.1.

Determination of Intermediate Variables

Background does not account for much of the variation in the intermediate variables. Mark in English is influenced mainly by intelligence although the small effects of X, V and S are of the expected sign. Of course, the present assumption that X, V and S influence E directly is not intended to supplant our earlier conclusion that family status affects course marks via its influence on achievement. Family status and intelligence are weak predictors of membership in organizations, but slightly less so in the case of girls than of boys. In both sexes the net effect of X on O is of the same size as its net effect on E, and the net effect of V on O is intermediate in size between the effects of V on Z and on E. There is a sex-related interaction in the relationship of S with O; thus, for girls, number of siblings has a modest negative net effect on memberships which is nearly identical in magnitude to the net effect of S on E. For boys the small negative correlation of S with O is probably reproducible from the net effects of X, V and Q on O and the relationships among them, and there is a trivial positive net effect of S on O.

The dependence of Z on the background variables is surprisingly weak, given its interpretation as a measure of parental encouragement. That is, were we to assume Z perfectly valid, we should conclude that paternal encouragement of his offspring's ambitions for status has little connection with a father's own level of social achievement. Then, given the substantial effect of Z on aspirations, we would come to a conclusion which seems to run counter to intuition: that a primary effect of paternal aspiration is to

Figure 7.3.—Two-stage within-school model of the determination of boys' educational and occupational aspirations based on average correlations, white public secondary school students: Davidson County ring, 1957

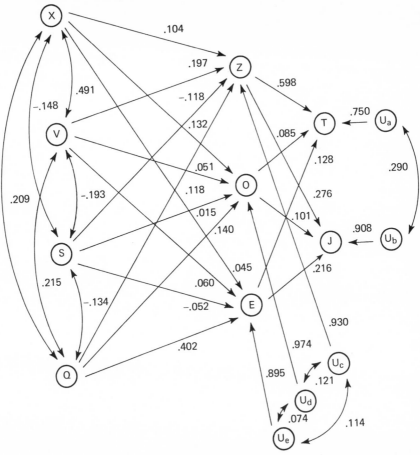

Note: Item identifications are: X-Father's occupation; V-Father's education; S-Number of siblings; Q-Intelligence; Z-Father's educational aspiration; O-Organizational membership; E-English mark; T-Student's educational aspiration; J-Student's occupational aspiration; U_a-Unmeasured determinants of T; U_b-Unmeasured determinants of J; U_c-Unmeasured determinants of Z; U_d-Unmeasured determinants of O; and U_e-Unmeasured determinants of E.

reduce the extent to which status is perpetuated. While the background variables are slightly better predictors of Z than of T for boys, the finding is reversed for girls (compare these results with Figure 7.1). However, in the case of boys the net effects of Q on Z are smaller in relation to those of X, V and S than in the determination of T or J. This is at least a minor indication of validity, since one might expect parents to be less sensitive than their children to the bearing of performance in school on later achievement.

Figure 7.4.—Two-stage within-school model of the determination of girls' educational and occupational aspirations based on average correlations, white public secondary school students: Davidson County ring, 1957

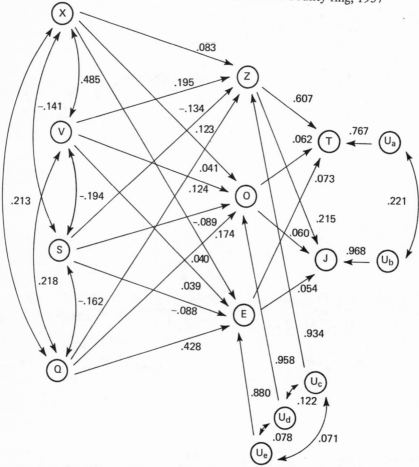

Note: Item identifications are: X-Father's occupation; V-Father's education; S-Number of siblings; Q-Intelligence; Z-Father's educational aspiration; O-Organizational membership; E-English mark; T-Student's educational aspiration; J-Student's occupational aspiration; U_a-Unmeasured determinants of T; U_b-Unmeasured determinants of J; U_c-Unmeasured determinants of Z;. U_d-Unmeasured determinants of O; and U_e-Unmeasured determinants of E.

The background variables fail to account for the relationships among the intervening variables. While the relationships among the disturbance terms, U_c, U_d and U_e in Figures 7.3 and 7.4, are not large, neither are they small, relative to the observed correlations among the variables. The boys' correla-

EDUCATIONAL AND OCCUPATIONAL ASPIRATIONS

tions, r_{ZO}, r_{ZE} and r_{OE}, are .184, .219 and .153, in that order, while the correlations implied by the determination of the intermediate variables by X, V, S and Q are .075, .124 and .088. The girls' observed correlations are .208, .184 and .189, while the implied correlations are .122, .071 and .078. Thus, the determination of the intermediate variables by the background variables accounts for about one-half of each relationship among the former.

Two modifications of the interpretation could be made to reduce or eliminate the correlations among U_c, U_d and U_e. First, additional variables with the same causal priority as X, V, S and Q could be introduced. Second, we could make assumptions about the causal priority of Z, O and E. However, neither of these would change the results with regard to the transmission of the effects of background through the intermediate variables, and for that reason we have no interest in proposing an ordering among the intermediate variables.

Determination of Aspiration

Even if we assume the effect of Z on aspiration is valid, the intermediate variables do not account for the relationship between T and J: for boys r_{TJ} is .456, and for girls, .329. The correlations implied by the analyses of Figure 7.3 and Figure 7.4, .258 and .168, respectively, are only about half the size of the observed correlations.

We might have failed to account for r_{TJ} because we lacked a direct measure of parents' occupational aspiration as powerfully related to J as Z is to T. For example, if we set $r_{ZJ} = r_{ZT} = .642$ in the boys' data, the implied value of r_{TJ} would be .437, and the effects of the intermediate variables on the two aspirations would be symmetric. Such a procedure would indeed be a more consistent analytical treatment of students' perceptions of parental aspirations. However, rather than providing greater insight into the role of background factors in the determination of aspiration it would simply shift the explanandum from the relation between two measures of student aspiration to that between two measures of perceived parental aspiration. We know that in twelfth-grade students the latter relationship involves a correlation of .35 to .45, but the correlation between two measures of parental aspiration implied by student background would be about as large as the coefficient of determination of Z on X, V, S and Q, which is only .127 for boys and .135 for girls. Moreover, in order to account for the roughly equal effects of father's education and occupation on each of the measures of the student's aspiration, we should have to believe that father's occupation and education had similar net effects on his educational and occupational aspirations while the latter had grossly unequal effects on the educational and occupational aspirations of his child. It would be much easier to be convinced of the occupation- and education-specific content of paternal aspirations, if student's aspirations were asymmetrically related to father's education and occupation.

Parental Encouragement and Ambition

The several indications that students' reports of their parents' aspirations are affected by their own aspirations suggest the strategy of modifying the data and assumptions to generate a more plausible quantification of the role of parental encouragement in the formation of aspirations.

We start from the model in Figure 7.2, where a hypothetical variable, ambition, was postulated to account for the relationship between educational and occupational aspirations. The final models with path coefficients from the average data are presented in Figure 7.5 and Figure 7.6. The background variables influence O and E as in Figure 7.3 and Figure 7.4 and also affect G, an unmeasured variable representing the true level of parental encouragement. Parental encouragement, membership in organizations and mark in English influence ambition, which mediates the effects of the other variables on educational and occupational aspirations. The crucial feature of the model is the assumption that Z, the student's perception of father's educational aspiration, is determined by T and G, the student's own educational aspiration and the hypothetical measure of his parents' encouragement. For the sake of brevity we ignore the details of the process of estimation, which is similar to those used earlier in over-identified models containing unobservable variables (see Hauser, 1968:306-316). The correlations involving the unobservable variables, G and H, are presented in Table 7.3, and for ease in comparison the table also reproduces the observed correlations involving Z. Considering the large number of overidentifying restrictions and the crude procedures used in estimation, the fit of model and data is fairly good. The point of worst fit is accounted for by the model's inability to reproduce the effect of intelligence on aspirations—a defect which can be remedied by using a second indicator of academic achievement (Hauser, 1969c).

The major assumption of the model, which we apply to both boys and girls, is that $r_{GT} = .342$, the value of the correlation r_{ZJ} for boys. That is, we assume that a true measure of parental encouragement would be no more highly correlated with educational aspiration than is the student's report of father's aspiration with occupational aspiration. This yields a slightly conservative estimate of the effects of response bias in Z, since J is a better indicator of boys' ambition than is T. The same value was used for both sexes because J is a better indicator of boys' ambition than of girls'.

The correlations between reported father's educational aspiration and the hypothetical measure of encouragement are surprisingly low for both sexes (.434 and .446), and the path coefficient r_{ZT} is nearly twice as large as p_{ZG} for them both. This suggests some need for care in the use of students' reports of their parents' aspirations in studies of achievement. The correlations of G with other measured variables are roughly twice as large as the values of their corresponding correlations with Z. There are also substantial sex differences in the results. Among the girls parental encouragement is more highly correlated with both membership in organizations and mark

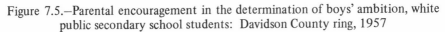

Figure 7.5.—Parental encouragement in the determination of boys' ambition, white public secondary school students: Davidson County ring, 1957

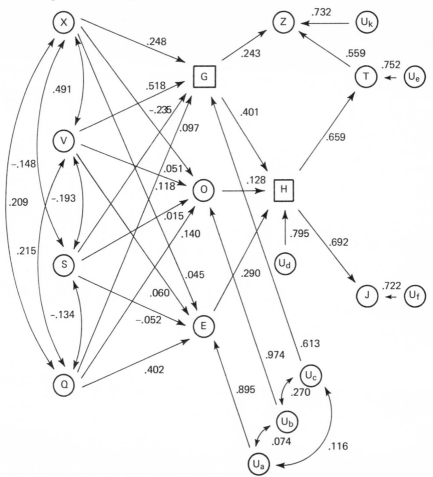

Note: Item identifications are: X-Father's occupation; V-Father's education; S-Number of siblings; Q-Intelligence; G-Parental encouragement; O-Organizational membership; E-English mark; Z-Father's educational aspiration; H-Ambition; T-Student's educational aspiration; J-Student's occupational aspiration; U_a-Unmeasured determinants of E; U_b-Unmeasured determinants of O; U_c-Unmeasured determinants of G; U_d-Unmeasured determinants of H; U_e-Unmeasured determinants of T; U_f-Unmeasured determinants of J; and U_k-Unmeasured determinants of Z.

in English than among the boys. The correlations of encouragement with father's occupation and education are higher for boys than for girls, and those with ability and number of siblings are higher for girls than for boys.

Despite the forced attenuation in the relationship between encouragement

SOCIOECONOMIC BACKGROUND AND EDUCATIONAL PERFORMANCE   125

Figure 7.6.—Parental encouragement in the determination of girls' ambition, white public secondary school students: Davidson County ring, 1957

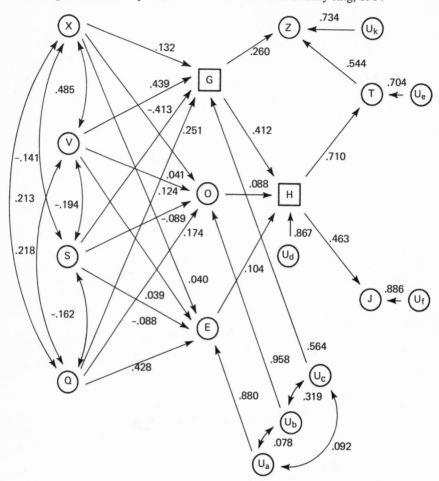

Note: Item identifications are: X-Father's occupation; V-Father's education; S-Number of siblings; Q-Intelligence; G-Parental encouragement; O-Organizational membership; E-English mark; Z-Father's educational aspiration; H-Ambition; T-Student's educational aspiration; J-Student's occupational aspiration; U_a-Unmeasured determinants of E; U_b-Unmeasured determinants of O; U_c-Unmeasured determinants of G; U_d-Unmeasured determinants of H; U_e-Unmeasured determinants of T; U_f-Unmeasured determinants of J; and U_k-Unmeasured determinants of Z.

and educational aspirations, parents' encouragement has a larger net effect on ambition in both sexes than does membership in organizations or mark in English. The net effects of parental encouragement for boys and girls are nearly equal in size, but the net effect of membership is one and a half times as large for boys as for girls, and the net effect of mark in English is

EDUCATIONAL AND OCCUPATIONAL ASPIRATIONS

Table 7.3.—Correlations of hypothetical variables in two-stage model of the determination of ambition by sex, white public secondary school students: Davidson County ring, 1957

Variable	Males			Females		
	H	G	Z	H	G	Z
G	.519	——	.434	.481	——	.446
O	.296	.308	.184	.271	.397	.208
E	.418	.268	.219	.256	.327	.184
X	.300	.558	.246	.269	.457	.223
V	.346	.707	.299	.315	.638	.288
S	−.259	−.385	−.189	−.152	−.557	−.204
Q	.383	.292	.212	.233	.442	.205

Note: Item identifications are: H-Ambition; G-Parental encouragement; Z-Father's educational aspiration; O-Organizational membership; E-English mark; X-Father's occupation; V-Father's education; S-Number of siblings; and Q-Intelligence.

nearly three times as large for boys as for girls. Thus, despite the lower correlation between H and G, parental encouragement of girls is relatively more important in the determination of their ambition. The sex differentials in the net effects of O and E are a consequence of both the girls' lower gross relationships of H with O and E and their larger correlations among G, O and E.

The effects of the background variables on ambition can be interpreted using expressions of the form

$$r_{Hi} = p_{HG}r_{Gi} + p_{HO}r_{Oi} + p_{HE}r_{Ei} + p_{Hd}r_{di}, \qquad (7.20)$$

where i varies over X, V, S and Q. These decompositions are shown in Table 7.4. The overall importance of parental encouragement and its greater relative importance among girls are evident in these results. The effect of each background variable via G is larger than that via O or E in every decomposition except that of the relationship in boys, between intelligence and ambition. The influence of each background variable via parental encouragement is larger in absolute value among girls than boys in two cases, and, disregarding the error terms, it is relatively larger for girls than for boys in the other two cases. In part, the importance of parents' encouragement is an artifact of our greater attention to the problems in its measurement than in the measurement of the other intervening variables. Yet, some efforts to inflate our estimates of the effect of academic performance have produced little change in the pattern of these results. We feel safe in concluding that parental encouragement plays a crucial role in the determination of ambition for social status.

Before leaving within-school models of aspiration we should mention an

Table 7.4.–Decomposition of correlations of ambition with student background by sex in two-stage model of the determination of ambition, white public secondary school students: Davidson County ring, 1957

Sex and correlations	Influence transmitted via			
	G	O	E	Error
Males				
r_{XH} = .300	.224	.017	.048	.011
r_{VH} = .346	.284	.022	.052	−.012
r_{SH} = −.259	−.155	−.004	−.036	−.064
r_{QH} = .383	.117	.022	.125	.119
Females				
r_{XH} = .269	.188	.013	.017	.051
r_{VH} = .315	.263	.018	.018	.016
r_{SH} = −.152	−.230	−.013	−.018	.109
r_{QH} = .233	.182	.020	.048	−.017

Note: Item identifications are: H-Ambition; G-Parental encouragement; O-Organizational membership; and E-English mark. Student background characteristics are: X-Father's occupation; V-Father's education; S-Number of siblings; and Q-Intelligence.

alternative ordering of our variables proposed by Turner (1964) and reformulated by Rehberg, Schafer and Sinclair (1970). Turner suggests that socioeconomic background influences ambition; both those variables influence intelligence; and all three influence class values. Rehberg, Schafer and Sinclair propose the same ordering, but substitute "mobility attitudes" for "class values" and a single measure, "educational expectations," for Turner's three-component index of ambition. Here, we have no interest in class values or mobility attitudes, but need consider only the contention that educational expectations (or in our case, aspirations) are causally prior to intelligence.

Rehberg, Schafer and Sinclair (1970:35, 45-46) agree with Turner's (1964:52) suggestion that, "The students who have the motivations and attitudes which lead to high ambition may be those who are accordingly motivated to learn the tasks which are measured by intelligence tests and motivated to make their best performance in the tests." Without attempting to exclude a motivational component in intelligence we note that Turner's formulation of the model uses only one measurement of intelligence. Thus, it ignores the impressive evidence (Bloom, 1964) that measured intelligence stabilizes to within the limits of its reliability by early adolescence. Implicitly, Turner suggests that an early measure of intelligence would have no net influence on current ambition and that current ambition would have a large net effect on later intelligence if early intelligence were controlled. Neither Turner's tentative formulation nor the more confident proposal of Rehberg, Schafer and Sinclair offers any evidence on these points.

Instead, their case is based on the specious dictum that a three-variable recursive model is ordered correctly when one of the partial relationships disappears. In both Turner and Rehberg, Schafer and Sinclair the argument is supported by the "finding" that a control for ambition reduces the partial relationship between socioeconomic background and intelligence more than a control for intelligence reduces the partial relationship between socioeconomic background and ambition. This "test" shows nothing beyond what it assumes. The model Turner and Rehberg, Schafer and Sinclair implicitly propose to estimate is shown in Figure 7.7, where a and b denote the non-zero paths in their theory and a, c, and d are non-zero in our formulation. One might think of verifying their theory by estimating a, b, c and

Figure 7.7.–Some possible paths among SES, intelligence and ambition

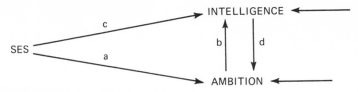

d from a sample and showing that the estimates of c and d do not differ significantly from zero. But such estimates cannot be made for this model, or, rather, an infinite number of estimates will fit *any* set of sample data because the model is underidentified. The model requires the estimation of four path coefficients to account for only three correlations, and it has no unique solution. Only if one of the coefficients a, b, c or d is set equal to zero (or some other constant) is there a unique solution. For example, the partial relationships examined by Turner and by Rehberg, Schafer and Sinclair are obtained by estimating the model twice, once assuming b = 0 and once assuming d = 0. That is, the non-zero coefficients in one theory can only be estimated by assuming the other theory false, so neither set of estimates carries any empirical implications about the truth of the other theory.

In fact, the model preferred by Turner and by Rehberg, Schafer and Sinclair (a ≠ 0, b ≠ 0, c = 0, d = 0) does not fit data very well. The partial relationships between status and intelligence are not reduced to negligible values in the data of Turner (1964:51-52), in those of Sewell and Shah, or in our data, though they are in the data presented by Rehberg, Schafer and

Sinclair (1970:41-42). Further, the fact that the partial relationship between socioeconomic background and ambition, controlling intelligence, does not disappear suggests nothing beyond the obvious conclusion that variables other than intelligence mediate the effect of socioeconomic background on ambition. Indeed, in the present context, following the consistent practice of Sewell and his associates, we have treated both socioeconomic background and intelligence as predetermined with respect to ambition, and we have demonstrated that the effects of those variables on ambition are mediated largely by academic performance, membership in organizations and parental encouragement.

Net School Differences in Aspirations

School differences in aspirations have received a great deal of attention from sociologists (Boyle, 1966a; Meyer, 1970; Michael, 1961; Sewell and Armer, 1966a; Simpson, 1962; Turner, 1964; Wilson, 1959, 1963, 1967). The present treatment differs from most others in that we recognize the limited variability of aspirations among schools (see Table 4.1), and we are explicitly concerned with the implications of within-school models for school differences in aspiration. As in preceding chapters we examine the extent to which differences among schools on the dependent variables are consequences of a fixed relationship within schools between that variable and one or more of its antecedents and the varying composition of student bodies on the antecedent variables. That is, the net effect of composition on any antecedent variable or combination of such variables depends both on the strength of the within-school effects and on the amount of variation between schools in the antecedent variable or variables. Further, the interpretation of school differences is complicated by the fact that composition effects are correlated with other sources of differences between schools. As in the previous chapter, we aggregate the decompositions over the grade subgroups in order to produce a stable set of results.

In the within-school analysis we have argued that the student's background affects aspirations through intermediate variables: father's educational aspiration, membership in organizations and mark in English. The decomposition of between-school variance in the intermediate variables attributable to composition on X, V, S and Q are shown on the first three lines of Table 7.5. About a third of the between-school variance in Z is accounted for by the composition of schools in respect to X, V, S and Q. That is, a large share of school differences in reported levels of paternal aspiration is explained directly by the mechanism of residential segregation. Also, there is positive overlap of the effects of background composition and those of the unmeasured determinants of father's aspiration. Students report higher than expected levels of Z where background composition is favorable and lower than expected levels where it is not. Despite the substantial compositional and joint effects, the residual is the largest component of between-school variance in Z.

Table 7.5.—Decompositions of between-school variance in aspirations and related variables by sex, white public secondary school students: Davidson County ring, 1957

Dependent variable	Predetermined variables	Male				Female			
		Composition	Joint	Residual	Total	Composition	Joint	Residual	Total
Z	X,V,S,Q,	31.0%	24.2%	44.8%	100.0%	31.6%	30.5%	37.9%	100.0%
O	X,V,S,Q,	5.7	−10.3	104.6	100.0	9.3	−20.2	110.9	100.0
E	X,V,S,Q,	22.0	−10.4	88.5	100.0	37.2	−24.9	87.7	100.0
T	Z,O,E,	57.8	18.9	23.3	100.0	50.3	28.4	21.3	100.0
J	Z,O,E,	20.7	26.9	52.4	100.0	10.3	14.4	75.3	100.0
T	X,V,S,Q,	34.8	22.5	42.7	100.0	24.5	31.9	46.3	100.0
J	X,V,S,Q,	32.0	17.2	50.8	100.0	12.2	16.3	71.5	100.0

Note: Item identifications are: Z-Father's educational aspiration; O-Organizational membership; E-English mark; T-student's educational aspiration; J-Student's occupational aspiration; X-Father's occupation; V-Father's education; S-Number of siblings; and Q-Intelligence. Figures may not add to 100 percent because of independent rounding. The figures differ from those published elsewhere (Hauser, 1969b) because of changes in the definition of the study population.

Composition accounts for little of the variance in membership in organizations among schools. There is a tendency for the overlap of composition and residual terms to be negative. That is, membership is higher than expected where the composition of student bodies is unfavorable to it and lower than expected where it is favorable. In this respect membership is similar to course marks; the observed differences in membership among schools are smaller than one would predict from knowledge of the student characteristics which predict membership. One might argue there is a fixed complement of roles in extra-curricular organizations in any school and that all the roles are filled, irrespective of the aggregated predispositions of the student body. At the same time a set of student characteristics influences the extent of individual membership in organizations in much the same way within any school. However, a comparison of the second and third lines of the table makes it clear that negative overlap is not so large in the case of memberships as it is for course marks.

Composition on Z, O and E accounts directly for more than half the between-school variance in T but for only from ten to twenty percent of the between-school variance in J. That is, if one accepts Z as a measure of parental encouragement, it becomes much easier to account for differences between schools in educational aspiration. The decompositions of between-school variance in J may be more indicative of what would be found for T with an unbiased measure of parental encouragement. The effects of composition on the intermediate variables overlap other school variables affecting aspiration. Again, because of the known defects of the within-school models on which the decompositions are based and because of the equivocal content of the residual school variable, we do not offer a specific interpretation of the joint effects.

In the decompositions presented up to this point only the combined effects of composition on all of the antecedent variables have been shown. However, we can show the effect of composition on each of the antecedent variables and examine each relationship with the residual term. The separate effects of Z, O and E on between-school variation in J are presented in Figure 7.8 for the combined subgroups of boys and girls. We omit the similar model for T because of the bias in Z (see Hauser, 1968: 323-324). The net effect of each of the composition terms is positive by virtue of the positive sign of the corresponding regression coefficient in the within-school analyses. However, the total effect of each variable need not be of the same sign, nor is it necessary for all the components of a positive between-school correlation to be of the same sign.

There are marked differences in the determination of the between-school components of the educational and occupational aspirations of boys and girls. The between-school correlation of each of the intermediate variables with boys' occupational aspiration is positive although the gross relationships of both E and O with J contain negative components. In the case of membership in organizations, the negative component is a result of the negative between-school correlation between it and average grade: while the boys with high marks are likely to belong to more organizations in any given school, there are more organizational memberships in schoools where marks reach a lower average. For example we write:

$$r_{OJ} = p_{JO} + p_{JE}r_{EO} + p_{JZ}r_{ZO} + p_{JR}r_{RO} \quad (7.21)$$

$$\text{(gross)} \quad \text{(direct)} \quad \text{(via E)} \quad \text{(via Z)} \quad \text{(via R)}$$

or $\quad .418 = .090 - .085 + .082 + .331 .$

Figure 7.8.—Decomposition of between-school components of occupational aspirations on father's educational aspiration, organizational membership and English mark by sex, white public secondary school students: Davidson County ring, 1957

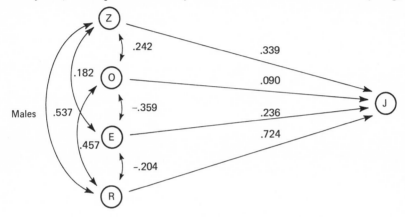

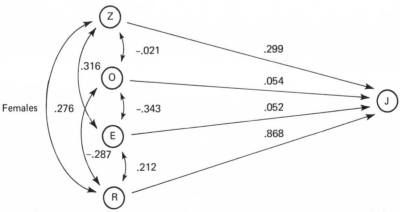

Note: Variables are school means on: Z-Father's educational aspiration; O-Organizational membership; E-English mark; R-Unmeasured variables; T-Student's educational aspiration; and J-Student's occupational aspiration.

Schools with high levels of membership among boys tend also to be those with low average grades, and this offsets the positive net effect of membership. It is only the positive association of membership with average levels of father's aspiration and the disturbance term which gives r_{OJ} a positive value.

The correlation between mark in English and boys' aspirations has two negative components, since both r_{OE} and r_{RE} are negative. We can write:

$$r_{EJ} = p_{JE} + p_{JO}r_{OE} + p_{JR}r_{RE} + p_{JZ}r_{ZE} \quad (7.22)$$

| (gross) | (direct) | (via O) | (via R) | (via Z) |

$$\text{or} \quad .118 = .236 - .032 - .148 + .062 \ .$$

The negative indirect effects of E on the between-school component of J via O and R are large enough to make the gross relationship, r_{EJ}, half as large as the net effect, p_{JE}. The average level of boys' marks in a school is a worse indicator of the school's average level of aspiration than would be expected from the direct relationship between the two variables. While a boy who earns high marks is rewarded in terms of aspiration, the average marks in his school are only weakly related to the school's level of aspiration because of their counter-balancing relationships with other determinants of aggregate aspirations. If there were negative correlations between average school marks and background and academic achievement, differences in average school marks would dampen the relationships between those antecedent variables and average levels of aspiration. However, we found (Chapter VI) that, while the direct effects of background and achievement composition on average marks are substantial and positive, their gross effects are small and unstable. Thus, variation in average school marks has no net effect on the gross relationship between background composition and aspiration.

The interpretation of the role of marking practices in the formation of aspirations is modified in the case of girls by the fact that E is positively associated with the residual determinants of average aspirations. We may write the decomposition of equation 7.22 as

$$r_{EJ} = .312 = .052 - .019 + .184 + .095.$$

| (gross) | (direct) | (via O) | (via R) | (via Z) |

While the direct effect of composition on E here is less than one-fourth the size of its effect for boys, the negative indirect effect via membership in organizations is also smaller, and the positive indirect effect via the residual variable is the largest component of the relationship. Thus the gross relationship between E and J is larger for girls than for boys. Still, a between-school correlation of $r_{EJ} = .312$ is hardly earth-shaking, and among both boys and girls the correlation is largely to be interpreted in terms of measured composition.

The findings of this and the preceding chapter lead to quite a different interpretation of the role of marking in the formation of aspirations from that offered in Wilson's article of 1963. As we noted in Chapter VI, Wilson argued that course marks are devalued in schools with low-status, low-achieving students, resulting in unrealistically high aspirations which are shattered when students come to face the demands at higher levels of the educational system. The findings reported here suggest that school differences in marking ultimately have little impact on students' aspirations. Like Wilson, we have found that marks are devalued in schools with low-achieving students, but the data do not support the hypothesis that their socioeconomic composition accounts for the devaluation. Further, there is so little gross variation in average marks between schools that the admittedly larger variation in marking, net of socioeconomic composition or achievement, has little impact on the individual student's course marks. Further, differences in marking can act on other variables only through the average marks assigned in a school. While the latter have a modest direct effect on the school's level of aspiration, with whose other determinants they are also negatively correlated, their overall effect on the school's level of aspiration is small.

Finally, differences in marks among schools can affect the aspirations of individuals only by way of the school's level of aspiration, and we have found little variation in aspiration among schools. Thus the relationship between marking and the student's aspirations is both weak and highly indirect. While the intervening relationships may be of substantive interest, the covariation of marks and aspirations from school to school is of little importance. To make that point absolutely clear we present the within- and between-school components of the total correlation between mark in English and educational and occupational aspirations for the grade-sex subgroups in Table 7.6. Clearly, variation in marks within schools is vastly more important than variation between schools in the overall relationship between marks and aspirations.

The aggregate relationship of membership in organizations with level of aspiration is quite different for boys and girls. Replicating the interpretation of equation 7.21 for girls we obtain

$$r_{OJ} = \underset{\text{(gross)}}{-.219} = \underset{\text{(direct)}}{.054} - \underset{\text{(via E)}}{.018} - \underset{\text{(via Z)}}{.006} - \underset{\text{(via R)}}{.249} .$$

While the net effect of membership on the average aspiration levels of girls is positive by definition, its indirect effects via Z, E and R are negative and the overall relationship is dominated by those three terms. This and the result of equation 7.21 suggest the need of conceptual precision in discussions of the role of organizational activity in the high school in the determination of educational outcomes. With respect to the outcomes treated here, it appears necessary to consider at least three consequences of membership in organizations: (1) For both boys and girls taken individually, involvement in extracurricular activity makes a modest positive contribution to levels of aspiration. (2) For both sexes, and to a marked degree among girls, the aggregate relationships are affected by negative relationships between levels of organizational involvement and other determinants of aspiration. The mechanisms underlying these complex relationships are

Table 7.6.—Between- and within-school components of correlation between English mark and educational and occupational aspirations by sex and grade in school, white public secondary school students: Davidson County ring, 1957

Sex and grade	Educational aspirations			Occupational aspirations		
	Total	Between	Within	Total	Between	Within
Males						
12	.246	.078	.168	.312	.067	.245
11	.324	.089	.235	.364	.063	.301
10	.308	.063	.245	.328	.056	.272
9	.360	.061	.299	.330	.066	.264
8	.330	.081	.249	.321	.060	.261
7	.272	.014	.258	.251	.020	.231
Females						
12	.157	.005	.152	.169	.005	.164
11	.266	.051	.215	.181	.024	.157
10	.177	−.006	.183	.071	−.012	.083
9	.264	.041	.223	.089	.012	.077
8	.214	.060	.154	.076	.014	.062
7	.188	.033	.155	.060	.011	.049

problematic. Both the degree and the specific character of involvement of students in extracurricular activities should be considered in further approaches to the problem. (3) None of the evidence presented here bears on the larger issue of the implications for levels of aspiration of the pervasive characteristics of extra-classroom activities in all high schools (Coleman, 1961a). Sex differentials in the aggregate relationships of organizational involvement with aspiration provide indirect evidence that the issue is not amenable to blanket treatment.

Decompositions of between-school variance in T and J directly on the background variables are displayed on the bottom two lines of Table 7.5. Composition on the background variables accounts directly for one-third of the between-school variance in educational and occupational aspirations of boys and for one-fourth and one-eighth, respectively, of the between-school variance in educational and occupational aspirations of girls. Among both boys and girls composition has a greater net effect on occupational aspiration in the decomposition on the background variables than in the decomposition on the intermediate variables. These substantial effects of background composition may appear anomalous in view of the larger effects of the intermediate variables in the within-school models. The explanation of this result lies in the greater variation in background than in the intermediate variables (save Z) among schools. The direct effects of composition depend on both the within-school effects of the control variables and their variability among schools.

In view of one recent suggestion that the schools' average levels of ability have a negative effect on aspiration, net of their socioeconomic levels, we examined the details of the effect of the boys' backgrounds. Meyer (1970: 62-65) suggests that levels of aspiration are formed relative to the local level of competition, so aspirations are lower where average ability (i.e., level of competition) is high. Further, he argues that the positive effect of the schools' socioeconomic context is enhanced when the negative effect of ability is controlled. In our treatment of course marks we have already found evidence of negative components in the between-school correlation of ability with aspiration. However, Meyer seems to go beyond this in suggesting that the entire partial effect of ability, net of status, is negative.

Our interpretation of Meyer's proposed contextual analysis is shown in Figure 7.9, where the path coefficients pertain to the boys in the Davidson County ring. The diagram refers *only* to between-school variation in aspiration, which accounts for about 14 percent of the total variance among boys. Rather than depicting R, the unmeasured school influences on aspiration, as merely correlated with composition on the background variables, X, V, S and Q, we assume those variables affect R directly. We take this assumption to characterize the differences between our equivocal approach and that of contextual analysis (Hauser, 1970a:662). The direct effects of the background variables would be the same in the absence of the contextual assumption; they represent the effect of composition one would expect from the within-school model.

Figure 7.9.—"Contextual" model of variation in boys' educational aspiration between schools, white public secondary school students: Davidson County ring, 1957

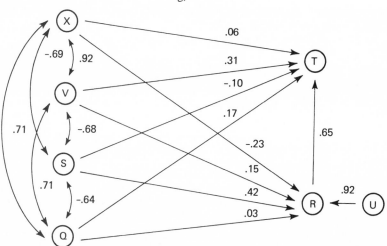

Note: Variables are school averages of X-Father's occupation; V-Father's education; S-Number of siblings; Q-Intelligence; T-Student's educational aspiration; R-other school factors; and U-School factors uncorrelated with X, V, S, Q.

Of course, the path coefficients for the direct effects of X, V, S and Q on T have the same sign as their effects within schools. If we have interpreted Meyer's theory correctly, we would expect to find coefficients of the same sign for the effects of X, V and S on R and a reversal (i.e., a negative sign) for the effect of Q on R. Clearly, Meyer's findings are not replicated here; in contrast, the effect of Q on R is small and positive, with a reversal in sign for one of the socioeconomic variables. In the Nashville data we find no evidence that the average level of ability in a school has a depressing effect on aspiration net of the socioeconomic composition of the student body.

The model in Figure 7.9 clarifies one other point that is often missed, namely, that composition on the measured control variables does not explain much of the variance in the contextual variable. Here, the assumption that X, V, S and Q affect the contextual variable, R, accounts for less than 16 percent of the variance in R. Most of the influence of R on T must be attributed to U, which is uncorrelated with X, V, S and Q by assumption. If we carry out the implications of the model in Figure 7.9, we find that composition (X, V, S, Q) accounts directly for 35 percent of the variance in T; that inseparable joint effects of composition (X, V, S, Q) and the residual (R) account for 23 percent; that the effects of unmeasured variables (U) via the residual (R) account for 36 percent of the variance; and finally, that the effects of composition (X, V, S, Q) via the residual (R)—the contextual effect—account for 7 per cent of the variance in T between schools. In short, by making the dubious assumptions entailed in a contextual analysis, we end up "explaining" a small component of the variance in a variable which does not explain much in the first place.

In interpreting school differences in aspiration sociologists have also emphasized normative features of the organization of adolescent activities which are only partly coincident with the academic resources and organization of the school. The peer society, rather than marking or ability, has been the focus of most analyses of school contexts, and its effects have frequently been identified with those of the "socioeconomic context" ("climate," "atmosphere," "structure" and "subculture" are alternative terms). The common content of these orientations appears to be a concern with the role of adolescent peer groups in the formation of life-styles and life-goals, and the validity of identifying the effects of peers with differences among schools rests on the extent to which the social contacts of the adolescent are limited by the school he attends.

We have argued that identification of the correlations between various aspects of the student body's composition and unmeasured school influences on aspiration with effects of the peer society is implausible. Indeed, we have just seen that it does not accord those organizational features much explanatory power; for that reason alone one might be suspicious of identifying effects of context with effects of the peer group.

Where, then, does the peer society fit into our interpretation? In one respect we have already taken it into account. If the society of grade or age peers is a pervasive aspect of the organization of the school, its influence is represented in the observed relationships among variables within schools and the direct effects of composition on those variables which we have already examined. In the light of that argument, differences among schools in adolescent life-styles might appear as differences in relationships among variables from school to school, though we have found few differences of that kind in the Nashville data. Further, differences in the organization of the peer society may be involved in those differences between schools which are unrelated to the student body's composition. While those effects are not large relative to the total variability in aspirations, they are substantial in comparison with the variability explained by the contextual analysis. Of course, the latter argument would require one to assume that the relevant differences in peer organization are not class-based.

This is not to argue that the adolescent subculture does not exist or that it is not relevant to the mechanisms by which aspirations are formed. On the contrary, it is quite consistent with the argument that peer groups exert pervasive influence, but it suggests that the organization of those groups is much the same from one school to another. If that is the case, then a disaggregated treatment of peer effects will be far more useful than continued efforts to identify them with school differences (Campbell and Alexander, 1965; Rhodes, Reiss and Duncan, 1965; Duncan, Haller and Portes, 1968). Indeed, a serious effort to identify peer effects within schools may be of some help in the interpretation of school differences (Duncan, Featherman and Duncan, 1968:207-221). Certainly, our earlier findings leave no doubt that our within-school models of aspirations are in need of elaboration and refinement.

As for the observed correlations between the composition of the student body and the other school factors influencing aspirations, the most one can say is that in schools with favorable composition aspirations are higher than expected and in schools with unfavorable composition they are lower. There is no clear basis for a causal interpretation of the joint effects. Because of our inability to identify the content of the other school factors we can argue with equal plausibility that bright, student bodies, high in status, lead to the development of characteristics of the school which are conducive to the formation of high aspirations (as in Figure 7.9) or that a school with real or reputed quality attracts bright, high-status students. Rather than yielding clearly interpretable social facts, supposed effects of school contexts represent gaps in our own understanding of the schooling process.

Neighborhood Status and Aspirations

The treatment of neighborhood socioeconomic levels in studies of the effects of schools has sometimes been indistinguishable from the treatment of school's socioeconomic contexts; that is, both have been misinterpreted as global indicators of school organization. Here, keeping in mind that school and neighborhood are not distinct as units of aggregation and that both "school" and "neighborhood" processes are best studied by dis-aggregating them, we attempt to interpret the gross correlations between the neighborhood's socioeconomic levels and the school's levels of aspiration. In short, we are concerned with the extent to which school levels of aspiration are explicable as consequences of "residential segregation of social classes."

In each school district we take the proportion of the adult population with at least a high-school education as an index of neighborhood status. We examine in turn (1) its association with the composition of the student body; (2) its association with other school factors influencing aspiration; and (3) its ability to account for the positive overlap of compositional and residual determinants of school levels of aspiration. The last part of the analysis simply involves a test of the proposition that $r_{CR} = r_{CD}r_{RD}$, where D is neighborhood status, C is a composition term, and R is a residual term. The results of these analyses are displayed in Table 7.7.

Neighborhood status is strongly associated with background composition, and its association with composition on the intermediate variables is only slightly weaker. The associations of neighborhood status with the residual terms are uniformly much weaker than those with the composition terms. Neighborhood status comes very close to explaining the correlation between composition and residual terms in four of the analyses in Table 7.7, and there are no very large discrepancies in the other cases. It may well ac-

Table 7.7.—Neighborhood status effects on student body composition and other factors influencing school aspiration levels by sex, white public secondary school students: Davidson County ring, 1957

	Educational aspiration				Occupational aspiration			
	r_{CD}	r_{RD}	r_{CR}		r_{CD}	r_{RD}	r_{CR}	
Sex			Observed	Implied			Observed	Implied
A. Controlling for background composition (X,V,S,Q)								
Males	.881	.224	.291	.197	.876	.239	.213	.210
Females	.907	.470	.485	.427	.857	.190	.276	.163
B. Controlling for intermediate variables (Z,O,E)								
Males	.738	.190	.157	.140	.709	.456	.350	.323
Females	.761	.442	.336	.336	.727	.252	.283	.184

Note: Item identifications are: C-Compositional term; R-Residual term; D-Proportion of high school graduates in the adult populations of the school district; X-Father's occupation; V-Father's education; S-Number of siblings; Q-Intelligence; Z-Father's educational aspiration; O-Organizational membership; and E-English mark.

count for the relationship between the student body's composition and the residual determinants of aspiration. Of course, we have not specified the mechanisms by which neighborhood status accounts for the residuals. Presumably, they include effects on the composition of student bodies with respect to variables not measured here and effective demand for quality in education. Also, neighborhood status need not account for much of the variance in the residual in order to explain the relationships between composition and residual terms, for these relationships are not large enough to require it. The largest value of r_{RD} is .47, which is to say that neighborhood status accounts for no more than 22 percent of the variance in the residual school factors influencing aspirations. As we found earlier in the case of academic achievement, neighborhood status leaves most of the variance unexplained in this aspect of the quality of schools.

Whether neighborhood status adds anything to the explanation of aspirations by the students' characteristics has been a matter of some controversy (Sewell and Armer, 1966a, 1966b; Turner, 1966; Boyle, 1966b; Michael, 1966). It takes an unusual form here because the explanation of between-school variance in aspirations is technically complete without introducing neighborhood status into the analysis. The results above indicate that the residual term does mediate some effects of neighborhood status upon aspirations and we can quantify its role by writing

$$r_{TD} = p_{TC}r_{CD} + p_{TR}r_{RD}. \tag{7.23}$$

Table 7.8.—Interpretation of relationships between neighborhood status and school levels of educational and occupational aspiration by sex, white public secondary school students: Davidson County ring, 1957

Variables and sex	Decomposition					
	r_{TD}	$= p_{TC}r_{CD}$	$+ p_{TR}r_{RD}$	r_{JD}	$= p_{JC}r_{CD}$	$+ p_{JR}r_{RD}$
Background variables:						
All males	.666	.520	.146	.666	.496	.170
All females	.760	.449	.311	.460	.300	.161
Intermediate variables:						
All males	.666	.564	.102	.666	.331	.335
All females	.760	.530	.230	.460	.246	.214

Note: Item identifications are: T-Student's educational aspiration; J-Student's occupational aspiration; C-Compositional term; R-Residual term; and D-Proportion of high school graduates in the adult populations of the school district.

To the extent that the relationship between neighborhood status and T or J results from influence of the former on the residual term, it may be said that neighborhood status influences aspiration beyond its effect on the social composition of the high school. The interpretations of the correlations r_{TD} and r_{JD} provided by equation 7.23 and its analogue in J are shown in Table 7.8 for the combined grade subgroups. About one-third of the relationship between neighborhood status and aspiration is attributable to the influence of neighborhood status on the residual terms. Considering the less than elegant explanation achieved in the within-school models to which the decompositions correspond, small importance need be accorded to neighborhood status, beyond its influence on the composition of student bodies. Residential segregation is an important mechanism differentiating schools levels of aspiration, but its effect is largely mechanical; that is, it functions primarily to segregate students who are predisposed toward different levels of aspiration.

VIII

SUMMARY AND CONCLUSIONS

Many persons who are interested in the determination of educational performance may be unfamiliar with our statistical model, the analysis of covariance, and our major expository device, path analysis. Not only are our analyses lengthy and complicated, but many of our findings and interpretations conflict with those of other studies. For these reasons the conceptual framework and analytic strategy of the study are reviewed in this chapter, and major findings are presented with a minimum of references to method. It should be understood that this recapitulation omits many necessary qualifications, and the results are no more credible than our methods of analysis and the assumptions underlying the use of those methods.

Orientation of the Study

This has been a study of home, school and neighborhood factors which influence academic achievement, course marks and aspiration, three educational performances which we interpret as part of a sequential process of stratification or socioeconomic life-cycle. The cycle begins with the position of the family of origin, and unfolds through processes of childhood socialization, schooling, job-seeking, occupational achievement and the formation and functioning of a new family of procreation.

This study has been concerned with the initial stages of that process, in which family origins condition performance in the educational system. In Chapter I a distinction was drawn between two kinds of educational outcomes: educational attainment and educational performance. The former refers to the number of years of schooling completed, or the quantity of schooling, and the latter refers to the demonstrated capacity to perform certain tasks, or the quality of schooling.

We know a good deal about the role of educational attainment in the process of stratification in the United States. Except in some minorities, educational attainment serves both to transmit the advantages or disadvantages of status of origin and to weaken the relationship between it and subsequent achievement. On the one hand, the most important way in which families influence the adult achievement of their offspring is by their effect on their children's educational attainment. On the other hand, privileged birth is no guarantee of high educational attainment: the rewards of education go to those who are educated, and for many persons of lowly origin educational attainment is the high road to success.

If educational performance, like educational attainment, were measured at the time when the individual completed his schooling, there is every indication that its role in the process of stratification would be much like that of educational attainment. However, investigations of educational performance such as ours have usually measured performance at some earlier point. For this reason, such studies can best be viewed as specifying some of the mechanisms by which status of origin affects ultimate educational outcomes.

In our study population neither the effects on ultimate outcomes of origin status nor those of the measured educational performances are known, but we assumed that the former are not so large, nor the latter so small, as to reduce to trivial proportions the role of educational performance in mediating the impact of status of origin on educational outcomes. Further, we argued that in many studies these contingencies had not been recognized.

Beyond these observations, we voiced three specific criticisms of earlier studies of educational performance. First, such studies had examined numerous indicators of educational performance without specifying the relationships among the indicators, i.e., without producing an overall interpretation of schooling. Second, extended interpretations were often based on no more demanding a criterion of explanatory adequacy than the mere existence of an expected relationship between measures of family background and educational performance. Third, disproportionate attention was devoted to variation in educational performance among schools, to the exclusion of variation within schools.

The analytic strategy of this study was conceived to avoid these criticisms. First, an incremental strategy of model building was used in an effort to generate explicit and internally consistent multivariate interpretations of the determination of educational performance. It was assumed that family background and intelligence influenced academic achievement; that background, intelligence, and achievement influenced course marks; and that all these factors influenced educational and occupational aspirations. In addition it was assumed that parents' aspirations for the achievement of their offspring developed in the course of schooling, and that this and other facets of the child's participation in the life of the school affected his aspirations. Further, it was assumed these relationships might differ with respect to sex and grade, and parallel analyses were conducted by sex and grade. Within this causal framework the analytic strategy called for an effort to generate parsimonious recursive interpretations; that is, it was assumed wherever the data allowed it, that variables at earlier stages in the sequence influenced variables at later stages by way of intermediate variables.

Second, to serve as an explicit criterion of explanatory adequacy two indicators of each educational performance had been ascertained. An explanation of each kind of performance was deemed adequate only if the interpretation could account for the common content of the indicators. Where it could not be explained by prior measured variables, the criterion was used as a basis of quantitative speculation about the processes by which that content might have been determined.

Third, the total variation in educational performance was partitioned into orthogonal within-school and between-school components, whose interpretation could be examined separately. When we rejected the possibility that relationships among the variables differed from school to school, we constructed within-school models of the determination of performances, following the causal scheme we have just outlined. The gross school differences in educational performance were then adjusted to take account of the effects of differing compositions of student bodies on the variables assumed to influence performance within schools. This procedure made interpretation difficult because composition on measured variables was generally correlated with the other factors producing differences between schools. Finally, we made an effort to interpret the compositional and residual determinants of the between-school differences as consequences of urban patterns of residence.

Data and Methods

The analyses were carried out on the population of white students enrolled in regular grades of the secondary schools in the City of Nashville and the remainder of Davidson County, Tennessee in 1957. Parallel analyses were carried out for the students of each sex in the six grades from seven to twelve. We drew upon the data files of the Nashville school survey, which contained a variety of information ascertained from group-administered questionnaires and school records. For the present secondary analysis these data were supplemented by population characteristics of the school districts in 1960 and by putative school feeding patterns, both of which we ascertained by using the school district boundaries of 1957.

Coverage of the study population was reportedly excellent, and the rates of response to questionnaire items were generally good. For some of the school record items rates of ascertainment were low; exploratory analyses indicated that there was probably little danger in estimating relationships in the total population from the pairwise-present cases. Further, there was no problem in assuming linearity of the postulated relationships among variables.

The analysis had two major methodological features. The first was the use of path analysis. Developed half a century ago by the geneticist, Sewall Wright, path analysis has only recently been used in sociological research. It uses a combination of graphically displayed causal networks and linear equations to interpret multivariate systems of relationships among variables.

The second feature was the use of the analysis of covariance in the interpretation of within- and between-school differences in educational performance. Much effort has been devoted by sociologists to the detection and interpretation of supposed "contextual" effects on educational performance of student body composition on socioeconomic or other antecedent variables. We suggested that the analysis of covariance is an appropriate model for interpreting differences between schools and that several defects of contextual analysis become evident when the covariance model is adopted. In the analysis of covariance each variable is partitioned into orthogonal within-group and between-group components. Provided the relationships among the variables are the same in every group, "average" within-group relationships can be used in the interpretation of within-group variation in the dependent variable. By a process of adjustment to the grand mean of each antecedent variable, the net differences among the groups on a dependent variable can be measured. Where individuals have not been assigned randomly to groups this strategy may not fully account for the between-group relationships among the measured variables.

This method of analysis had several advantages: (1) It was possible to measure both the gross and net variation in educational performances which could be attributed to the school attended. (2) All the relationships involved in the determination of an educational performance could be represented in a single statistical model. (3) The model made it clear that the effects of school context or composition were attributable either to differences in relationships among variables from school to school or to correlated error resulting from lack of randomization. (4) From these developments we argued that the popular interpretations of contextual effects are of doubtful validity.

Determination of Educational Performances

What follows is a summary of the major findings of Chapter IV through VII. Rather than recapitulating them in the order in which they were developed initially, we present separately the results of each of the four segments of the analysis of the covariance model: (1) gross school effects, (2) within-school variation, (3) net school effects, and (4) neighborhood effects.

Gross School Effects

It should be kept in mind that "school effect" refers to the unique contribution of the school attended to the determination of educational performance and not to the effect of being in school. There are two kinds of gross school effects: (1) school differences in average levels of educational performance and (2) school differences in relationships among variables, or nonadditivity.

Between-School Variance

The maximum possible influence on the individual student's performance of factors associated with the school he attends is described by the proportion of variance in educational performance which lies between schools. A review of previous studies of school effects suggests that gross differences in educational performance among schools almost invariably account for less than one-third of the total variance in educational performances. The upper limit is much smaller than one-third of the total variance in populations where school differences are not confounded with racial differences and it is essentially the same whether the population sampled is urban, metropolitan, regional, or national in scope. Even in studies of schools selected to represent extreme variations in community type and educational organization the gross variation in educational performance among schools has been found to be small in comparison with the individual variability within schools. In most of the studies reviewed the between-school variance in measures of ability or academic achievement is about twenty percent of the total; the between-school variance in educational aspirations ranges from ten to twenty percent; and the between-school variance in course marks is even smaller.

The gross differences in educational performance among schools in Nashville are comparable to those observed in other populations. Over the grade sex subgroups the percentages of common variance in academic achievement lying between schools ranged from fifteen percent to thirty percent; the percentages of common variance in course marks lying between schools ranged from close to zero to seventeen percent; and the percentages of common variance in aspirations lying between schools ranged from ten percent to twenty-two percent. The proportions of variance lying between schools in the separate measures of educational performance were of about the same size, or perhaps a little smaller.

The proportions of variance in student background characteristics lying between schools were also ascertained for the Nashville population. About twenty percent of the variance in intelligence was found to lie between schools, as was about one quarter of the variance in father's educational attainment and occupational status. These findings were interpreted as presumptive evidence that some part of the gross differences between schools in educational performance was accounted for by the differing composition of schools and the within-school relationships between student's background and performance. On the other hand, they did not provide much support for the idea that patterns of urban residence segregate the social classes very rigidly.

The hypothesis that the effect of the school attended on educational performance might have been obscured by the student's having moved from school to school was considered, but when students who had not moved within four years were analyzed in many of the ways just described only a small increase was found in the effect of the school they attended.

By treating students in different grades who were in the same geographic feeding channel as a synthetic cohort, we found that averages of school performance persisted in moderately strong degree from year to year—in fact, persistence from grade seven to grade twelve was generally greater than that predicted from the persistence for each of the intervening years. However, persistence in school composition on the student background factors was even stronger than that in educational performance, and the latter may have been attributable to the former.

Nonadditive School Effects

It has often been suggested that there are interactions of the school attended with other variables affecting educational performances, that is, that the relationships among variables in achievement differ from school to school. Nowhere has this hypothesis been subjected to intensive scrutiny in a representative population of schools and students. The evidence on this point from previous studies is fragmentary and inconclusive.

In the course of the Nashville study this problem was broached in three different ways: (1) We calculated variance ratios for each of the relationships we had examined to determine whether there was statistically significant interaction of the school attended with other variables—and found little evidence of any. (2) For six relationships the proportions of variance explained by average within-school regression lines were compared with those explained by fitting a separate regression line for each school and we found in each case that the additional proportion of variance explained was three percent or less. (3) For these relationships, the treatment as a synthetic cohort was applied to determine whether there was any persistence from year to year in the regression slopes of the several schools. Unlike the case of the average levels of school performance, there was here no evidence of persistence.

Hence we assumed for the remainder of our analyses that the effects of interest to us do not interact with the school attended. Thereby we made it possible to compare net differences between schools in educational performance by the process of covariance adjustment. Just as important is the added weight these results lend to the implication of the preceding subsection. Even on a gross basis the school attended is a minor factor in the determination of cross-sectional differences in educational performance.

Within-School Variation

In the light of the earlier evidence that relationships among variables were additive, we used average within-school relationships of each grade-sex subgroup to interpret differences in educational performance within schools. Within-school relationships were generally strongest in the lower grades, but differentials by grade proved difficult to interpret because students in the upper grades were presumably less representative than students in the lower grades. Further, the small number of cases in some of the subgroups made observed relationships unstable. For these reasons exploratory and summary within-school analyses were carried out with simple arithmetic averages of within-school correlation coefficients for the subgroups.

Academic Achievement

The analysis began with the assumption that father's educational attainment and occupational status influence achievement in reading and mathematics, and it did show that each of the two variables has modest positive effects. Despite some problems with measurement which should have resulted in an overestimate, we found that intact family has no effect on academic achievement, net of father's education and occupation. In consequence of this and other evidence intact family was dropped from the analysis. In contrast, the number of the student's siblings exerts a mild depressing effect on academic achievement. When this explanation of academic achievement was judged by our criterion of explanatory adequacy, the ability to explain the common variance in achievement in reading and in mathematics, it was found utterly inadequate.

At this point, intelligence was added as a variable to the model. Intelligence makes a substantial contribution to the explanation of academic achievement, net of the effects of family background, and it is almost possible to say that the effects of background on achievement are due entirely to its association with intelligence. Still, with intelligence added, the model explains only about half the relationship between the two measures of achievement. At the same time, the relationship between socioeconomic background and intelligence is not strong enough to support the theory that intelligence testing effectively discriminates against the poor; most of the effects of intelligence on achievement are unrelated to socioeconomic background.

At this stage of the analysis, our first efforts at quantitative speculation were undertaken. We assumed that an unmeasured variable, quality of teaching, accounted for that part of the relationship between achievement in reading and in mathematics which could not be explained by intelligence, and we examined the relationships between family background and this new variable under alternative assumptions about the relationship between it and intelligence. The assumption that quality of teaching accounts for the remainder of the relationship between achievement in mathematics and in reading implies that there are small net effects of family background on teaching. Even if highly intelligent students are favored by teachers the effects of family background and quality of teaching must be small.

Finally, we estimated effects of socioeconomic background and intelligence on achievement under the assumption that achievement in mathematics and in reading mutually reinforced each other. We found that achievement in mathematics had virtually no effect on achievement in reading, while if high levels are reached in reading, it does improve mathematics. Family background has almost no influence on mathematics but does contribute modestly to success or failure in reading. As in the earlier recursive models, intelligence has substantial effects on both reading and mathematics achievement.

Course Marks

Within schools family background is weakly associated with course marks. Still, students from small families or those with high status tend to obtain higher course marks. When intervening variables, intelligence and achievement, are controlled, the association between family background and course marks disappears. Thus, there is no evidence of gross discrimination by family background in the allocation of course marks within schools. Further, when it is assumed that intelligence influences achievement in reading and in mathematics, it follows that most of the influence of family background on course marks is mediated by intelligence.

The relationships among intelligence and the family factors, academic achievement and course marks are paradoxical. On the one hand, the relationships between the family factors and intelligence are far from perfect, and the assumption that the first cause the second leaves almost all of the variance in the latter unexplained. If schools use intelligence tests to discriminate on the basis of family background, the effort is notably unsuccessful. On the other hand, intelligence plays a crucial role in bringing about the relationships between family background and achievement and course marks in that those relationships are almost entirely attributable to the association of family background with intelligence.

The assumption that intelligence and academic achievement influence marks in arithmetic and in English directly accounts for only about one half the relationship between them. Therefore, factors other than background, intelligence and achievement must be of great importance in the allocation of course marks within schools. By assuming that success (as measured by course mark) in one course influences success in the other, and *vice versa,* it is possible to account for the relationship between the two without adding more measured variables to the model. When we conceive of the allocation of course marks within schools in this way, the reciprocal influences of marks are of about the same size as the net effects of ability and achievement on marks. There are marked asymmetries in the relationships between specific measures of ability and achievement and the two course marks. These can be summarized by the statement that

SUMMARY AND CONCLUSIONS

to achieve a high mark in English is a more complex task than to achieve a high mark in arithmetic. That is, we found: (1) that ability has a smaller direct effect on arithmetic mark than on English mark; (2) that achievement in mathematics has substantial direct effects on both arithmetic mark and English mark; and (3) that achievement in reading has no direct effect on arithmetic mark.

Educational and Occupational Aspirations

Students from families with high status who have few siblings or high intelligence tend to have high educational and occupational aspirations. A modest interaction of sex with these variables was detected; intelligence was relatively more important and family background relatively less important in the case of boys than of girls; still, family status was more important than intelligence in the determination of the aspirations of both.

Educational and occupational aspirations might be specific to the occupational and educational level of the student's family; or they might be indicators of a general level of ambition. If the former hypothesis were correct, we would expect that ambition could not mediate all the effects of father's occupation on occupational aspiration and all the effects of father's education on educational aspiration. But if the latter hypothesis were correct, we would expect that nearly all the effects of background on aspirations could be accounted for by the effect of background on ambition and of ambition on aspirations. Our estimates tended to confirm the latter view. Other techniques might reveal more differentiated goals among high-school youth, but our data are consistent with the conclusion that reported aspirations toward achievement in education and occupation are no more than reflections of social ambition.

The interpretation of aspirations was elaborated by the assumption that performance in school, participation in school-related activities and parental aspiration intervene between background and aspirations. When the three intervening factors are operationalized as English mark, number of memberships in organizations and perception of father's educational aspiration, respectively, family background and intelligence are found to exert very little influence on educational aspirations and only a modest influence on occupational aspirations beyond that mediated by the intervening variables. The relationships between the intervening and background variables are far from perfect, and background does not account for the relationships among the interviewing variables. Still, the intervening variables, like the background variables, do not account for the common content of the measures of aspiration.

There is a marked difference in the correlations of perception of father's educational aspiration with educational and occupational aspirations. This seems incongruous because father's educational attainment and occupational status were not asymmetrically correlated with educational and occupational aspirations. Also, perceived father's educational aspiration was only weakly related to the family's status. For these and other reasons, we reconsidered the two-stage model of educational and occupational aspirations, assuming that perceived levels of father's educational aspiration were contaminated by the student's own aspiration. In reconstructing the model we also assumed that the background and intervening variables acted on aspirations only through ambition. However, the crucial aspect of the reinterpretation was the postulation of an unmeasured level of parental encouragement rather than the original report of father's aspiration as the third intervening variable. Our fear that the reports of father's aspiration would be contaminated was confirmed by the reinterpretation; the effect of the student's own aspiration on father's aspiration as he reported it was nearly twice as large as that of the "true" measure of parental encouragement. However, the substance of the reinterpretation is much like that of the original two-stage model: (1) parental encouragement is the most important of the three intervening variables; (2) parental encouragement is relatively more important in the case of girls than of boys; and (3) the intervening variables mediate most of the effects of family background and intelligence on ambition and aspirations.

Net School Effects

The results presented up to this point were used to interpret the net effect of the school on educational performance. We had found (1) that there is gross variation among schools in educational performance; (2) that variation in antecedent factors within schools affects educational performance; (3) that these effects are much the same in any school; and (4) that there is variation in the composition of the student body on the antecedent factors. Thus, some portion of the gross variation in educational performance among schools must be attributable to the combination of constant within-school relationships and differing student body composition on the antecedent factors. Further, the procedure of adjusting gross differences between schools for composition requires no causal assumptions beyond those implicit in the construction of within-school models; in fact, the adjustment for composition is strictly implied by such models.

There are two difficulties in decomposing gross variation among schools into net effects of composition and net effects of the school attended: (1) The procedure of adjusting for composition implies a favorable judgment of the explanatory adequacy of the within-school model on which a decomposition is based. However, simple assumptions about the determination of educational performance by measured variables are not adequate to explain the common content of educational performances, and all of our decompositions are based on such inadequate within-school models. Thus, the net effects of composition here reported are minimal estimates of the variation in levels of school performance which might be explained by composition. (2) There is no reason for the net effects of composition on antecedent variables to account completely for the observed relationships between those variables and educational performance in the between-school segment of the model. That is, a two-component decomposition of gross effects of the school into net effects of the student body's composition and of other school characteristics cannot generally be made because composition on the antecedent factors is associated with other, unmeasured school characteristics. In view of the first observation made in this paragraph, this is hardly surprising.

It is just such associations of the student body's composition with other school variables that have been interpreted elsewhere as effects of the school's context or climate. Contextual interpretations of net school effects require one to accept within-school models which we have found inadequate. They require also the operational identification of the school context or climate with the residual school differences. This is not a convincing operation when the within-school model is inadequate or when the specific mechanisms identified with the contextual variable might readily be studied at the disaggregate level. Moreover, contextual interpretations require the equivocal assumption that composition causes the other school factors. In short, such interpretations lack scientific merit. At the same time, if one does accept the contextual interpretations, they turn out not to explain much variation in educational performance.

Net Effects of Composition

Moderate proportions of between-school variance in educational performance were attributed directly to the student body's composition in each of the analyses we performed. In Chapter IV we made a brief effort to determine the net effects of the school attended on educational performance from published tabulations in other studies of the effects of schools. By imposing one or two controls we were able to account for a large share of the reported effects of schools. In the Nashville data we found that the three family factors and intelligence account for from 6 percent to 56 percent of the between-school variance in academic achievement of the several grade-sex subgroups. Composition on the family factors accounts for less than 10 percent of the between-school variance in course marks but composition on ability and achievement accounts for about a quarter of it. Composition on father's educational aspiration, membership in organizations and mark in English accounts for about half the between-school variance in educational aspiration and for from 10 to 20 percent of the between-school variance in occupational aspiration. Composition on background and intelligence accounts for a third of the between-school variance in educational and occupational aspirations of boys, for a quarter of the between-school variance in girls' educational aspirations and for 10 percent of the between-school variance in the latter's occupational aspirations. However inadequate these simple within-school models may be as theories of educational performance, they do account for a significant share of the variation in educational performance among schools.

Covariation of Composition with Other Factors

While composition does have substantial direct effects on school performance, it does not follow that the net effect of the school attended is decreased in the same proportion. That is, the relationship between the composition of the student body and the other factors determining the school's levels of educational performance may be positive or negative, and the net effect of the school attended may be smaller or larger than the gross variation among schools.

In the decompositions of academic achievement on the family factors and intelligence the overlap of student body composition on the effects of other school factors was generally small and positive in the upper grades and small and negative in the lower. That is, in the upper grades achievement is higher than would be expected from composition in schools with favorable composition, and in the lower grades it is lower than would be expected from composition in schools with favorable composition. The latter results are suspect because of possible errors in the ascertainment of average levels of school achievement, and no firm conclusion was drawn about the relationships between the schools' composition and the other determinants of their academic achievement.

In the decompositions of educational and occupational aspirations on background and intelligence and on the intermediate variables there was a moderate degree of positive overlap of composition on the other factors influencing school levels of aspiration. Thus, aspirations are higher than expected in schools where composition favors higher aspirations, and the net effect of the school attended is lower than the gross effect. Quite the opposite was the case with the determination of average school marks. When average school marks were regressed on ability and achievement and, to a lesser extent, on the family factors, we found a negative over-lap of student body composition on the other factors influencing average course marks. That is, average course marks are generally lower than expected in schools with composition favoring high marks, and the net effect of school marking are larger than the gross variation in average marks among schools. At the same time the gross variation in marks among schools is so small that the larger net variation is still small in comparison with the total variability in marks. The negative overlap of composition and school marking standards is clearly not a class-based devaluation of standards. More probably, it is an artifact of the differences in ability and achievement and the similarity in letter-grade distributions from school to school.

Neighborhood Effects

Census data on the composition of the population of school districts were assembled, and the relationships between these characteristics and the compositional and residual determinants of school performance were examined. These were not intended to represent "neighborhood effects" like social interaction occurring outside the school. Neighborhood var-

154   SUMMARY AND CONCLUSIONS

iables were used in the analysis to interpret student body composition and the other determinants of school performance as consequences of urban residential segregation. In particular, we asked whether neighborhood composition could account for the association between the student body's composition and other school factors, and whether the other school factors were instrumental in bringing about the association between neighborhood composition and school levels of performance.

Of several indicators of neighborhood composition which we used, the neighborhood's educational composition was as powerful a predictor of school levels of performance as any reasonable combination of indicators. In general, the neighborhood's educational composition is more highly related to the student body's composition than to the other determinants of school levels of performance, and the influence of the neighborhood on the school's composition is more important than its effect on other school variables in bringing about the association between neighborhood composition and school performance. The results of our efforts to explain the correlation between compositional and residual determinants of school performance using neighborhood composition were encouraging. Neighborhood composition can account for most of the relationships between the compositional and residual determinants of academic achievement and of educational and occupational aspirations. The first of these points is the most important; that is, the effect of the neighborhood on school quality is largely limited to its influence on the social composition of student bodies.

Concluding Remarks

Our results present a picture of the relationships between family origin and educational performance quite different from that which sociologists sometimes draw. The contrast is one between a relatively loose process of stratification, in which achievement is the primary mode of ascent or descent, and a rather tight process in which ascriptive treatment, sometimes thinly disguised as meritocratic, perpetuates past inequalities. The present results appear to substantiate the view of the process of stratification as rather loose. Given the recent increments in our knowledge about stratification in the United States, it would hardly be necessary to point to the present results in this context, were it not for sociologists' disposition to interpret almost any social fact as evidence of great or increasing rigidity.

There are three interrelated areas in which this study may have added to the body of sociological knowledge. One primary contribution is to method. As noted in Chapter II, the analysis of covariance, which we used in the interpretation of school differences, is well suited to the more general problem of interpreting differences among social groups. Application of this statistical model to other problem areas might well reduce the difficulties in interpretation to which such efforts have been susceptible in the past.

A second area in which some advance may have been made is in the construction of multivariate models for the determination of educational performance within schools. Of course, one may choose to differ with one or another of the causal assumptions which we made or with our choice of variables. However, it is difficult to conceive how we might arrive at an adequate understanding of the process of schooling without considering models of at least the complexity of those developed here. Simple testing of hypotheses is not enough. The models proposed here have at least the virtues of being constructed to satisfy an explicit criterion of explanatory adequacy and of being easily modified or rejected.

A third area in which some advance may have been made is the conceptualization and interpretation of the role of the school attended in the process of stratification. Educational performances like those we have studied are no more than intervening variables in the process of educational achievement, yet even with respect to these variables, the school attended plays a relatively minor role. The alleged effects on educational performance of school contexts, on which social scientists have recently pinned their hopes for scientific advance and social reform, are statistical artifacts which involve only part of the variation in performance which is associated with the school. If there is any scientific or practical reward in cross-sectional studies of the determination of educational performance, it will be gained by learning more about what happens in school, and not in further efforts to detect effects of the school.

REFERENCES

Abrahamson, Stephen.
   1952a "Our status system and scholastic rewards." *Journal of Educational Sociology* 25(April):441-450.
   1952b "School rewards and social class status." *Educational Research Bulletin* 31(January):8-15.

Alexander C. Norman, Jr., and Ernest Q. Campbell.
   1964 "Peer influences on adolescent aspirations and attainments." *American Sociological Review* 29(August):568-575.

Bachman, Jerald G., Clagett G. Smith, and Jonathan A. Slesinger.
   1966 "Control, performance, and satisfaction: an analysis of structural and individual effects." *Journal of Personality and Social Psychology* 4, 2:127-136.

Blalock, Hubert M., Jr.
   1960 *Social Statistics.* New York: McGraw-Hill.
   1961a *Causal Inferences in Nonexperimental Research.* Chapel Hill: University of North Carolina.
   1961b "Theory, measurement, and replication in the social sciences." *American Journal of Sociology* 66(January):342-347.
   1967a "Path coefficients versus regression coefficients." *American Journal of Sociology* 72(May):675-676.
   1967b "Status inconsistency, social mobility, status integration, and structural effects." *American Sociological Review* 32(October):790-800.
   1969 "Multiple indicators and the causal approach to measurement error." *American Journal of Sociology* 75(September):264-272.
   1970 "Estimating measurement error using multiple indicators and several points in time." *American Sociological Review* 35(February):101-111.

Blau, Peter M.
   1957 "Formal organization: dimensions of analysis." *American Journal of Sociology* 63(July):58-69.
   1960 "Structural effects." *American Sociological Review* 25(April):178-193.

Blau, Peter M., and Otis Dudley Duncan.
   1967 *The American Occupational Structure.* New York: John Wiley.

Bloom, Benjamin S.
   1963 "Testing cognitive ability and achievement." Pp. 379-397 in N. L. Gage (ed.), *Handbook of Research on Teaching.* Chicago: Rand McNally and Company.
   1964 *Stability and Change in Human Characteristics.* New York: John Wiley.

Bogue, Donald J., and Dorothy L. Harris.
   1954 *Comparative Population and Urban Research Via Multiple Regression and Covariance Analysis.* Oxford, Ohio: Scripps Foundation, Miami University.

Boocock, Sarane S.
   1966 "Toward a sociology of learning: a selective review of existing research." *Sociology of Education* 39(Winter):1-45.

Bordua, David J.
   1960 "Educational aspirations and parental stress on college." *Social Forces* 38(March):262-269.

Bowles, Samuel, and Henry M. Levin.
   1968 "The determinants of scholastic achievement—an appraisal of some recent evidence." *The Journal of Human Resources* 3(Winter):3-24.

Boyle, Richard P.
   1966a "The effect of the high school on student's aspirations." *American Journal of Sociology* 71(May):628-639.
   1966b "On neighborhood context and college plans (III)." *American Sociological Review* 31(October):706-707.

Brown, Alan F., and John H. House.
1967 "The organizational component in education." *Review of Educational Research* 37(October):399-416.

Brownlee, K. A.
1960 *Statistical Theory and Methodology in Science and Engineering.* New York: John Wiley.

Burkhead, Jesse, Thomas Fox, and John W. Holland.
1967 *Input and Output in Large City Schools.* Syracuse, New York: Syracuse University Press.

Cain, Glen G., and Harold W. Watts.
1970 "Problems in making policy inferences from the Coleman Report." *American Sociological Review* 35(April):228-242.

Campbell, Ernest Q., and C. Norman Alexander.
1965 "Structural effects and interpersonal relationships." *American Journal of Sociology* 71(November):284-289.

Central Advisory Council on Education.
1967 *Children and Their Primary Schools: Volume I, The Report; Volume II, Research and Surveys.* London: Her Majesty's Stationery Office.

Charters, W. W., Jr.
1963 "The social background of teaching." Pp. 715-813 in N. L. Gage (ed.), *Handbook of Research on Teaching.* Chicago: Rand McNally and Company.

Clark, Burton R.
1961 "The 'Cooling-out' function in higher education." Pp. 513-523 in A. H. Halsey, Jean Floud, and C. Arnold Anderson (eds.), *Education, Economy, and Society.* New York: The Free Press.

Cleveland, Stuart.
1962 "A tardy look at Stouffer's findings in the Harvard mobility project." *Public Opinion Quarterly* 26(Fall):453-454.

Cohen, David K.
1968 "Children and their primary schools: volume II." *Harvard Educational Review* 38(Spring):329-340.

Cohen, Elizabeth G.
1965 "Parental factors in educational mobility." *Sociology of Education* 38(Fall):405-425.

Coleman, James S.
1959 "Academic achievement and the structure of competition." *Harvard Educational Review* 29(Fall):330-351.
1961a *The Adolescent Society: The Social Life of the Teenager and its Impact on Education.* Glencoe, Illinois: The Free Press.
1961b "Comment on three 'climate of opinion' studies." *Public Opinion Quarterly* 25(Winter):607-610.
1961c *Social Climates in High Schools.* Cooperatvie Research in Monograph No. 4. Office of Education, U. S. Department of Health, Education, and Welfare. Washington, D. C.: U. S. Government Printing Office.
1964 *Introduction to Mathematical Sociology.* Glencoe, Illinois: The Free Press.
1967 "Toward open schools." *The Public Interest* (Fall):20-27.
1968 "Equality of educational opportunity: reply to Bowles and Levin." *The Journal of Human Resources* 3(Spring):237-246.

Coleman, James S., Ernest Q. Campbell, Carol J. Hobson, James McPartland, Alexander M. Mood, Frederic D. Weinfeld, and Robert L. York.
1966 *Equality of Educational Opportunity.* Office of Education, U. S. Department of Health, Education, and Welfare. Washington, D. C.: U. S. Government Printing Office.

Conant, James Bryant.
1961 *Slums and Suburbs.* New York: McGraw-Hill.

Coombs, Robert H., and Vernon Davies.
1965 "Social class, scholastic aspiration, and academic achievement." *Pacific Sociological Review* 8(Fall):96-100.

Costner, Herbert L.
1969 "Theory, deduction and rules of correspondence." *American Journal of Sociology* 75(September):245-263.

David, Martin H., Harvey E. Brazer, James N. Morgan, and Wilbur J. Cohen.
1961 *Educational Achievement: Its Causes and Effects.* Survey Research Center Monograph Series, 23. Ann Arbor, Michigan: Institute for Social Research.

Davis, Allison, and Robert Hess.
1963 *Relationships Between Achievement in High School, College, and Occupation: A Follow-Up Study,* CRP542, U. S. Office of Education. Chicago: University of Chicago Press, Chapter VII.

Davis, James A.
1961a "Compositional effects, role systems, and the survival of small discussion groups." *Public Opinion Quarterly* 25(Winter):575-584.
1961b *Great Books and Small Groups.* Glencoe, Illinois: The Free Press.
1966 "The campus as a frog pond: an application of the theory of relative deprivation to career decisions of college men." *American Journal of Sociology* 72(July):17-31.

Davis, James A., Joe L. Spaeth, and Carolyn Huson.
1961 "A technique for analyzing the effects of group composition." *American Sociological Review* 26(April):215-226.

Dubin, Robert.
1969 *Theory Building.* New York: The Free Press.

Duncan, Beverly.
1965 *Family Factors and School Dropout: 1920-1960.* Cooperative Research Project No. 2258, Office of Education, U. S. Department of Health, Education, and Welfare. Ann Arbor, Michigan: The University of Michigan.
1967 "Education and social background." *American Journal of Sociology* 72(January):366-368.
1968 "Trends in output and distribution of schooling." Pp. 601-674 in Eleanor Bernert Sheldon and Wilbert E. Moore (eds.), *Indicators of Social Change.* New York: Russell Sage Foundation.

Duncan, Otis Dudley.
1959 "Human ecology and population studies." Pp. 678-716 in Philip M. Hauser and Otis Dudley Duncan (eds.), *The Study of Population: An Inventory and Appraisal.* Chicago: The University of Chicago Press.
1964 "Social organization and the ecosystem." Pp. 37-82 in Robert E. L. Faris (ed.), *Handbook of Modern Sociology.* Chicago: Rand McNally and Company.
1966 "Path analysis: sociological examples." *American Journal of Sociology* 72 (July):1-16.
1967 "Discrimination against Negroes." *The Annals,* 371(May):87-89.
1968a "Ability and achievement." *Eugenics Quarterly* 15(March):1-11.
1968b "Social stratification and mobility: problems in the measurement of trend." Pp. 675-719 in Eleanor Bernert Sheldon and Wilbert E. Moore (eds.), *Indicators of Social Change.* New York: Russell Sage Foundation.

Duncan, Otis Dudley, Ray P. Cuzzort, and Beverly Duncan.
1961 *Statistical Geography.* Glencoe, Illinois: The Free Press.

Duncan, Otis Dudley, and Beverly Davis.
1953 "An alternative to ecological correlation." *American Sociological Review* 18(December):665-666.

Duncan, Otis Dudley, David L. Featherman, and Beverly Duncan.
1968 *Socioeconomic Background and Occupational Achievement: Extensions of a Basic Model, Final Report, Project No. 5-0074 (EO-191),* Contract No. OE-5-85-072. Washington, D. C.: U. S. Department of Health, Education, and Welfare, Office of Education, Bureau of Research.

Duncan, Otis Dudley, Archibald O. Haller, and Alejandro Portes.
1968 "Peer influences on aspirations: a reinterpretation." *American Journal of Sociology* 74(September):119-137.

Duncan, Otis Dudley, and Robert W. Hodge.
1963 "Education and occupational mobility." *American Journal of Sociology* 68 (May):629-644.

Duncan, Otis Dudley, W. Richard Scott, Stanley Lieberson, Beverly Duncan and Hal H. Winsborough
1960 *Metropolis and Region.* Baltimore: Johns Hopkins Press.

Duncan, Otis Dudley, and Albert J. Reiss, Jr.
1956 *Social Characteristics of Urban and Rural Communities, 1950.* New York: John Wiley.

Duncan, Otis Dudley, and Leo F. Schnore.
1959 "Cultural, behavioral, and ecological perspectives in the study of social organization." *American Journal of Sociology* 65(September):132-153.

Durkheim, Emile.
1951 *Suicide.* Glencoe, Illinois: The Free Press.

Dyer, Henry S.
1968 "School factors and equal educational opportunity." *Harvard Educational Review* 35(Winter):38-56.

Eckland, Bruce K.
1965 "Academic ability, higher education, and occupational mobility." *American Sociological Review* 30(October):735-746.
1967 "Genetics and sociology: a reconsideration." *American Sociological Review* 32(April):173-194.

Edwards, T. Bently, and Alan B. Wilson.
1961 *A Study of Some Social and Psychological Factors Influencing Educational Achievement.* Final Report of Project SAE 7787. California: Department of Education, University of California (June).

Flanagan, John C., J. T. Dailey, Marion F. Shaycoft, D. B. Orr, and I. Goldberg.
1962 *A Survey and Follow-Up Study of Educational Plans and Decisions in Relation to Aptitude Patterns: Studies of The American High School,* Cooperative Research Project No. 226. Pittsburgh, Pennsylvania: Project Talent Office, University of Pittsburgh.

Flanagan, John C., F B. Davis, J T. Dailey, Marion F. Shaycoft, D. B. Orr, I. Goldberg, and C. A. Neyman, Jr.
1964 *The American High School Student.* Cooperative Research Project No. 635. Pittsburgh, Pennsylvania: Project Talent Office, University of Pittsburgh.

Folger, John K., Helen S. Astin, and Alan E. Bayer.
1970 *Human Resources and Higher Education.* New York: Russell Sage Foundation.

Folger, John K., and Charles B. Nam.
1967 *Education of the American Population.* Washington, D. C.: U. S. Bureau of the Census.

Ginsburg, Eli.
1961 "Education and national efficiency in the U. S. A." Pp. 68-79 in A. H. Halsey, Jean Floud, and C. Arnold Anderson (eds.), *Education, Economy, and Society.* New York: The Free Press.

Goldberger, Arthur S.
1964 *Econometric Theory.* New York: John Wiley and Sons.

Goodman, Leo A.
1953 "Ecological regressions and behavior of individuals." *American Sociological Review* 18(December):663-664.
1959 "Some alternatives to ecological correlation." *American Journal of Sociology* 64(May):610-625.

Goodman, Paul
1964 *Compulsory Miseducation and The Community of Scholars.* New York: Vintage Books.

Gordon, Robert A.
1968 "Issues in multiple regression." *American Journal of Sociology* 73(March): 592-616.

Goslin, David A.
1963 *The Search for Ability: Standardized Testing in Social Perspective.* New York: Russell Sage Foundation.

Gottlieb, David.
1964 "Sociology of education." *Review of Educational Research* 34(February):62-70.

Haller, Archie, and C. E. Butterworth.
1960 "Peer influences on levels of occupational and educational aspiration." *Social Forces* 38(May):289-295.

Hauser, Philip M., and Otis Dudley Duncan (eds.)
1959 *The Study of Population: An Inventory and Appraisal.* Chicago: The University of Chicago Press.

Hauser, Robert M.
1968 *Family, School, and Neighborhood Factors in Educational Performances in a Metropolitan School System.* Unpublished Ph.D. dissertation, Department of Sociology, University of Michigan.
1969a "On 'social participation and social status' ". *American Sociological Review* 34(August):549-554.
1969b "Schools and the stratification process." *American Journal of Sociology* 74(May):587-611.
1969c "Measurement problems in a causal interpretation: parental encouragement and adolescent ambition." Paper presented at a joint session of the American Sociological Association and the Rural Sociological Society.
1970 a "Context and consex: a cautionary tale." *American Journal of Sociology* 75(January):645-664.
1970b "Educational stratification in the United States." *Sociological Inquiry* 40(Spring):102-129.

Hauser, Robert M., and Arthur S. Goldberger.
1970 *The Treatment of Unobservable Variables in Path Analysis.* Social Systems Research Institute Workshop Paper EME 7030 (August).

Havighurst, Robert J., and Bernice L. Neugarten.
1957 *Society and Education.* Boston: Allyn and Bacon, Inc.

Havighurst, Robert J., Paul H. Bowman, Gordon P. Liddle, Charles V. Matthews, and James V. Pierce.
1962 *Growing Up in River City.* New York: John Wiley.

Havighurst, Robert J., and Robert R. Rodgers.
1952 "The role of motivation in attendance at post-high-school educational institutions." Pp. 135-165 in Byron S. Hollinshead (ed.), *Who Should Go to College.* New York: Columbia University Press.

Heise, David R.
1969 "Problems in path analysis and causal inference." Pp. 38-73 in Edgar F. Borgatta (ed.), *Sociological Methodology, 1969.* San Francisco: Jossey-Bass.

Herriott, Robert E.
1963 "Some social determinants of educational aspiration." *Harvard Educational Review* 33(Spring):157-177.

Herriott, Robert E., and Nancy Hoyt St. John.
1966 *Social Class and the Urban School.* New York: John Wiley.

Hodgkinson, Harold L.
1962 *Education in Social and Cultural Perspective.* Englewood Cliffs, New Jersey: Prentice-Hall, Inc.

Hollingshead, A. B.
1949 *Elmtown's Youth.* New York: John Wiley.

Jacobs, James N.
1959 "Aptitude and achievement measures in predicting high school academic success." *Personnel and Guidance Journal* 37:334-341.

Jencks, Christopher.
1968 "Social stratification and higher education." *Harvard Educational Review* 38(Spring):277-316.

Johnston, J.
1963 *Econometric Methods.* New York: McGraw-Hill Book Company.

Kahl, Joseph A.
1953 "Educational and occupational aspirations of 'common man' boys." *Harvard Educational Review* 23(Summer):186-203.

Kendall, Patricia L., and Paul F. Lazarsfeld.
1950 "Problems of survey analysis." Pp. 186-196 in Robert K. Merton and Paul F. Lazarsfeld (eds.), *Continuities in Social Research: Studies in the Scope and Method of "The American Soldier."* Glencoe, Illinois: The Free Press.

Krauss, Irving.
1964 "Sources of educational aspirations among working-class youths." *American Sociological Review* 29(December):867-879.

Land, Kenneth C.
1969 "Principles of path analysis." Pp. 3-37 in Edgar F. Borgatta (ed.), *Sociological Methodology, 1969.* San Francisco: Jossey-Bass.

Lavin, David E.
1965 *The Prediction of Academic Performance.* New York: Russell Sage Foundation.

Layton, Wilbur L.
1954 "Socioeconomic status and after-high school plans." Pp. 178-192 in Ralph F. Berdie (ed.), *After High School, What?* Minneapolis: University of Minnesota Press.

Lazarsfeld, Paul F.
1955 "Interpretation of statistical relations as a research operation." Pp. 115-125 in Paul F. Lazarsfeld and Morris Rosenberg (eds.), *The Language of Social Research.* Glencoe, Illinois: The Free Press.
1958 "Evidence and inference in social research." *Daedalus,* 87, 4:99-130.
1959 "Problems in methodology." Pp. 39-80 in Robert K. Merton, Leonard Broom, and Leonard S. Cottrell, Jr. (eds.), *Sociology Today: Problems and Prospects.* New York: Harper and Row.

Levin, Martin L.
1961 "Social climates and political socialization," *Public Opinion Quarterly* 25 (Winter):596-606.

McDill, Edward L., and James S. Coleman.
1963 "High school social status, college plans, and interest in academic achievement: a panel analysis." *American Sociological Review* 28(December):905-918.
1965 "Family and peer influences in college plans of high school students." *Sociology of Education* 38(Winter):112-126.

REFERENCES

McDill, Edward L., Edmund D. Meyers, Jr., and Leo C. Rigsby.
1967 "Institutional effects on the academic behavior of high school students." *Sociology of Education* 40(Winter):181-199.

McDill, Edward L., Leo C. Rigsby, and Edmund D. Meyers, Jr.
1969 "Educational climates of high schools: their effects and sources." 74(May): 567-586.

Meltzer, Leo.
1963 "Comparing relationships of individual and average variables to individual response." *American Sociological Review* 28(February):117-125.

Menzel, Herbert.
1950 "Comment on Robinson's 'ecological correlations and the behavior of individuals'." *American Sociological Review* 15(October):674.

Merton, Robert K., and Alice S. Kitt.
1950 "Contributions to the theory of reference group behavior." In Robert K. Merton and Paul F. Lazarsfeld (eds.), *Continuities in Social Research: Studies in the Scope and Method of "The American Soldier."* Glencoe, Illinois: The Free Press.

Meyer, John W.
1970 "High school effects on college intentions." *American Journal of Sociology* 76(July):59-70.

Michael, John A.
1961 "High school climates and plans for entering college." *Public Opinion Quarterly* 25(Winter):585-595.
1966 "On neighborhood context and college plans (II)" *American Sociological Review* 31(October):702-706.

Moore, Wilbert E., and Eleanor Bernert Sheldon.
1966 "Monitoring social change: a conceptual and programmatic statement." Pp. 144-149 in *Proceedings of the Social Statistics Section, 1965.* Washington, D. C.: American Statistical Association.

Moynihan, Daniel P.
1968 "Sources of resistance to the Coleman Report." *Harvard Educational Review* 38(Winter):23-36.

Nam, Charles B., and James D. Cowhig.
1962 "Factors related to college attendance of farm and nonfarm high school graduates: 1960." *Farm Population,* Census Series ERS (P-27) No. 32(June):1-18.

Nam, Charles B., and John K. Folger.
1965 "Factors related to school retention." *Demography* 2:456-462.

Nasatir, David.
1963 "A contextual analysis of academic failure." *The School Review* 71(Autumn): 290-298.
1968 "A note on contextual effects and the political orientation of university students." *American Sociological Review,* 33(April):210-219.

Office of Policy Planning and Research, United States Department of Labor.
1965 *The Negro Family: The Case for National Action.* Washington, D.C.: United States Government Printing Office (March).

Parsons, Talcott.
1959 "The school class as a social system: some of its functions in American society." *Harvard Educational Review* 29(Fall):297-318.

Perucci, Robert.
1967 "Education, stratification, and mobility." Pp. 105-155 in Donald A. Hansen and Joel E. Gerstl (eds.), *On Education-Sociological Perspectives.* New York: John Wiley.

Pettigrew, Thomas F.
  1968 "Race and equal educational opportunity." *Harvard Educational Review* 38(Winter):66-76.
  1969 "The Negro and education: problems and proposals." Pp. 49-112 in Irwin Katz and Patricia Gurin (eds.), *Race and the Social Sciences.* New York: Basic Books, Inc.

Rehberg, Richard A.
  1967 "Adolescent career aspirations and expectations: evaluation of two contrary stratification hypotheses." *Pacific Sociological Review* 10(Fall):81-90.

Rehberg, Richard A., and Walter E. Schafer.
  1968 "Participation in interscholastic athletics and college expectations." *American Journal of Sociology* 73(May):732-740.

Rehberg, Richard A., Walter E. Schafer, and Judie Sinclair.
  1970 "Toward a temporal sequence of adolescent achievement variables." *American Sociological Review* 35(February):34-48.

Rehberg, Richard A., and David L. Westby.
  1967 "Parental encouragement, occupation, education and family size: artifactual or independent determinants of adolescent educational expectations?" *Social Forces* 45(March):362-374.

Reiss, Albert J., Jr., Otis Dudley Duncan, and Paul K. Hatt.
  1961 *Occupations and Social Status.* New York: The Free Press of Glencoe.

Reiss, Albert J., Jr., and Albert Lewis Rhodes.
  1959 *A Sociopsychological Study of Conforming and Deviating Behavior Among Adolescents.* Final report of the Cooperative Research Project No. 507 (8133), Office of Education, U. S. Department of Health, Education, and Welfare. Iowa City, Iowa: The State University of Iowa (October), Ditto.

Rhodes, Albert Lewis, Albert J. Reiss, Jr., and Otis Dudley Duncan.
  1965 "Occupational segregation in a metropolitan school system." *American Journal of Sociology* 70(May):682-694.

Riley, Matilda White.
  1964 "Sources and types of sociological data." Pp. 978-1026 in R. E. L. Faris (ed.), *Handbook of Modern Sociology.* Chicago: Rand McNally.

Robinson, W. S.
  1950 "Ecological correlations and the behavior of individuals." *American Sociological Review* 15(June):351-357.

Rogoff, Natalie.
  1961a "American public schools and equality of opportunity." Pp. 140-141 in A. H. Halsey, Jean Floud, and C. Arnold Anderson (eds.), *Education, Economy, and Society.* New York: The Free Press.
  1961b "Local social structure and educational selection." Pp. 241-251 in A. H. Halsey, Jean Floud, and C. Arnold Anderson (eds.), *Education, Economy, and Society.* New York: The Free Press.

Rosenthal, Robert, and Lenore Jacobson.
  1968 *Pygmalion in the Classroom: Teacher Expectation and Pupils' Intellectual Development.* New York: Rinehart and Winston.

Ryder, Norman B.
  1965 "The cohort as a concept in the study of social change." *American Sociological Review* 30(December):843-861.

Schnore, Leo F.
  1961 "The myth of human ecology." *Sociological Inquiry* 31, 2:128-149.

Schuessler, Karl.
  1969 "Covariance analysis in sociological research." Pp. 219-244 in Edgar F. Borgatta (ed.), *Sociological Methodology, 1969.* San Francisco: Jossey-Bass.

Sewell, William H.
1964 "Community of residence and college plans." *American Sociological Review* 29(February):24-38.
1967 "Review symposium: 'Equality of Educational Opportunity'." *American Sociological Review* 32(June):475-479.

Sewell, William H., and J. Michael Armer.
1966a "Neighborhood context and college plans." *American Sociological Review* 31(April):159-168.
1966b "Reply to Turner, Michael, and Boyle." *American Sociological Review* 31(October):707-712.

Sewell, William H., Archibald O. Haller, and George W. Ohlendorf.
1970 "The educational and early occupational status attainment process: replication and revision." *American Sociological Review* 35(December):1014-1027.

Sewell, William H., Archbald O. Haller, and Alejandro Portes.
1969 "The educational and early occupational attainment process." *American Sociological Review* 34(February):82-92.

Sewell, William H., Archie O. Haller, and Murray A. Straus.
1957 "Social status and educational and occupational aspiration." *American Sociological Review* 22(February):67-73.

Sewell, William H., and Alan M. Orenstein.
1965 "Community of residence and occupational choice." *American Journal of Sociology* 70(March):551-563.

Sewell, William H., and Vimal P. Shah.
1967 "Socioeconomic status, intelligence, and the attainment of higher education." *Sociology of Education* 40(Winter):1-23.
1968a "Parents' education and children's educational aspirations and achievements." *American Sociological Review* 33(April):191-209.
1968b "Social class, parental encouragement, and educational aspirations." *American Journal of Sociology* 73(March):559-572.

Sexton, Patricia.
1961 *Education and Income: Inequalities in Our Public Schools*. New York: The Viking Press.

Shaycoft, Marion F.
1967 *The High School Years: Growth in Cognitive Skills*. Pittsburgh Pennsylvania: American Institutes for Research and School of Education, University of Pittsburgh.

Simpson, Richard L.
1962 "Parental influence, anticipatory socialization, and social mobility." *American Sociological Review* 27(August):517-522.

Spaeth, Joe L.
1968 "The allocation of college graduates to graduate and professional schools." *Sociology of Education* 41(Fall):342-349.

Stouffer, S. A., Edward A. Suchman, Leland C. DeVinney, Shirley A. Star and Robin Williams, Jr.
1949 *Studies in Social Psychology in World War II, Volume I, The American Soldier During Army Life*. Princeton, New Jersey: Princeton University Press.

Taeuber, Karl E., and Alma F. Taeuber.
1965 *Negroes in Cities*. Chicago: Aldine Publishing Company.

Tannenbaum, Arnold S., and Jerald G. Bachman.
1964 "Structural versus individual effects." *American Journal of Sociology* 69 (May):585-595.

Taves, Marvin J.
1950 "The application of analysis of covariance in social science research." *American Sociological Review* 15(June):373-381.

Turner, Ralph H.

1961 "Modes of social ascent through education: sponsored and contest mobility." Pp. 121-139 in A. H. Halsey, Jean Floud, and C. Arnold Anderson (eds.), *Education, Economy, and Society.* New York: The Free Press.

1964 "The Social Context of Ambition. San Francisco: Chandler.

1966 "On neighborhood context and college plans (I)." *American Sociological Review* 31(October):698-702.

U. S. Commission on Civil Rights.

1967 *Racial Isolation in the Public Schools,* Volume I and II. Washington, D.C.: U. S. Government Printing Office.

Walker, Helen M., and Joseph Lev.

1953 *Statistical Inference.* New York: Henry Holt.

Warner, W. Lloyd, Robert J. Havighurst, and Martin B. Loeb.

1944 *Who Shall be Educated?* New York: Harper and Brothers.

Wiley, David E., and James A. Wiley.

1970 "The estimation of measurement error in panel data." *American Sociological Review* 35(February):112-117.

Wilson, Alan B.

1959 "Residential segregation of social classes and aspirations of high school boys." *American Sociological Review* 24(December):836-845.

1963 "Social stratification and academic achievement." Pp. 217-236 in A. Harry Passow (ed.), *Education in Depressed Areas.* New York: Columbia University.

1967 "Educational consequences of segregation in a California community." *Racial Isolation in the Public Schools, Volume II.* U. S. Commission on Civil Rights. Washington, D. C.: U. S. Government Printing Office, Appendix C3.

1968 "Social class and equal educational opportunity." *Harvard Educational Review* 38(Winter):77-84.

1969 *The Consequences of Segregation: Academic Achievement in a Northern Community.* Berkeley: The Glendessary Press.

Wolfle, Dael.

1961 "Educational opportunity, measured intelligence, and social background." Pp. 216-240 in A. H. Halsey, Jean Floud and C. Arnold Anderson (eds.), *Education, Economy, and Society.* New York: The Free Press.

Wolking, William D.

1955 "Predicting academic achievement with the differential aptitude and the primary mental abilities test." *Journal of Applied Psychology* 39:115-118.

Yinger, J. Milton.

1968 "Recent developments in minority and race relations." *The Annals,* 378 (July):130-145.